# The Ritual Abuse Secrets

## of

## The

by

ArchAngel

© 1998 2ndEmpireMedia

All rights reserved. No part of this publication may be reproduced, distributed, or transmitted in any form or by any means, including photocopying, recording, or other electronic or mechanical methods, without the prior written permission of the publisher, except in the case of brief quotations embodied in critical reviews and certain other noncommercial uses permitted by copyright law. For permission requests, write to the publisher, addressed "Attention: Permissions Coordinator," at our website.
www.2ndEmpireMedia.Com

Printed in the United States of America

## WARNING!!!

If you are a survivor of ritual abuse, please be aware that reading about it may be triggering.

Please take care of yourself, and be in a safe place before reading these pages.

# Ritual Abuse:
# The Under-Recognized Problem

The word conjures up images of people in robes, chanting, or perhaps a grade D horror flick.
But what is the reality?

First, let's look at a definition of ritual abuse: Ritual abuse is the systematic, repetitive abuse of both children and adults by either an individual or a group.

It may involve psychological, sexual, physical and/or spiritual abuse, and the effects are devastating on the individual who undergoes it.

Often survivors of this type of extreme abuse cope by dissociating, and as adults may continue the cycle of amnesia and abuse.
The key word here is: repetitive.

Ritual abuse is done repetitively, in a consistent pattern, over time. This may be done in the name of a religious belief, or simply out of patterned cruelty.

Any ideology can and has been used to justify the pattern of abuse. Most of the victimization begins in early childhood, and is done by adults who were themselves abused. The cycle continues because people often do not realize that they can stop it; often, they feel "trapped" in the pattern of abuse.

What is the incidence of ritual abuse today? Statistics vary, depending upon the source. When I lived in a large metropolitan city in the Southwest, population close to 2,000,000 , the group that I was affiliated with, known as the Illuminati, had 24 sister groups.
Each group had roughly 50 members, so they had approximately 1,200 members in this area.

These numbers are reflected across the United States and European countries.
And this was only one group.

In the next few months, I will be sharing different perspectives on the reality of ritual abuse. I hope to address the following questions:

1. What kinds of groups engage in what is known as ritual abuse? What motivates them?
2. How do these groups maintain their "cloak of secrecy?" How do they operate?
What kind of security do they use?

3. How do they program their followers? Why? How does a person break free from this kind of programming?

4. What is the opinion of experts in the field?

5. Has there been documented, physical evidence that ritual abuse occurs? What evidence?

6. What about spouses and friends: what can they do to help survivors of ritual abuse? What is helpful, and what isn't?

7. What can the general public do to help?
These are all valid points that need to be addressed in order to understand ritual abuse.

As a survivor of ritual abuse myself, as well as a former cult programmer, or trainer, I have a vested interest in sharing both from my own experience, and the wealth of published information about ritual abuse that is available now.

I also hope to be able to share some survivor stories (with names changed to protect the people involved) about the reality of ritual abuse, and the ongoing effects that it causes in the life of the survivor, as well as things that have helped them in their healing journey.

I will be sharing internet links that relate to the topics that I have addressed. They are there, and are well worth reading for the person who desires to learn more, and is willing to approach this subject objectively.

God Bless,
**Archangel**

# Ritual Abuse:
# Modern Hysteria or Ancient Practice?

*If you are a survivor of ritual abuse, please be in a safe place before reading the following article, as it mentions groups that practice ritual abuse as well as the historical groups that they are descended from.*

In this chapter, I will be discussing ritual abuse in a historical context. Later chapters will share about ritual abuse from the perspective of its effects on the survivor as well as significant others.

Ritualized forms of abuse have been practiced since the dawn of human history.
Violence in the name of a religious or ideological belief is not new; it has been practiced for thousands of years.

Here I will discuss a few groups that have been documented as practicing secret, esoteric, or abusive rites to place modern ritual abuse in a historical context.

Please be aware that this is only some of the documented ritualized abuse that we know of from ancient until modern times, and is by no means complete.

The ancient Assyrians and Phoenicians worshipped the sun god, **Baal**, who they depended upon for the continuance of their crops. The antiquity of the worship of the god or gods of Baal extends back to the 14th century BCE among the ancient Semitic cultures.

Worship of Baal extended from the Canaanites to the Phoenicians who also were partially an agricultural people. Baal, the sun god, was fervently prayed to for the protection of livestock and crops, and the rites also included animal and human sacrifice.

Another co-current deity was **Molech**, whose rituals were also costly to human life.
(Excerpted from Alan G. Hefner).

Many of these rituals were adopted by the ancient Hebrews, as mentioned in the Bible

(Leviticus 20 and 2 Kings 23). These rituals were carried out for over a thousand years, both openly and secretly.

Ancient Babylonia also practiced Mystery Religions, which involved worship of the sun god, and sacrifices to this deity.

In Europe and Indo-asia, the ancient Druids also were known to engagein human sacrifice and rituals before the coming of Christianity to the areas occupied by the celts in Europe and Britain.

*Caesar commented upon this practice:*
"The whole nation of the Gauls is greatly devoted to ritual observances, and for that reason those who are smitten with the more grievous maladies and who are engaged in the perils of battle either sacrifice human victims or vow to do so, employing the Druids as ministers for such sacrifices. " (Gallic War, 6, 16)

By the medieval ages, Christianity had entered Europe, and groups were formed who practiced rites that were the antithesis of the organized religion of the day.

Many of these groups claimed roots founded in the rites of the ancient druids and
Canaanites. The Knights Templar were one such order. They were founded by medieval lords and barons to protect pilgrims who visited Jerusalem, which had been captured during the First Crusade.

They were also quite wealthy, and financed the leading kings of Europe at the time, creating the modern banking system of lending at interest. They were disbanded in the early 1300s by the Pope and the King of France because of fear due to their power, as well as their esoteric religious practices.

The Knights Templar began corrupting their Catholicism, and incorporating elements of mystery religions, which included rituals with candles around the body of a young virgin, and homosexual practices.

They also began summoning demons during these rituals. Although officially disbanded, the Templar knights continued practicing their rites in secret, founding the thirteen orders, each with their own symbol.

Rosicrucianism. This group was publicly founded in the 17th century in Germany, supposedly by an individual in a novel known as Christian Resenkrutz.

The order was based on the traditions of the "Rose Cross" order. This group emphasized the need for "enlightenment" through following certain spiritual principles, and had both a public and covert philosophy.

Meanwhile, in South America and Mexico, the Incas and Aztecs were also performing rituals which involved the taking of human life. This has been documented in the annals of the early Spanish conquerors Up until modern times, esoteric, hidden practices have continued around the world.

Brutality, and sacrifices in the name of religion are not limited to one locality or one time in history.
In Africa, ritual murder is still ongoing, and has been extensively documented.
See articles by Oke (1989) for more information.

In Thailand, India, and Malaysia, sacrifices and rituals are still conducted, similar to those of ancient times, and have been documented in numerous articles.
See Newton (1993) and Constantine (1995).

Modern Europe has also reported incidences of ritual murder in recent years
See articles by Newton, 1993a for discussion of cases of ritual murder that have been convicted in Dusseldorf and Spain.

In strife-torn Peru, human sacrifice remains a daily fact of life, dating back to the time of the Incas. For some practitioners, the ritual offering of human lives is believed to insure bountiful crops, control the weather, and prevent such natural catastrophes as floods and earthquakes.

These rituals, called "paying the earth," are also employed by wealthy businessmen, including mine owners and beer distributors, to insure continued prosperity.

In neighboring Chile, human sacrifice is such an established tradition that the courts recognize "compulsion by irresistible psychic forces" as grounds for acquittal in cases of ritual murder. (Tierney, 1989)

There is much, much more evidence of documented continuing ritual sacrifice around the world. It would take a strong denial system to refute both the historical and circumstantial evidence that ritual abuse has been a reality throughout the ages, and continues to be until this day.

Why am I sharing about the history of ritual abuse?

One of the things that often perplexes survivors of ritual abuse is the denial with which their memories or accounts are often met.

They are told: *"ritual abuse is a modern-day witch hunt,"* *"Things like that don't happen in this day and age"* (as if man's entering the Industrial Revolution changed human nature), or *"I don't believe you."*

Comments like these can be devastating both to the survivor of ritual abuse, who often WISHES the memories were not true, and the family and support people for the individual, who know the individual, and that they are NOT lying.

Comments like these only reinforce what the individual was told by the cult group:
"If you tell, no one will believe you," or *"You will be laughed at, or shunned."* The survivor courageous enough to not only remember, but then disclose their abuse, will be faced with a society that often appears in denial. *"Why isn't anyone doing anything about this?"* the survivor wonders, as they share the atrocities. *"Why isn't it stopped?"* *"Why do more children have to be hurt?"*

Societal denial is complex. People often do not want to think about or hear about painful topics. Thirty years ago, teenage girls who shared that their middle class father was sexually abusing them were told that they were *"lying"*, or worse, *"delusional"*.

Twenty years ago, medical professionals who suspected that battered children were being seen from not only the poverty levels of society, but also the middle class and well to do, were told it wasn't possible. Society closed its eyes to the facts before it, until enough people finally came forward and disclosed the truth.

Hopefully, placing ritual abuse in a historical context will help the reader see that:

Ritual abuse is NOT a *"new"* phenomenon, or a modern day *"hysteria"*. Human beings have been capable of great cruelty throughout the ages, and to believe otherwise refutes the historical record

Those who are abused tend to abuse.

Why would this well-known psychological fact be different in the context of familial, generational ritual abuse? Where the abuse has been passed down for generations, in a codified manner?

That ritual abuse is occurring around the world. It is NOT a phenomenon limited to the United States, or to people *"recovering memories"* through therapy. Newton, Ryder, and Lockwood ("Other altars") have researched and proven this.

My hope is that at the least, this article has helped raise some questions about a topic that is often overlooked and highly misunderstood.

**References:**

Crowley, Aleister. The Book of Lies (Weiser, 1988)
Howard, Michael The Occult Conspiracy (1989)
Shaw, Jim and McKenney The Deadly Deception (1988)
Ryder, Daniel ; article: Satanic Ritual abuse: The evidence surfaces: . (1999)
Newton, Michael: Excerpt from essay published in the Journal of Psychohistory 24 (2) Fall 1996."BLOOD ATONEMENT" IN 19TH-CENTURY AMERICA
Out of Darkness: Controversy over Satanism and ritual abuse: Sakheim, Devine (1998)
Smith, Margaret: Ritual Abuse; (1993)
James, Simon: The World of the Celts (1993)
The Book of Illumination (age unknown)

Most people associate satanic rituals with the stuff of Hollywood horror movies and tabloids as you will see in upcoming chapters truth is far more shocking.

# Cults That Abuse

**Groups that abuse**
Before I address survivor's stories in later articles, I believe it is important to understand how groups that ritually abuse operate.

Cults can be abusive or non-abusive, and there are many fairly benign cult-like groups that exist today. But for the purposes of my article, I want to look at cults that abuse, specifically, in the sense of ritual abuse.

What are the characteristics of an abusive cult? There are many studies that have defined controlling cults. Dr. Margaret Singer, Phd, U.Ca. Berkley, has written one of the definitive articles on cults that employ mind control and their characteristics (1).

She states that thought reform, as employed by controlling cults, involves the entire
Anthropological/social spectrum of behavior, including language use, social environment, and influence of the leader and peers on the member. This often involves attacking the person's self-concept.

I would like to take *the six conditions* that she has identified as being pre-requisites to exerting mind control, and compare them to experiences of survivors in ritualistically abusive groups. The two correlate completely.

**1. CONTROL OVER TIME:** This is Singer's first condition. The cult group must get some of the person's time, as much as possible, and have the individual think about group ideology.

Survivors report spending time during the week in contact with the cultic groups that abuse them. Contact is by phone; by verbal discussion, or going to meetings.

Survivors state that group meetings often occur weekly, monthly, or as frequently as two to three times a week for intensive training sessions.

The group that I was involved in (the Illuminati) met two to three times a week for normal teaching times, and had large group meetings on a monthly basis ("ritual times") as well as leadership meetings once a month to plan the activities for the next few weeks.

**2. CREATE A SENSE OF POWERLESSNESS:** Most groups involved in ritual abuse do this to the *nth degree*. Through pain, degradation, tying up victims, and experiences created to show there is "no escape" from infancy on, the victim of cult control soon comes to believe that he/she is trapped, can never break free, and should just "give in" to what is asked of them.

## 3. MANIPULATE REWARDS, PUNISHMENTS & EXPERIENCES IN ORDER TO SUPPRESS OLD SOCIAL BEHAVIOR

*BEHAVIORS THAT ARE REWARDED:* Participation, conformity to ideas/behavior, zeal, personal changes

*BEHAVIORS TO BE PUNISHED:* criticalness, independent thinking, non-conformity to ideas/behavior From earliest childhood in generational ritual groups, to later childhood or adulthood in other groups, the use of rewards and praise, as well as punishment all have a name: **"*training*"**.

Cult type groups believe strongly in the use of praise if the person does well, including merit badges, ceremonies of reward, and high status if the person conforms to the expected behavior, and severe punishment, even death is threatened if the person refuses to perform. Often, the more abusive and coercive type groups will take this concept to its outermost extremes.

## 4. MANIPULATE REWARDS, PUNISHMENTS & EXPERIENCES IN ORDER TO ELICIT NEW BEHAVIOR:

Models will demonstrate new behavior conformity through dress and language and behavior using group language will eventually quiet the thinking mind.

I will discuss this from the point of view of my experiences in the Illuminati in San Diego, Ca.

Again, "training" in the Illuminati and other highly controlling groups (outside people call it *"programming"*) is meant to create behavior that helps the group to continue. The goal is a member who is absolutely committed to the group; who never questions leadership, who strives to excel, and who scoffs at the weak.

*Weakness* is the displaying of emotion during ritual events; the refusal to perform an act, or the inability to keep up with others in the group during activities. *"Weak"* members are brought forward, and punished in full view of everyone.

During military exercises (my group had a strong military basis, with forced marches at night, and mock "battles" and "hunts" ) if a member did well, they were highly praised and rewarded.

This could be being excused from a difficult maneuver, or sexual rewards, or moving up in status at the next award time.

Members were highly conscious of their standing in the group, and were constantly seeking to "move up."


## 5. MUST BE A TIGHTLY CONTROLLED SYSTEM OF LOGIC:

There must be authoritarian leaders in control, who inspire confidence and punish questioning behavior.

In San Diego, as well as several other Illuminati groups that I belonged to across the country, the leadership looked like a "pyramid", with the top person being head of *"leadership council",* with a group of two *"advisors"* below him.

Below these two were six *administrators* who coordinated finances, meeting times, and running the groups logistically. Below them were six head trainers.

Underneath were the *"sister groups"* of about 50 members each, with priests/priestesses, and others. All aspired to a leadership role, to being allowed to move up the rigid hierarchy.

Questioning of leadership was unthought of, and considered quite dangerous. From earliest childhood on, members were taught that seeking to leave, or questioning the group's philosophy, would mean isolation, beratement, punishment, and possible death, with "mock deaths" often being staged to convince children of this reality.

Survivors of groups outside the Illuminati have also reported similar activities to control members, with a hierarchy of leadership and leaders being given the right to severely punish or discipline nonconformers.

**6. PERSONS BEING THOUGHT REFORMED MUST BE UNAWARE THAT THEY ARE BEING MOVED THROUGH A PROGRAM TO MAKE THEM DEPLOYABLE AGENTS**: A person is hard to manipulate if they KNOW they are being manipulated. That is why techniques used by ritualistically abusive groups are often based on a sophisticated knowledge of human behavior and psychology.

The member's peers including family, closest friends, and spouse are ALL members of the group in generational cults. These people all reinforce for the member that the group is good; has the member's "best interests" at heart, no matter how abusive the behavior. That they want to "help" the member.

Trainers and behavior programmers also use these techniques, including "bonding" with the victim, convincing the victim that they "care for them", that *"no one else could possibly understand them the way their 'family' (the name the Illuminati go by) does"*, etc.

As a former trainer in this group, I used those phrases frequently during sessions. At one time, I even believed them myself, until I began questioning what I was doing (this will be discussed in further detail in upcoming chapters).

Surrounded by members who all dress alike, act alike, the person in an abusive cult will often question themselves instead of the cult group, *if they question* at all. After all, in generational cults, this is the ONLY reality the person has known, from infancy on, and rarely does anyone think to question what happens to them.

Coming up in later chapters, I will incorporate first hand survivor accounts of the types of groups involved in this kind of abuse.

On a personal note, the group that was involved in my ritual abuse was known as the Illuminati, although day to day they called themselves "family", "the Order", or "the Society" depending on the given circumstances.

For thirteen years, at times my abuse occurred in a Masonic temple in Alexandria, Virginia and some of the abusers were Masons, although most of the membership of that group had no idea that some of the members were using the temple for that purpose.

All Masons are NOT abusers, most are not, but SOME in my experience were members of the Illuminati and abused me in that context. I was also abused in a small abandoned Baptist church in the country in northern Virginia.

One of my abusers was a deacon in a local Baptist church. Again, all Baptists are NOT abusers, but in this one instance, some members of the local church were members of a group that abused during the night hours.

In the daytime, these people were respected members of the community, churchgoers, and appeared benevolent. This shows that a person's daytime "persona" can be quite different from how they act at night or in a different setting.

All of the members of the group that abused me were generational themselves, and had been abused in the same way when they were children.

This shows how the cycle of abuse, if not healed, will continue generation after generation in some families.

**References:**
(1) Singer, Margaret T. "Conditions for Thought Reform"

Anton Szandor LaVey was an American author, musician and occultist.
He was the founder of the Church of Satan and the religion of LaVeyan Satanism.

# Why The Cult Doesn't Get Caught

When confronted with the possibility that ritual abuse may occur, one of the first questions people ask is:
*"But if it's real, why aren't they caught?"*

In other words, how can an organized society meet and execute rituals in secret, yet not leave any incriminating evidence which may lead to a conviction? How can such secrecy possibly be maintained in this day and age? Surely they would leave behind a 'trail' that would alert others as to what was happening.

I will address these questions from my own experience with one cultic group and also provide a link to articles about other ritually abusive groups who HAVE been
*'Caught in the act'* and subsequently convicted in court.

I would first, however, like to discuss one other secret society that has continued to operate in the US since the early 1920s. A secret society that commits acts of brutality including not only physical beatings, but also cold blooded murder. A criminal group that engages in a variety of illegal activities. An organization with members who are born into it and thus can be termed 'generational'. One who prior to the 1970s enjoyed the official FBI position of non-existence, despite those who were reporting its reality (sounds much like ritual abuse today, doesn't it?). I am referring, of course, to **'La Cosa Nostra' aka 'The Mafia'**.

In **'Who Is The Mob Today?'**, Writer Peter Maas quotes FBI Director Louis J. Freeh admitting the terrible past mistake made by the FBI in rejecting accounts of the Mafia's existence: For decades under the late J. Edgar Hoover, the FBI's official position was that the existence of Cosa Nostra was a myth.

"We cannot allow the same kinds of mistakes to be made today", Freeh told Congress.
"The failure of American law enforcement, including the FBI permitted the development of a powerful, well-entrenched organized crime syndicate (that required) 35 years of concerted law-enforcement effort and the expenditure of incredible resources to address."

The current 'official' position of the FBI is that organized, secretive societies that ritually abuse and participate in illegal activities do not exist, despite overwhelming evidence to the contrary. The bureau appears to have a consistent track record in this department.

What kind of evidence?
Ritual abuse does occur and is being successfully prosecuted in courts today, despite the claims of those who deny this fact.
Evidence such as pentagrams and assorted paraphernalia IS being found in many of these instances.

## Survivor memories:

More and more survivors are coming forward and sharing memories of ritual abuse. These accounts are specific in terms of dates, times, individuals present and events which transpired. Such disclosures have been made by both children and adults from around the world.

How security is maintained: One group's methods
In the remainder of this article I will share my knowledge of how one group operated its internal security in order to prevent detection. I cannot speak of other groups or their security measures.

As previously stated, I was a member of the
Illuminati for the first 38 years of my life, spanning from 1957 to 1995. Based on this experience I will now discuss exactly how security was maintained both in Northern Virginia and San Diego, Ca.

**1. Telephone Tree:** General meetings were scheduled by the leadership council well in advance (usually several months) during their private meetings.

In turn, these dates were then given to ranking leaders in the group who, several days prior to a meeting, would activate a *telephone tree*.

Higher members first called their peers, then those beneath them in the group hierarchy. Those at the lowest level were notified just one night before the meeting date, since they were considered 'higher security risks'.

**2. Conditioning To Remain Silent:** From the age of 24 months, ALL children in the group were taught the importance of not discussing group activities during the daytime.

Teaching methods included 'set-ups', in which a member 'told' and was then 'punished' through the administration of torture.

Set-ups were designed to look very realistic, with the 'betrayer' loudly screaming throughout his 'punishment' – which may have included drowning, burning or even murder.

This graphic experience of what happened to those who 'snitch', served as an unforgettable lesson to young children. Other methods included beating the child if he spoke of night-related activities in the daytime.

The adults around the child also modeled this behavior by NEVER discussing night activities the following morning. If the child mentioned something he would be told *"you were dreaming"* and to *"forget it"*.

Severe and brutal physical punishment of children was also used. Set-up scenarios such as fake burials, where the child is then retrieved from a coffin and told he will stay below ground forever should he even think of talking about group activities was done.

I was put through that scenario as a young child and in turn, as an adult, saw it perpetrated upon young children. The child is always screaming and swears to never ever tell.

Long held as a simple child's story featuring an alternate reality, the tale of Alice in Wonderland was actually written by 33rd Degree Mason Carroll Lewis and it's symbollogy is often used by mind control programmers to evoke programed alters within their victims.

**3. Expert Clean-up Crews:** Many rituals involving murder were set-ups (no, the cult was not murdering its children - however they did create very realistic set-ups that had powerful psychological effects on the children present).

More commonly, an animal was used during spiritual rituals (as I will discuss in another article, there were many other kinds of meetings.

*Spiritual* was but one of six areas of group
activities, the others being *military, sciences, scholarship, leadership…* and *government*).

\* intuitive readers will immediately understand that these special fields were purposely selected to create future "influencers" within high ranking positions within these chosen fields to further illuminati agendas.

Members were trained in post-meeting clean-up techniques from childhood. Wooden tables were taken apart, bleached, cleaned and then loaded into vans. Clothes were folded in preparation for laundering later. If the site was outdoors then the area was raked clean. If inside a large private home then the site was thoroughly washed down.

**4. Restriction Of Meeting Size:** In order to avoid overly large meetings, the San Diego group was divided into 24 sister groups (each approx. 60 members) that met on alternating days at alternating sites. Some groups met on Mondays and Thursdays, others on Tuesdays and Fridays, and yet others on Wednesdays and Saturdays.

Usually two groups (occasionally three) would meet together at one site. Only at major annual meetings would large numbers congregate. As mentioned earlier, meeting times were always coordinated by telephone trees.

**5. Clandestine Times:** Meetings were held between 12:30am and 2:00am and on occasion were extended to 4:00am. Traffic would be light.

Members often lived in communities where everyone was a member of the group (oh yes, there are 'cult communities' because *like attracts like*, and often whole neighborhoods are comprised exclusively of cult members).

People would leave quietly in the night, with car lights off until they were out on the street. The adult non-driver would be the 'watcher', checking that they were not being followed.

Each family had a cover story to be used in the event of an outsider catching them leaving. Typically the story would involve an urgently hospitalized relative, which would satisfactorily explain the lateness of the hour and the presence of small children.

Normal clothes were worn enroute to the meeting and people would change once on-site. In my family we would sometimes go to sleep in our clothes, which saved time when we got up in the middle of the night. I never considered it unusual to go to bed in my clothing two or three nights a week.

**6. On-site Security:** The group had several security perimeters around meetings.
The first checkpoint (outermost perimeter) was at the five mile mark.

There were always at least two roads leading into the meeting site and both would be manned by members possessing a list of approved license plate numbers.

All vehicles (incoming and outgoing) were checked. Vehicle flow was minimized as families often car pooled.
In the event of an unauthorized vehicle breaching the perimeter, a hidden security person (they would stand behind a tree, watching) would radio ahead and the meeting was immediately packed-up and the people quickly dispersed.

Meanwhile, the incoming vehicle would be delayed by the non-hidden security who would pretend to be stranded and in need of assistance. They were taught how to engage the outsider for several crucial minutes. If that ploy failed then they would alert the next perimeter where logs would then be positioned to block the roadway.

Of the three-man security team, one would be responsible for alerting members while the other two executed delaying tactics if required.

This security procedure was repeated at both the three mile and one mile perimeters, meaning members had to pass through a total of three checkpoints before arriving at the meeting.

To avoid boredom or staleness, security members were rotated on a bi-monthly basis.
Often, on private property, indoor meetings or trainings would occur on large multi-acred estates appointed with securely fenced perimeters.

The site would be located in a downstairs basement which could be closed-off from the rest of the house by a false wall.

These estates usually had at least one private roadway at the rear and the customary security perimeters in place. As you may by now appreciate, it would be extremely difficult to *'crash a meeting'* considering the security measures utilized by the group.

Given that an outsider was able to discover the time and date of a meeting, he would then have to travel in a vehicle with approved plates. Short of breaking the law, this would require the cooperation of an active group member (which is quite difficult to arrange as they are taught to report to their leader anything like this).

The above has been shared with police departments and they have said that I describe a "highly sophisticated security system". It is the only one I ever knew while part of this group.

# What about the bodies?

As mentioned above, the reality is that many of the 'ritual killings' (although not all) were set-ups. Fake. Some involved filling a corpse (obtained prior to the ritual) with warm blood.

A child would be allowed to play with a living infant before a ceremony, then a switch would be made while the child was away in a room 'preparing'.

Children *NEVER* question set-ups (they are simply too frightened) and truly do believe they actually witnessed a murder. The group wants them to believe this because the perpetrator guilt will then bind the child to them, and make it less willing to disclose group activities.

The child is told it is *now a murderer* and will go to jail for life should it ever talk about the meetings. There *are* real ritual killings, but I believe that set-ups inflate the figures somewhat. Homeless people, and runaways were also used on rare occasions.

At times animals are used, however they usually belonged to group members.
While living in San Diego I had four cats and three dogs mysteriously 'disappear' as well as most of my chickens (I lived in the country). These pets were undoubtedly used in ceremonies. After that I quit having pets - the trauma was simply too great.

Goats, chickens, cattle and deer are all used on these occasions. The carcasses are subsequently torn-up, buried or thrown to the dogs in order to make the killings appear to have been done by wild dogs. Sometimes the skins are incinerated and the ashes buried.

It is not my intention to be gruesome. I am merely attempting to explain the mechanics of how this group maintained its secrecy. No doubt other groups use different methods.

In closing this chapter, I would like to offer a comparison upon which to ponder. The Mafia, comprised of thousands of members and openly killing people, maintained its secrecy for over fifty years in the US.

Today nobody doubts their existence, yet those same people question that other groups could successfully remain secret.

Secrecy is not difficult. The Mafia used their own code of silence - *'Omerta'*. The Illuminati cult also maintains its own silence to this day.

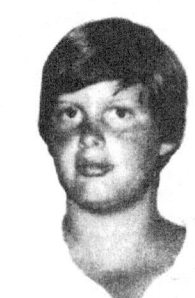

# KIDNAPPED
## JOHN DAVID GOSCH

Taken 81/82 School Year     Fair Photo '82

**Composite Of Suspect**
5'9", 175 lbs. dark eyes, black eyebrows, older, early to mid 40's, black hair, combed back, full in back, black mustache, heavy beard or unshaven appearance. Latin appearance. This man may be driving a two tone blue car, real dark top and light blue bottom -mid size - 79 to 81 model -clean inside and outside - no vinyl top -plush interior -Iowa plate.

DESCRIPTION: Age: 13 years old, D.O.B.: Nov. 12, 1969, Ht.: 5'7" Wt.: 145 lbs. Hair: light brown, Eyes: blue, Complexion: medium Teeth: gaps between front teeth, Shoe Size: 9½-10, Marks/Scars: freckles, large birthmark upper left chest, horseshoe shaped scar on tongue, large lower lip. Stature: At 13 years old, John has the physical appearance of a boy 15 or older.

John David Gosch was last seen on Sunday, September 5, 1982 at approximately 6:06 A.M. He was believed to have been kidnapped when starting his paper route at 42nd and Marcourt Lane in West Des Moines, Iowa.

John was believed to have been wearing a white sweat shirt with the words KIM'S ACADEMY on the back of it along with black warm up pants and blue rubber thongs. Missing also with John is his yellow paperbag and wire cutters.

## REWARD

A $90,000.00 REWARD has been offered for the safe return of John David Gosch in addition to a $10,000.00 REWARD for information leading to his whereabouts.

Anyone having information to John's whereabouts, please call: LOCAL F.B.I. OFFICE or INVESTIGATIVE RESEARCH AGENCY, INC. (404) 563-8467 or John's parents JOHN and NOREEN GOSCH at (515) 225-7456.

Sponsored by the Help Find Johnny Gosch Fund, Inc.

The Famous case of West Des Moines, Iowa Paperboy Johnny Gosch remains unsolved some 30 years later, yet occasional reports of sightings of him as an adult still surface from time to time.

# Survivors Speak Out On Remembering: Part One

A significant aspect of the ritual abuse subject is the testimony of survivors - those who are seriously engaged in the healing process.

The uninitiated reader can scarcely begin to comprehend the journey upon which many such people from around the world have embarked.

They are all ages, both male and female. They are working hard at exchanging old belief systems for a different world-view and an entirely new way of life.

This is the first in a series of assembled articles based on survivor responses to a questionnaire I distributed.

All quoted passages herein have the express permission of the respective survivor and, for obvious reasons, I have substituted pseudonyms in order to protect their true identities.
These are, however, very real people and each has a genuine story to tell.

Memory retrieval is a strenuously debated topic. There are groups (well chronicled in the mass media) who assert that repressed memories cannot be accessed as an adult, while other groups or professionals argue that yes, it is possible and does in fact happen.
I thought it wise to go to the source - the survivors themselves – and discover what their first-hand experience has been. They know best how they remembered.

My hope is that upon experiencing what is shared here, you will be inspired by their sincerity, truthfulness and conviction. These are NOT people "fabricating memories" as is sometimes alleged. Several people have always remembered at least some of their abuse.

These are people whose determination to escape from an abusive environment (both receiving abuse and inflicting it upon others) has cost them dearly. They are paying a very high price for living in a culture which continues to wallow in a state of collective denial. Here, survivors speak out for the first time on how they remembered:

**Joanne, a survivor of generational abuse, states:** I was about 12yrs old when I realized what was going on wasn't "normal" but I never came out and said anything, I was the typical abused kid who acted up, but no-one would believe me when I first tried to say anything at the age of 16yrs.

The memories, well some I have always known, generally the more traumatic the event the better recall of them that I have, although there are still some major injuries that I remember having but can't recall what lead up to the injuries, I know when and where they took place but as to what precipitated the actual injury, I don't remember.

**Ellen, another survivor, did not dissociate her memories:** I was in a cult which started in 1994 evolving from alleged apparitions of the Virgin Mary in my area of the country.

These apparitions, called *Our Lady of Light*, I now believe to be luciferian in nature. There was a visionary who claimed to be receiving messages from Jesus to renew the Church and the world with a particular emphasis on the priesthood.

A *Jesuit* theologian became the spiritual director of this group through messages from Our Lady of Light. I was deeply involved in this cult from its inception in 1994 until I was able to escape in June of 1998.

I don't have *Dissociative Identity Disorder* (*also known as D.I.D*), but I do feel as though I was well on my way by the time I left. I remember feeling as if there were 2 different realities while I was in that cult………. I dared not remember my former life………. but glimpses would come through at times which I would quickly shut down.

It was not until after I left that cult and began healing and studying that I came to the realization of the symbolic satanic rituals involved in this cult. My understanding would come little bits at a time.

The depth of the evil was so intense that I could only have tolerated little pieces at a time. If I would have come to a full understanding immediately, I do believe that I would have shattered or died. I just knew that I had to keep battling for the truth.

It was through my struggle to sift out the truth from the lie that I came to the understanding of the nature of the evil of the group.

**Children as well as adults have remembered abuse. Vicky, a 15 year old, shares:** I had bad dreams at night. I would dream that I was going somewhere and things happened, but the next morning, everything was normal.
I didn't really start remembering until I went to be with my Mom, after she got out, and it was safe.
They don't let you remember, you get hurt if you do. I didn't want to get hurt.

I started remembering, and inside people started sharing stuff. But most of the time, I try to ignore it. I'm busy at school, and being a teenager. It happened, but I try not to think about it. Except at night I get scared because then I can't help but think about it. That's when my Mom and Dad would wake me up, they were all cold and impersonal, and get me and my brother out of bed to go to a meeting.

I have trouble sleeping at night, I keep waking up all night to make sure I'm safe and at home even now.

Aleister Crowley -Born Edward Alexander Crowley; *Dubbed the most evil man who ever lived*, Crowley was an English occultist, ceremonial magician, poet, painter, novelist, and mountaineer. He founded the religion of Thelema, identifying himself as the prophet entrusted with guiding humanity into the Æon of Horus in the early 20th century.

# Survivors Speak Out On Remembering: Part Two

Survivors of ritual abuse come from all over the world. This is not a phenomenon limited to the United States or Europe.

**John, a survivor outside the U.S., shares his process of remembering:** I did not always remember. As with many sexual assault survivors and because of the violence and threats done to them, I was not able or allowed to remember. In 1974 I was 16 and I saw the movie, The Exorcist.

It triggered an uncomfortableness and because of the brainwashing and lies "my family would be killed" I couldn't get consciousness and clarity. I ran away though on this subconscious and yet still powerful fear.

I then got brainwashed again and it blotted out all my memory and the abuse that was happening then. In 1992, I met a ritual abuse survivor in an incest survivors group and after about six months of listening to her, I realized that I had been, and was then also being, ritually abused.

The brainwashing was so strong that it took six months of listening to another survivor to assist me to have consciousness and clarity.

**Abigail is another survivor who has always remembered some things:** We always had part memories indicating such things, though we didn't know how to label it, for example, going to grade school and then my father would show up with an excuse to take me out of school.

He would take me to the grocery store he worked at and sit me in the cooler room to sort numbers for pricing. Even though it was very cold in that room, he would tell his co-workers that I was sick and he was taking me to the Doctor.

We would leave at noon time and then there would be no memory for the next 3 days. I know it was 3 days because the note my mother wrote for me to give my teacher always said that I was absent with a 3 day flu.

Other things were almost life-long inexplicable fears and reactions to things that are otherwise pretty much commonplace. I still can't light a match but do ok with a lighter.

The fear with an unlighted match in my hand is overwhelming panic and terror feeling very young.
There are many others, too long to list here but they are this specific rather than general.

Recognition of ritual abuse came later in adulthood during a support group for sexual abuse survivors. We, as a group of survivors, were reading and working out of a book together.
There were lists for identifying sexually abused girls and boys and then a chapter and list for identifying ritual abuse.

All our fears were listed, our reactions, our body pains. All never had explanation before were now explained within the context of ritual abuse and as things fell into place, things began to make sense. Our reaction to this was more, *"Oh no, no, that can't be so!"* then it was the *"Ahhh, now it makes sense."*
For us, memories have surfaced more in an age-based chronological order with only few exceptions, i.e. related issues at a later age.

**Ian, an eleven year old child, shares his experience:** I always knew I had inside people.
I could see them and talk to them. One time, I remembered something, and two nights later, one of my inside people told my leader that I remembered, it was an inside kid who "squealed" on me.

They hit me, and then they shocked me, yelling at me I was to never remember, ever, or it would be worse for me. They then made me run, shooting bullets over my head, and laughing. I was really afraid then, when I first remembered again, when I got away from them. I was sure someone was going to come and get me, or hurt me. In fact, at night, I need someone with me so I can fall asleep. Night is the worst, because that is when we would go to meetings. Daytime is great for me.

**I also remembered gradually:** I had struggled with depression all of my life, but without a reason. I was labeled "endogenous" depression.

My ex-wife and I entered marriage counseling for conflicts. One day the therapist told me, "Won't it be good when the tremendous guilt that I see in you is gone." Guilty was out then, and I ran to a corner and crouched, saying "But if the guilt is gone, then I will be gone."

I then had a spontaneous memory of being hurt. The counselor had no idea what it was, and neither did I. That night, when I got home, while washing the dishes, I remembered my father abusing me.

I ran into my bedroom, stuffed a pillow in my mouth, and screamed as the memory came out. The rage, the hurt, the pain were all there. As time went on, other memories came forward, all spontaneously, usually at home.

I had always remembered my family's dysfunctionality: that my stepfather was an alcoholic, that my mother would beat her children, that my sister and brothers and I all tried to commit suicide many times growing up.

They had to cut my 8 year old brother down when he tried to hang himself. But other things I had blocked, because it hurt too much until I felt safer and was older, able to deal with it.

**Frank remembers:** I knew I was different. I would find things in my room that I had never bought, or would wake up in a strange city with no idea how I got there, would find out I had a job for several months, a bank account, even a girlfriend!

I moved around a lot, was afraid to get close to anyone, or they would find out my "secret". But one day, I was in drug rehab several years ago, and it happened...

My grandfather, one of my biggest perpetrators died, and I had flashback after flashback about him. I was given his masonic ring, and just looking at it, I remembered more. I went into therapy, and right away inside other people came out and started talking too. They figured that once he was dead, it was safe to talk.

**Alex, a survivor from the West Coast, shares:**
I had no idea that it was happening until last year when I started to remember.

I'm over 50, so there's a lot to remember! I don't talk about this with my family, I don't want to hurt them. I have all of this stuff about my life growing up that makes sense now.

I always knew my family wasn't normal, that things weren't right. I always had a lot of rage, I would throw things against the wall and scream and yell without knowing why.

But now, I'm finding out where the rage came from. I am getting better now, and feel better than I ever had in my life, because before all that rage was bottled up inside, and now it is getting released and healed.

Someday I will tell my sister, because I want her to get out too, but it isn't time yet. I need to heal more.

As clearly illustrated by these accounts, many survivors HAVE remembered some things all of their life - or had indications that something traumatic happened. Others have progressed through a more gradual process of remembering.

All, however, are courageously working at dealing with some of the most overwhelming abuse that a young child or adult can experience (and still survive): Ritual Abuse.

I am greatly inspired by their courage and honesty in sharing here.

# Survivors Speak Out On Dissociation: Part One

One of the most lingering effects of ritual abuse in a survivor's life is the reality of dissociation. Dissociation can take many forms, and describes a complex continuum of methods to cope psychologically with intense pain.

Ritual abuse is some of the most horrendous psychological pain and trauma that a human being can face and survive. Often coping with its effects manifests in the form of P.T.S.D. (*post-traumatic stress disorder*) and D.I.D (dissociative identity disorder, formerly known as M.P.D).

DID has caused some controversy in the media: is it real, does it exist? The DSMIV (Diagnostic and Statistical Manual of Mental Disorders, fourth edition, published by the American Psychiatric Association) certainly recognizes it as a reality, and defines it as: The presence of two or more distinct identities or personality states (each with its own relatively enduring pattern of perceiving, relating to, and thinking about the environment and self). At least two of these identities or personality states recurrently take control of the person's behavior. Inability to recall important personal information that is too extensive to be explained by ordinary forgetfulness.

The disturbance is not due to the direct physiological effects of a substance (e.g., blackouts or chaotic behavior during Alcohol Intoxication) or a general medical condition (e.g., complex partial seizures).

Note: In children, the symptoms are not attributable to imaginary playmates or other fantasy play. Dissociative Identity Disorder is also referred to as Multiple Personality Disorder.

*Note: I find it extremely interesting that supposed "syndromes" such as "false memory" are not listed in the largest book for diagnosing psychological disorders in the world; perhaps because there is absolutely NO objective evidence for the reality of this supposed syndrome?

But what is it like to live with the lasting effects of trauma? In my survey, I asked survivors to share what the reality is like for them, as they deal with DID in their life.

I believe that their insights and experiences as well as courage in coping with the effects of ritual abuse in day to day life speaks far more than any scholarly definitions.

**Ellen, a survivor of cult abuse**, is not DID but describes the symptoms of PTSD that she experienced when first getting out of a cult group: When I was initially out of the cult I would feel waves of terror going through my body.

There was nothing that I could do to relieve this. I just had to wait it out. These terror waves would come often during the times that the cult was "praying". I slept very little the first year that I was out and still have trouble getting quality sleep.

That first year I would doze and then awaken in terror with the programming of the cult going through my mind……the warnings of disaster and hell, etc. I would sometimes experience darkness surrounding my bed. I was terrified of the cult coming to kidnap me or to harm my daughter.

It was difficult for me to focus with all of this going on. I would have floating episodes and lose touch with what was happening around me. I had been programmed to never speak of the inner workings of the cult or any peculiarities with the leaders. To talk was quite a battle. Once I told someone, I would be up all night trying to work through the fear from breaking the silence which had been imposed upon me. I would often be in a state of full blown panic. I had also been programmed to "never leave my post"……. so I tended to isolate.

It was a major battle to go anywhere. When I did go anywhere, I was fearful of running into a member of the cult. I was programmed to perform ritualistic "prayers" every hour.

I no longer performed these rituals; but had to work through lots of guilt feelings and the fear of Satan attacking me because I did not do as told. The doubts that maybe I had left the only group to lead the Church and the world into the new era would flood me.

I could almost hear the voice of the leader telling me why the bizarre things that were done in the cult were valid. I had to work hard to function since my thoughts were scattered and confused. It took a long time before I could shed some of the props of this cult……. like wearing a rosary with a crucifix around my neck. I feared that if I took them off that Satan would attack.

**Joanne, another survivor**, describes her reaction to her recent diagnosis of DID: Just been diagnosed with it recently and still coming to terms with it, and having a lot of problems with it too, can't even admit to people who know and are aware (like psychiatrists) of what is going on. Nobody other than my therapist and psychiatrist know of my diagnosis, but will only talk about it with my therapist as I know she doesn't judge me in any way.

My alters (and I hate that word too) have only just begun to make their presence before other people, usually it's when I'm just with my kids or by myself (especially driving), although for a number of years I have been aware of the voices inside my head and I thought I was going crazy.

Constantly asked about voices but always denied it because I felt that it was a sign of madness basically, but they were always referring to schizophrenia voices as in auditory hallucinations and not the voices in my head.

Sketch drawn by an alter of a girl rescued from a life inside the Illuminati

# Survivors Speak Out On Dissociation Part Two:

**Frank, a male survivor of ritual abuse both in the U.S. and Canada**, shares what being DID means to him: Being DID has made me feel distrustful of people at times. There was so much hurt to me, and that's why I dissociated, so my protectors don't trust a lot.

It has made me hate God at times, too, since I wonder why I have to have this inside, why I have to deal with it. It isn't always easy, trust me.

One good thing: at work, I can work longer and harder than most people, because there are more of me! I work outside in the hot sun, so that helps. Also, I have lots of interests, more than you would expect, since so many inside people like different things. It's never boring, never, inside.

I have always had a valley inside, since I was little, peopled with animals, dragons, and people that comforted me when I was going through the worst times.
The animals inside still have trouble believing that they are part of a human being; they protected me through so much that it was easier pretending that I was an animal than a person.

**Abigail, a survivor of ritual abuse**, discusses the effects of being DID in her life: We were preliminary diagnosed with DID in 1993 and then officially in 1995. Up until diagnosis, nothing made much sense. We would have what we called circle days where you start your day doing something and at the end of the day you're right back where you started.

We suffered more from the lack of knowledge and understanding and were the target of much verbal abuse, loss of friends, lacked defenses against abuse to even recognize it, extremely low self-esteem, couldn't account for time or things said or done or not done and suffered much verbal degradation and recrimination for 'mistakes'. What couldn't be explained was taken on as something that was our fault.

After the diagnosis, a lot of this has remained the same except, now I recognize abuse and will fight to get to the position to stand up against it. When I've lost time, etc. internal communication helps me put the pieces together. We (me and my others) don't regularly work cooperatively together but we do more of that now and days go much smoother for the most part. Circle days are becoming rarer, especially as integration takes place.

Self-esteem is at a better level but not where it needs to be to be called healthy. but it's getting there.
Strategies to cope/help are making sure I listen to my others and communicate with them. Making time for my others to orient with the present and find or fulfill a dream of theirs before they integrate.

Notes and keeping calendars especially. I keep a calendar on the wall in my room. Those write on kinds. I keep a small calendar with me to write appointments in when I'm at therapy, drs. etc. I keep an organizer to keep track of everything, calendar, lists, phone numbers, expenses, etc. and I keep a calendar and note pad in my car.

At the end of the day or beginning of the day, I review all these to update them and then list out what my day holds even to the most minute detail such as 6am - take a shower.

My struggles are identifying boundaries and maintaining them. I have a very demanding wife and very demanding children who are adults but living at home. I struggle with the perception of everything having to be perfect and perfectly done because I fear punishment, rejection, verbal abuse, emotional detachment, etc. from others.

I'm like a tightly wound clock just about every day. I can't think of any joys being DID outside of finding people through the internet that are like me and we can share and identify with each other, encouraging each other as we heal. Humor? Well after my diagnosis and telling my husband and kids about it and what it means.

About a year later, my son was cleaning his closet and decided that he didn't have enough room, nor did he want any of his friends to see that he had a couple of suits in his closet. So he put them in mine.

Learning some of the signs of multiplicity, varying clothes being one of them, you can imagine my expression and reaction at finding a couple of men's suits in my closet! I was completely flabbergasted!

My son, seeing my distress, quickly told me what he had done and why they were there. That provided some relief except for a male alter about my son's size took a real liking to the suits, shoes included. I have more female alters so out in public, we over power his desire so we don't look completely out of whack!

**Christine, a survivor of ritual abuse**, discusses her DID: I have been working hard to bring everyone together. I admire what my people took for me so much. If they hadn't been there, I would never have survived, I would be a blithering idiot or psychotic.

I have told them thank you many, many times. It's hard, though, when parts who were so invested in the cult, in working for them and thought they had moved up the ladder, got pissed at me for leaving.

Or when untrusting parts try to sabotage therapy, or friendships, because some of them to this day don't trust ANYONE and probably never will. I am co-conscious with most, if not all, of them, though, and they cooperate so I can work and be a Mom.

I think some of them are really cool, especially Brogan. He's my favorite, he has an Irish accent and is really smart and helps me out if I need good advice. It's neat to be able to ask myself for advice when I need it, and get an answer!

Not all survivors of ritual abuse dissociate or become DID.

**In response to the question "If present, how has dissociation affected you" Eric responds**: N/A.
Although the cracks are there, I never fragmented in a significant way.

**Ian, an eleven year old survivor of ritual abuse**, shares a younger perspective: My protectors are cool. When I was in California, Jason, one of my inside people who was taught to fight by the cult, could beat ANYONE in a fight. I got into lots of fights at school, because if someone teased me or upset me, Jason would come out.

Now, I don't fight as much, I get along with people better. I'm the one who goes to school and does stuff, and he doesn't have to step in for me.

But I worry that I'm getting weaker, that I can't fight as good since he doesn't come out as much. I also have someone inside, Mei, who can do karate. It is awesome when he comes out, because I never learned it, but he sure does. He won't let anyone ever beat me up.

# How The Cult Programs People: Part One

This chapter is a very difficult one personally.
Why? Because it touches on some of the things that I am most ashamed of in my own life. I used to be a cult programmer, or "trainer" as they are called, and here I will share some of what I did and/or witnessed while in that role. I also went through these things as a child, so this article is also quite autobiographical as well.

Autobiography can be a moment of boasting, of quiet joy, or intense pain. Mine falls deeply into the latter category, to say the least. But I am hoping with all of my heart that sharing my pain will help others avoid this pain, or will help society better understand what survivors go through.
This article will in no means be a complete treatment of the subject.

Cult programming is a complex subject, one that would fill volumes and volumes if dealt with beyond a surface description. Also, I can only write from my own experiences with the Illuminati, which is one of several groups operating today, and about the techniques used in the Washington, DC area and in San Diego, Ca. Other localities might use very different techniques.
This article does NOT take the place of advice from a qualified therapist, and is meant to be informative only.

If you are a survivor of cult abuse, please be aware that this article and the subject it covers could be extremely triggering, and keep yourself safe.

Why does the cult train or program people? In earlier articles, I have mentioned the goals they have of:
- making money
- total secrecy
- & unquestioning loyalty in their members

Programming, or training, is one method that the cult has found that will ensure that these goals are met.
In the Illuminati, the programmers are called "trainers" because the belief is that they are not abusing, but "training" the future generation.

The trainers actually believe that they are doing a good thing, "strengthening" the children, helping them to get in touch with their "potential."

Some of these methods have been around for hundreds, perhaps thousands of years. I will divide cult programming into five major categories, and address each one separately:
1. training to be silent
2. training to be strong
3. training to be loyal
4. training for jobs in the group
5. spiritual training

The first category, **training to be silent**, begins at a very early age, frequently even pre-verbal. This is accomplished in several ways, depending upon the child and the trainer, and can include:
Being asked after a ceremony what the child saw and heard.

The very young child may just say "bad things", and is punished severely and brutally, and told that no, they didn't really see those things. This is repeated at frequent intervals, until the child learns to block the ceremonies.

*Often, a "protector" or "guardian" alter will be created from the abuse, whose job is to ensure that the child will not remember what is seen.*

This protector is told that if the child does remember, brutal punishment will follow.

Another method involves electroshocking the child, and placing them into a deep hypnotic trance, where they are told that they will not remember what they have seen or heard, that it is all "just a bad dream." The child WANTS to forget, and will be eager to agree.

Psychological torture may be used: mock burials, being placed in cages, abandonment, being hung over a bridge, with the child later being "rescued" and told that if they ever tell, they will be returned to the punishment.

Being forced to watch mock or real punishment or killing of a traitor who "told". When I was four years old, I was forced to watch a woman be skinned alive. Her crime: she disclosed to an outside person "family business". Talking to those outside the group is considered one of the worst crimes or betrayals a person can commit.

A "traitor's death" is one of the most horrifying imaginable, and will vary from crucifixion upside down, to other gruesome scenarios. Young children do not forget seeing these things, and they become convinced that not disclosing is the safest way to continue living.
These set ups are done to ensure that a young child will not disclose the criminal activities that they are seeing in the course of group activities, or even as an adult, when they are more actively engaged in them.

Another set up also is frequently done: The "no one will believe you scenario" (this is usually done with school age children). The child is told repeatedly that even if they DO disclose that no one will believe them. The child is taken by a mental hospital, or even taken to visit an inmate briefly.

Later, the child is told that people who disclose are considered "crazy" and sent to institutions, where they are punished severely and can never leave. These lies are told to reinforce once again the importance of not telling.

Another set up may include the "everyone is part of it" set up. The child is told that actually, everyone is secretly part of the group, but people are just good pretenders during the daytime.

The child will be taken to dinner at a member's house, where everyone acts normal, then later a ritual or ceremony follows. The child will then believe that there is no escape, since everyone is part of the group. Since most of the adults close to his/her parents are part of the group, there is no reason to question the logic of what they are told.

The set ups and psychological conditioning to not tell are endless, limited only by the cruel creativity of the adults around the child.

**Training to be strong:**
This type of training will also begin at a very young age, often in the toddler years.

The child is put through a series of conditioning exercises whose goals are to: increase the pain threshold, increase physical fitness, increase dissociative ability, force quick memorization of material (school age child), and create fear as well as the desire to please.

These exercises might include: mock military training, with marches, and playing "prisoner and guard"; shocking the child; physical abuse and torture, drugging the child or adult; placing the child into cages, where they are shocked; deprivation of food, water, or sleep; abandonment for varying amounts of time; forcing the child to watch brutalities and the abuse of others.

The child is taught to be completely silent during the training and to endure it without question. If the child screams, they are punished extremely, and told that this is "weakness". The child is taught to fear their own emotions, since they are quickly and mercilessly punished for expressing them. The scenes go on and on, these are just a few methods used.

**Training to be loyal**
The third area of training encompasses a broad area of behavior. Loyalty involves agreement with the group, espousing its doctrines and beliefs. This training is at times more subtle, but it also is one of the most powerful *pulls* to the group.

Adults in the group model complete loyalty to their children. Getting out, leaving, or questioning the group's beliefs are rarely or never seen, and the retaliation for questioning those in authority is quick and brutal.

A person seen questioning the rightness of things, or balking at doing their job might be sent in for "retraining", ie being shocked and tortured back into submission.

But often adults often believe the goals of the group are GOOD. They are convinced that they are helping the children, and in classes children are taught why these beliefs are good; about the coming agenda for the group, where they will be the new leaders.

Much discussion of the time when the group will "rule the world" is done, to show that they are actually ushering in a new order, when things will be "better for all."

*Status and leadership* are held out as carrots to group members to work harder and achieve. The rewards of leadership, of moving up, are real, and every member tries to advance themselves. Being higher means less abuse, being able to order others around, and more control in a life that has had precious little control.

Set ups, where a child is allowed to sit in a leader's seat, and is told that one day they, too, will lead, are often done, to increase the loyalty to the group. *Awards ceremonies*, where those who do well receive badges, jewels, or other rewards in front of others, are frequently done.

A child who works hard, who performs well, is praised and allowed to join the adults for coffee or a meal, while the other children look enviously on.

As the child progresses through the system, they do move higher, since adults are always higher than a young child. Now the child who is growing older can boss the younger children, can tell them what to do, can even abuse them with the approval of the adults around.

Being very young means being very abused and wounded in these groups; growing older means the chance to finally act out on the rage the abuse has caused.

The child begins to identify with the abusing adults, since they are hurt less, and becomes invested in a cult identity as a perpetrator. This is strongly encouraged, as long as the perpetration is not directed at members older or higher than the child or teen.

*This locks the child in*, as having become "*one of them*", like them, and the child is bonded to the group by his/her own guilt and shame, as well as the need for outlets for rage and pain that the group allows. The child may feel ambivalence, but also extreme loyalty.
The group or trainer will also tell the child that they are the only ones that really know the child, having seen them act out. That they are the only ones who could see this, and still love them, that *no one loves them the way "family" does.*

The child is *bombarded* with messages that the group truly accepts them, all of them, knowing the worst about them, to cement the loyalty.
The group uses sophisticated techniques based on behavioral psychology to ensure that the child/teen/adult will not even consider leaving the group.

Another form of loyalty programming is *"specialness programming"*. This is where the child is told by the adults or trainer that: they are "high", hidden royalty, or a "hidden" or "adopted" member of a high family line.

The child may be told that they will be a world leader who is hidden for now; a special CIA agent, or *"one in a thousand, a wunderkind"* who will lead as an adult. They may be told that there are very few like them;

that no one else can fill their special role; that they are of a special bloodline that is unbroken for thousands of years.

This is to increase the child's loyalty to the group. If the child believes that they are merely waiting now for the revealing of their "true, elevated status" one day, they will be much more likely to develop loyalty bonds to the group.

This is one of the cruelest tricks the group plays on children, since they have deprived them of normal love and caring, and instead replace it with a false sense of "specialness" or status.

Very few survivors getting out of these groups believe that they were low; almost all believe that they were high, or were adopted, but their real family is high, for this reason.

This was done to me as well, and as an adult, when I had to tell lies like this to children, I became more and more disillusioned with the group, one of many reasons I finally chose to leave it. I could no longer bear to listen to other trainers and scientists laughing about the gullibility of the people they worked with.

I had once been a child, eager to please, and gullible myself. I had believed the lies, and it was a rude awakening to find out I was NOT adopted from a royal line, as I had been told. That

I had been manipulated and deceived intentionally to increase my loyalty to the group.

# How The Cult Programs People: Part Two

**Training for jobs in the cult**
The fourth category of training or programming is towards doing a job in the cult.

Each person has a specific job(s) that they are given, from earliest childhood on in the Illuminati. Often, the child is tested at intervals during their early years for aptitude and ability. The parent's status, as well as the child's intelligence and dissociative ability, will also factor in to the final role.

- Jobs in the cult might include, but are not limited to: cleaners (clean up after ceremonies, set up)
- spiritual (lead meetings, high priest or priestess, or acolytes)
- punishers (punish members who are out of line or make mistakes)
- scholars (learn cult history, ancient languages, do readings and history set ups)
- prostitutes
- couriers
- assassins
- trainers
- scientists (trained in behavioral sciences)
- doctors, nurses, medical personnel military leader (for military exercises)

The list goes on and on. The Illuminati are a complex group, with interwoven roles.

The amount of training the child will need for their adult role will often depend upon the complexity of the final job. Sometimes, jobs overlap, or a person will be cross trained for several.
A child raised with child pornography may as an adult be taught to run a video camera, for example.
A nurse or doctor may also help as a trainer, or learn sciences.
A person trained as a military leader in the group will frequently also have assassin training (**MK-ULTRA**) as well.

These jobs are taught using *operant conditioning principles* from early childhood on. The child is shown how the role is done by an adult or older teen, this is known as "modeling", and the behavior is observed. The child will also see the jobs done in the course of being part of the group. After the behavior is modeled, the child is told that they will be learning it. Clear directions on what is expected are given.

**How it's done:**
*The job is broken down into steps*, and each step is put in sequentially.

The child may be shocked, or tortured, to create a "blank state" or *tabula erasa* personality who will do anything asked of them.

Then, the behavior is elicited. If the child does well, they are *praised and petted*. If they do not, they are punished severely. The child learns it is much less painful to demonstrate the asked for behavior.

Afterwards, once the behavior is shown, the trainer "bonds" with the child, praising them, telling them how valuable they are, and what a wonderful job they are doing for "family". The child is given the validation and caring that they so desperately crave, and a trauma bond is created.

*The personality state in the child will WANT to do well*, it has bonded with the trainer or adult, and seeks approval again and again. This bond will last into adulthood, and often the personality states that seek approval will stay in a young state inside of an adult body. After the "job" is done, they will come out and still ask for approval at times. Another reward for the adult will be perceived moving up in status if they do well.

**Spiritual Training**
At its foundation, the Illuminati are an intensely spiritual group. They worship ancient deities including those of Babylon and Assyria (***Baal and Ashtoth***) and of
Egypt (***Ra, Horus, Isis***, etc.).

They believe that the spiritual is the root that feeds its many manifestations today. Because of this, all children will undergo some form of spiritual training, or programming. This is to ensure their bonding to the group as well as coerce or frighten them into fearing leaving.

Spiritual programming begins with the first ceremony that an infant is taken to, when they are dedicated to a deity, or even prenatally, when the fetus may be dedicated in utero to the "mother of heaven" or other deities.

The young toddler's world will include seeing the adults around him/her going to ceremonies, and they will be forced to imitate the activities they see.

There may be blood baptisms, using animals. There will be many, many dedications and rites, including the passing on of familial spirits from mother or father or grandparent, to the young child. These can be intensely frightening experiences.

I do not want to argue the existence of the demonic here, but I will say that the group certainly does believe it is real, and that the manifestations I've seen at these rites go beyond that which can be explained scientifically or rationally!

As a child, I believed intensely that the demonic was real, as did all of the adults around me.
There will be ceremonies in which the demonic is invoked, and manifestations of power, including channeling, foretelling, or psychic slaying of animals. Objects may be moved, or a tree felled, using psychic abilities/demonic help.

Adults will be involved in power battles. "Reading" people will be done. And in all training/programming sessions, the demonic will be invoked to help the trainer, to guide them, or to give energy to the programming being done. Often, before important programming sessions, trainers will perform a ceremony asking for demonic aide.

*The child will be told that the demonic has been placed within them, and that if they ever try to leave, or break the programming, the demonic will "kill them."* The terrified child believes this.

"Psychic surgery" may be done, where *an "all seeing eye" is placed in the abdomen, and the child is told that the "eye" can see them wherever they go*, and will tell them if the child tries to escape or questions the group.

Implants may be placed, small thin metal rods, used to call up demonic forces. If the person tries to leave, or break programming, the implants are to cause intense pain or torment.

A child will be forced to participate in rites, including the mutilation or killing of animals or even an infant (although some of these are set ups, using a corpse, as mentioned in a previous chapter).

Visits to sacred groves or holy areas may occur,
One such famous grove visited by many of the rich and powerful is *Bohemian grove*, where statues to the deities are garlanded with flowers and robed followers chant before a rite.

In some groups, the child will be turned against Christianity with purposeful programming. Since Christianity is the antithesis of the dark occult practices of the Illuminati, they often will want their members to be unable to reach out for the hope that it offers.

Special sessions may include torturing a child. Often, the child will cry out for help, or to God. At that point, the programmer will tell the child, *"God has abandoned you, He could never love you! That is why you are being hurt. If He was so powerful, He could stop this."* They will even ask the child to ask God to stop it.

The child will, and then the trainer will hurt the child more. This will create a deep sense of hopelessness and despair in the child. He or she will truly believe they have been abandoned by God, that He has a deaf ears to their call for help.

The child may be tortured or shocked when the name "Jesus" is said, to create a barrier to hearing His name.

Hymns may be used in sessions, to create aversion.
Spiritual programming will cover a variety of areas. I have only briefly covered some of them here.

This has been an overview of some of the areas that the cult, specifically the Illuminati, program people in. It is by no means all-inclusive, and there will be many, many variations in specific techniques used. Also, I am sure that different groups use different methods.

If a survivor has memories that are *different* from what I have described here, they should believe their own memories. I am only sharing *what I do remember* about the Illuminati, the specific group that I was associated with, in the Washington, DC and the San Diego, Ca. areas from 1957 until 1995.

My hope is that this article will help those who work with survivors, or who wish to know more about how these groups operate, understand more about them. That it will increase compassion for the immense amount of suffering that a member of these groups undergoes and for the struggle, once they leave, to overcome years of conditioning from infancy on. It takes tremendous courage to leave such a group, to say "no" to the pull of all the person has known, to decide to question values that lay unquestioned for years. To look at the pain underlying the programming, and to grieve over the manipulations and betrayals that have occurred from infancy on.

# Breaking Free Of The Cult

One of the most important but also one of the most difficult steps that a survivor of generational cult abuse can make is the decision to leave the group that they were raised in.

Those who are naive, or don't understand the nature of being raised in a group may wonder, "Why would it be hard to leave abusers? Wouldn't a person WANT to get away?"

The reality is a little more complicated, and my hope is that this article will help both survivors, therapists, and support people as well as those who wish to understand ritual abuse have a better idea of the issues that survivors getting out face, as well as some helpful ideas on safety.

**BARRIERS TO GETTING OUT:**
I want to address these first. This is not to be discouraging, but to help identify the issues involved. If a person understands the obstacles to leaving, they can then begin developing a plan to overcome these problems.
Paramount is PERSONAL SAFETY. Threats against those who try to leave are real, and the person has been conditioned by witnessing the punishment of those who have tried to leave or even punishment for questioning the group or its leader.

The psychological intimidation built in over a lifetime is real, and the person must be assured of physical safety before they *will ever* consider leaving a group that could literally brutally punish them (or worse) for attempting to leave.

It is very, very difficult to consider leaving, or worse yet, to discuss leaving in therapy, then have reporter alters "telling on" the person to the group leaders. This happened to me in San Diego, and the results were devastating.

My inside parts who wanted to get out, who were working hard in therapy, were being physically brutalized at night to punish them for talking and remembering.

This created a great deal of what therapists call *"intrasystem conflict"*, to put it mildly. Some parts became hostile at other parts who wanted to leave, and they began punishing them as well. In addition, *suicide commands were put in by my head trainer!*

The reality is that if a person truly wants to break free, they may become "expendable" in the eyes of the cult, or considered a security risk, and will often be told to simply *commit suicide*.

In breaking free, a survivor and their support system needs to be ever vigilant of this reality.
To not be aware that this is/could be happening will cause therapy to be sabotaged.

Even if the person finds physical safety, other issues need to be addressed as well. One is ISOLATION. Often in transgenerational groups, the survivor's entire family of origin, as well as their closest friends, and spouse will be part of the group (the *Illuminati arrange almost 100% of their marriages*, I have never personally known of a person in the group whose spouse was not also involved, as well as the children.) These members of the immediate family will be the ones most likely to reaccess the survivor. I will give a personal example, again.

When I lived in San Diego, I was in therapy for DID. All that I remembered at the time was a period of three years of ritual abuse with my father and his mother. I *thought* my mother "rescued" me from him when she divorced him. But my therapy was at a standstill. The more I remembered, the WORSE I became, and decompensated.
I would go to therapy, talk, try to help my inside people, then would feel immense panic and fear, as well as suicidal urges afterwards.

It wasn't until later that I learned that my mother was my cult trainer the first five years of my life; that my wife was even taking me back to cult meetings where I was severely punished and programmed to NOT tell in therapy.

Once I had physical safety, and broke off contact with cult all members, I immediately began stabilizing psychologically. But the price was high.

My wife divorced me when I told her I remembered; I told her her cult name, mine and the children's, thinking she, too would want to get out.

Instead, I lost custody of my two children in a long and expensive court battle with a justice system whose attitude was that ritual abuse was a delusion! (Fortunately, 1 1/2 years ago, my ex decided to leave the group, in part because of seeing me alive and well and working full time; and I now have full custody of my children, who are doing well in therapy).

I am sharing this to help people be aware that the price of leaving a transgenerational group may include (although each situation is different): giving up contact with members of family of origin giving up contact with close friends (the survivor has often been surrounded by cult members in their social group, including at church; my five closest friends were all members of the Illuminati and I had no idea).

Often "cult twins" are best friends in day time life learning that a spouse and children are all members. The enormous psychological pain of giving up these relationships will often make it difficult for the survivor, but if they continue in them, the chances of being reaccessed are great.

MOST REACCESSING OF THE SURVIVOR COMES FROM MEMBERS OF THEIR IMMEDIATE FAMILY. This is one of the hardest tasks for the survivor to attempt as he or she learns good boundaries.

What those boundaries need to be will differ from person to person, and their individual situation.

Another real, and powerful pull back to the cult, will come from the perception that NEEDS inside the person are being met by the group. The person will likely be dissociative, if they have been raised in a transgenerational group, and they will often have alters inside who have never known or experienced the abuse, who will be considered "high alters" inside.

These part's reality is that they were praised and told that they were special, often unaware or not caring that other alters inside endured the abuse.

These higher alters may identify strongly with their perps and are often the alters that want recontact with the group and help drive internal recontact programming.

Frequently, when a person leaves a cult group, there is a real period of grieving. Social relations have been changed. Alters with special needs will feel that their needs are no longer being met, whether for belonging, for sexual activity, for power, or other personal agendas. The survivor needs to recognize this reality.

A person will often unconsciously recontact a group if they believe that deep needs are being met by this group. Teaching themselves to meet their needs in a healthy and appropriate way will take time and patience, working with a qualified safe therapist who understands ritual abuse.

There may be PROGRAMMING instilled to recontact the group. The survivor will need to identify if this is present, and take steps with the help of their therapist and support system to deactivate it.

## IDEAS ON BREAKING FREE
While breaking free can be difficult, as I have discussed above, it is possible to escape a cult group and maintain personal safety. I will share from both my personal experience and that of other survivor's things which have proven helpful in breaking free.

### 1. Safe outside accountability:
If the person attempting to break free can live with someone who is NOT a member of the group, who is a safe person, that will increase their own personal safety exponentially.

Cult members from groups such as the Illuminati will often hesitate to harass or try to access someone while they are with a safe person, one who is not dissociative. One of the most dangerous set ups is when a survivor is living alone, or in isolation, or if they talk long walks at night or in areas where there are no people around.

Abductions, kidnappings, or reaccessing may occur in these situations. The more safe outside accountability the survivor sets up around them, the less chance that this will occur.

This could mean a safe room mate who is not dissociative; staying with members of a church, finding a safe house, or even a women's shelter (although there are reports that some shelters and safe houses are being infiltrated by cult members as well; the survivor needs to be cautious in where they go and whom they trust).

One grievous problem today is the relative lack of safe houses for people trying to break free of the cult.

One precaution: often survivors will quickly make friends with other survivors, since they feel isolated and alone without the cult group. The survivor may want to exercise caution about rushing into friendships, since many survivors, especially at the beginning of their therapeutic process, may still be in contact with a cult group.

Each person will need to make decisions on an individual basis in this area to maintain safety.

**2. A good therapist:**
There are excellent therapists who specialize in working with ritual abuse. While qualifications among therapists will vary, a survivor can try locating one by contacting reputable people in the field for referrals, by contacting the ISSD, or by referral from people the survivor trusts.

Not all therapists who advertise that they work with DID are safe, but if the survivor checks out references and asks careful questions, their chances of finding a good therapist will be higher.

I have personally had therapists who worked with DID who ranged from:

- a pastor in San Diego who told me he could "integrate me" in 3 months if I had enough faith (this did NOT happen and was completely unrealistic);
- a therapist who was the referral for a national christian counseling group for DID who told me that her brother had tortured her as a child, and that I was not DID because she, the therapist, often "lost time" and went through personality changes and SHE wasn't DID
  (I stopped seeing her after two visits);
- a therapist associated with a ritual abuse and trauma program who was very knowledgeable, compassionate, and helpful!

The last one, needless to say, was the only helpful one in my healing process!

A good therapist will be knowledgeable about DID and ritual abuse; will BELIEVE the survivor and not discount memories shared; will help the survivor with achieving inter-system communication; and will have good boundaries.

A therapist like this is well worth the time and effort it will take to locate, and can help the survivor immensely in the process of breaking free of cult control.

### 3. Stopping telephone access:
The telephone is one of the first avenues used to access someone trying to leave the cult. Hang up calls; calls with tones played, or with a tape or hidden message, will be used.

Also, *survivors often have recontact programming to phone their trainer or family members*. One way to deal with this: take the telephone and lock it in the trunk of the car. This way, if a part of the survivor tries to get up in the middle of the night and make a phone call, they will have to find the car keys; unlock the trunk, plug the phone in, and make the call.

Hopefully, the survivor will have time to "switch out" another part who will stop the call, especially as they work in therapy to block cult access.

Use of caller i.d.; answering services, or an answering machine (calls can be checked with a therapist or support person present in case an access message is left) can also help prevent phone access.

Eventually, the survivor will find the parts inside with a vested interest in recontact, and can negotiate with them not to call or recontact.

An unlisted phone number may help for a short period of time. Phone numbers can also be blocked to prevent calls from certain numbers, such as those of known perps.

## 4. Alarm systems:
Some survivors will have alarm systems to prevent unauthorized entry into their home. Again, this is best combined with a safe living situation, as described above.
These alarm systems can also be coded by an outside safe person so that the survivor themself cannot decode it if internal parts try to leave in the middle of the night.

## 5. Share info with safe outsiders:
This could be a lock box with names of perps, and information, which the safe person will distribute if the survivor is harmed or access is attempted. The survivor can then mail a letter to this effect to known perps, to help prevent accessing or abducting of the survivor.

## 6. Go public
Some survivors have chosen to go public to maintain safety. The thought is that if they are harmed, they have shared enough info that an investigation will be done into the causes, and the cult group will risk further exposure, which they hate.

Sharing information with law enforcement, with legal advisors, therapists, social workers, and child protective services can all also help maintain safety, IF the law enforcement officers, etc. are not members of the group. The problem here is that at times, cult members will infiltrate legal and law enforcement organizations, even
CPS, to prevent cult members from escaping. The survivor will need to go to reputable, known safe people, if they choose to go this route.

### 7. Work on undoing recontact programming

This will take time, with a qualified therapist. It means looking at the trauma that placed the programming in, a difficult task psychologically. It will also mean addressing the powerful needs addressed above as well, and grieving when contact with cult members is stopped.

### 8. Prayer support

As a Christian, I believe that this can be a survivor's strongest protection. A strong, supportive faith system, and prayers for safety can protect the survivor during the spiritually and emotionally trying times while breaking free of the cult.

These are just a few ideas on breaking free. Many, many survivors have broken free, and have used their creativity and strength, as well as the help of noncult members who wish to help, to maintain safety.

My hope is that this article will be a beginning place for both survivors and their support people and therapists to look at maintaining safety. I welcome any comments or anecdotes' on ideas that other survivors and support people have found for maintaining safety.

# A Survivor's Testimony:

**Article by Kim Weston**
I wanted to share an article that I believe is both inspiring and courageous, by someone who is in the process of healing from ritual abuse.

This article is being reprinted here with the permission of the author, Kim Weston. My hope is that it will help educate as well as give hope to others.

**Note:**
**This article contains discussion of ritual abuse and Christianity.**

**A CASE REPORT OF DELIVERANCE**
My name is Kim Weston. I am a forty-four year old man living in Dallas, Texas. I am happily married; I practice medicine as a Physicians Assistant, and

I am a member of Hope Testimony Church. Over the past several years, I have also learned how very true it is that I am a Christian by choice.

In June 1997, I learned that I was DID. I learned almost immediately that I was born into a satanic family and was raised in the culture known as SRA. To say the least, my deliverance from this culture was a major test in my life. The past several years have been difficult, but I believe I was substantially resolved about three years ago.

But the crisis of my life has marked the beginning of an authentic faith in Jesus Christ as Redeemer and Lord of my life, something I have deeply desired but that has eluded me all my life.

This short essay is my testimony, which I first wrote in 1995. I want this to be an instructive piece for Shield of Faith Ministry of Nebraska, who has invited me to speak and share with them this coming May.

I, most of all, offer this as a testimony of the Lord God's love for me and for all the rest of the Body of His Son. I am utterly amazed at Him - Father, Son, and Holy Spirit - and His rightful commitment to His own glory as God, a glory that He delights to share with me as His son. Me, of all people!! *Amazing grace, indeed!*

In my satanic ancestry, I came from two families. My public family were hardy West
Texans who taught me how to tie my shoes, do arithmetic, be polite - all the normal things most parents do for their children.

A knowledgeable observer would have seen the depression, the switching, and the disordered attachment behaviors, but in a way I was fortunate. I escaped being misdiagnosed as ADD and placed on Ritalin. For all appearances, I was a typical (although very odd) child.

However, beneath this public veneer, I lived as a direct descendant of a very old culture, which has survived in an underground form for several thousand years, a culture as old as mankind itself.

In this culture, people worship Satan as God, and the form of the worship and the entire lifestyle, as old as it is, is steeped in deep violence. As a participant in this culture, I was exposed to every abuse, trauma, and demonization imaginable within Satanism.

The culture is unbelievably and ingeniously evil; virtually everything about this culture is humanly damaging. And I responded in the same way children do (and would) in this culture. I dissociated.

Over the course of my life I experienced trauma as an infant to sharpen my dissociative potential, coerced violence both as victim and perpetrator, high-tech medically-based mind control programming here in the US, often in government facilities and clinics, and at the Tavistock Institute in the UK, and participation (via indoctrination into the Kaballa, culminating in a series of occult initiations) into the oldest, most pristine form of Satanism, the old Sumero-Akkadian Babylonian mystery religion. Layer after layer, all these disaggregated identities were built and crafted to become my personality.

Inherent in this culture is the presence and power of demonic spirits, and they became an integral part of my life and even my being. In a culture addicted to power, demonic spirits offered the ultimate power trip. If, in American culture, people are addicted to comfort, status, and prestige, in satanic culture, people are addicted to demonic power.

Satanism has pervaded western civilization. Satanism is the foundation of all we would regard today as paganism in ancient and contemporary forms. It has been growing for thousands of years, quietly weaving its way through the very fabric of the culture and the power structures of the nations in the West. It has adherents in all walks of life, in all incomes, and all social strata. It has exerted a profound influence on the intellectual life of the west for the past several hundred years.

Their thoughts and writings have shaped Western civilization from the Greek philosophers through Augustine, Aquinas, the Christian mystics of the thirteenth century, and much of the charismatic movement of today.

Descartes, Spinoza, Kant, the philosophers of the Enlightenment. And many others arose from satanic culture. Polynesian religion, Animism, Spiritism, American Indian religion, Mayan and Incan culture, ancient Egyptian culture, and Greek religion all grew out of Satanism.

*To think that satanic culture is only about abuse is a fundamental misunderstanding of Satanism and the role of dissociation in human history.*

Satanism has influenced politics, economics, art and music, through the spiritual psychological process called dissociation, and dissociation is as old as human culture itself.

This was the culture in which I was born and raised. And to say the least, this culture is antithetical to the Kingdom of God, and I was born into the ongoing battle between these two cultures. Even though I was also a functioning Satanist, I was also a seminary graduate (M. Div. 1976).

While professing to be Christian, and my public life showed the discordance of living in irreconcilable cultures. My love for the Lord was hollow, as I wanted to love Him and be loved by Him deeply, but I was unable to resolve my fears and doubts as to His existence and character.

While my public life was filled with outward relative success, my spiritual and interpersonal life was marred with failure.

The emotional shock of learning of my SRA/DID was profound, but it launched me on a path which I could only call discipleship. For the first time in my life, being and becoming the Christian I wanted to be, took first priority in my life.

It would be very hard, very difficult work, but I knew that getting free of the occult and the dissociation was my work as a disciple of Jesus Christ and that I would have to do it as a Christian.

If I were to rely on the even best methods and techniques of psychology or psychiatry, neither I nor a traditional therapist would have enough money or lifetimes to work through this mess.

Even today I have yet to know of a traditional approach penetrating the deeper cores of an SRA personality. If I were to be free, I had no choice to be free except by Jesus Christ.

Because of this, I took my discipleship with Him extremely seriously. Time after time He called me to holiness and insisted on the power of His love - through the forgiveness in His Son - to deliver me from the power of sin.

Day after day, after work and in lieu of "living normally", I stayed home to read and pray, to exorcize demons and reclaim my humanity, to communicate and fuse with accessible self-states, and afterwards come to terms with the reality of my life. I read and went to conferences to learn all I could about MPD, ritual abuse, and the work of healing, so I could apply this to my own deliverance. I went to Church to hear from the Lord, since my Father chose to use "the folly of preaching" as the ultimate in cognitive restructuring.

I went to corporate prayer where the presence and the power of the Lord worked visible miracles in my and many other peoples' lives. And I scrutinized my entire life in the light of the Living Word of God. Every sin, whether from my conscious self or as passive influence from other self-states, was rigorously subjected to the sanctifying work of the Lord.

After all, SRA/DID is sin par excellence, and as a sinner, I needed repentance and forgiveness most of all. As it turns out for me, discipleship has been deliverance.

When I reached an impasse or when the obstacles were too difficult for me, I would schedule a session with my pastor, Doug Riggs, and the power and love of the
Lord God would come through this man.

Rather than do endless interviews with alters or focus on abreactive work, the Lord would lead us on deep penetrating raids down through my layers into the primal events of my personality. The work consisted of vigorous exorcism, prayer for my Father to connect me with my other self-states, and a Biblical existential counseling about the impact of SRA on my life in the light of the Person of Jesus Christ.

Through my pastor, the Lord could take me far deeper than I could go on my own. Through him, He could speak His specific, contemporary word of grace to me as a dissociated man. And through his voice and touch, my Father could be real to me. Many times the Lord gave my pastor knowledge or strategy that was essential in resolving those crises.

The Lord works though people like this (and many other great people in the Body of Christ) for people like me.
The Lord is not in the least intimidated by darkness; after all the Gospel is that He loved me while I was still in darkness.

The Lord has been doing all this in the setting of a small, apparently insignificant local Church of thirty or forty people (including children), most of whom are SRA or at least dissociative.

We had come together to live in such a way as to hasten the Lord's coming for His Bride, but we also had been constituted in the occult to frustrate the will of God for the Church and bring in the antichrist instead.

As Christians we have prayed for each other, counseled each other, and admonished each other, and as Satanists, we have controlled and done violence to each other.

In "working out our salvation with fear and trembling", many times we have been forced by the Living Word of God to remove planks from our own eyes while we fumbled to remove cinders from each other's eyes.

All this is the Lord's refining us into a repentant people. The Living Christ has worked in this Body Life, just like pre-crucifixion Capernaum or post- Pentecost Corinth.
So the Lord worked in the life of one of His disciples.

Bit by bit, my heavenly Father was progressively delivering me, literally, from the moral and demonic power of sin by the person of His Son, the Risen, and Living Jesus of Nazareth. All through the experience, I was becoming astounded at the grace and power of God through His Son.

After eighteen hard months of work and counseling, the multiplicity persisted. The Lord had told us to be bold. Both in what I read and in what I heard, I realized that my biggest obstacle was myself, not just the hidden internal me but the conscious external me.

Frankly, I was afraid to learn how bad I had been and perhaps still could be. So the Lord impressed me to confront those very things about myself that I feared the most.

It was worse than I had thought. My concept of SRA was that insane or frankly evil people took nice, good children and turned them into Satanists. I was wrong. Hiding under the surface layer that we had labored eighteen months to dismantle was the real, genuine core of my humanity as a Satanist.

The truth was that the defining reality of my childhood (perhaps fifty percent of my preschool waking hours) was being incested and indoctrinated into a Sodom and Gommorah culture within a brick West Texas two bedroom house; these aspects of myself had little need to be abused in ritual, as I already was living, growing, and worshiping in the 'normal' of an occult pagan culture.
All the splits and experiences I had recalled, renounced, and reconciled up to that point in the first eighteen months were but a window dressing - a protective, therapy-defeating maze to protect this central, substantial aspect of myself.

I had stepped into the living reality of my generational core of evil. It was more than merely a demonic deposit for me; it was my very world. In my being I was an historical descendant and perpetuator of my ancestors' incest, violence, and idolatry. And as such I was as intensely demonized as the worst of Canaanites.

The Lord's grace has been an amazing thing. Whether or not anyone else does, my God and Heavenly Father Himself absolutely believes in the efficacy of the sacrifice of His own Son on the cross for the totality of my evil.

As much as I have been repulsed and disgusted with myself, the Lord's love and kindness toward me did not change. Rather, it became richer, deeper, and more powerful.

The Lord Jesus refused to call my sin anything other than what it was; He allowed no excuses, He tolerated no irresponsibility on my part. He didn't need to cut me any slack or allow me to cut any for myself, since His sacrifice and new life was more than sufficient to deal with my sin.

So, I began to learn first-hand that evil isn't the greatest power in the cosmos. As the grace and power of God freed my faculties to hear and believe, I could grasp the larger picture of His relationship to me. Only with that encouragement could I continue looking at the truth of my life and continue on the path of deliverance.

This, then, was the structure the Lord uncovered. First was a surface presenter system, a "good me" of personalities that worked, functioned, learned, married, divorced, and lived as a Christian; this was also "the me" that committed to do the work of remembering. Next came the external dissociative shell; this was the residuum of all the violence and demonization that happened to the presenter to make the multiplicity more elaborate.

This was the part that would wear a therapist out, appearing to make progress but leaving the generational core undetected and undisturbed.

Deepest still was my ancestral, generational core, the historical continuation of a family and culture that had been living in Sodom and Gomorrah for generations completely oblivious but opposed to everything "the good (surface) me" had known as good, true, and real.

The attachment theorists would say that people are defined by their bonds, and I believe this is true. My core of identity has been marked by the emotional, affective attachments to the key figures in my life.

This core is my original identity, made up of the bonds and affective ties to those closest to me. My mother was indeed Lula Vieta Pauline Russell Weston, born 1917 in Farmersville, Texas, and died in 1977.

My real, biological father, was not the man I had known as my father. My true father, the man whom I loved and called father, was *Edouard Phillipe de Rothschild*, and I was his bastard son, named *Phillip Eugene*.

This man, Edouard, was my father and I, a product of occult incest, was one of the hundreds of thousands of both legitimate and illegitimate offspring of this powerful financial and occult family.

What was it like living in this household? During much of my childhood and adolescence, I lived with my father on his estate in France. I can remember his talking with me as a young boy, I remember his love of life and his passion for everything human.

In his soul he believed that humanity was god itself; he could talk for hours (and often did) about the phenomenal accomplishments of the human race. He would take me to his library and spend long periods displaying the miracles of being human. I loved his passion. I loved, too, the physical relationship we had, *held fast in the emotional power of incest*, which in this culture was "normal" and to be admired.

I listened to and adopted his lusts for power and even his hatred toward God. This man relished hating God, and I was his bastard son.

Such was the true generational core of my ancestral iniquity and, being a Rothschild descendant, it was maximally demonized.

**So how does a child of such a family become a Christian?**
A peculiarity of satanic families is that they introduce their own children to the Gospel, in order to attack the very relationship that is the emotional core of genuine faith.

I recall my father, with none other than *Herr Josef Mengele* himself coaching him over his shoulder, leading me to Christ.

His first awkward attempts often misfired, earning him (of all people) a tongue-lashing par excellence from *Herr Doktor.* But one day he succeeded; I saw the miracle of God as my Father, and my heart went out to the
Holy One as my Father, my "Abba".

Then by distorting the message of the Scriptures, they lead me to *"put the old man (the unregenerate human nature, in Pauline theology) to death".*

I did undergo death, an induced physical death followed by a medical resuscitation. Then I, a tender child just over two years old, was given the "choice" to love my Heavenly Father who led to death, or my earthly father who meant life. Over a protracted period, my father reinforced both yearnings - to be the Lord's and to be his.

He built in an incredible tension in me between these two diametrically opposed affective bonds, and I was not allowed to dissociate them to achieve a reconciliation. This was my core conflict – an attachment disorder of the first magnitude; out of this conflict emerged, through structured abuse and medically driven behavioral conditioning, everything that was my alter system.

Thus, the very origin of my identity as a Christian and the most wonderful and pristine experiences of my receiving the presence of the Holy Spirit and the Eternal Life of Christ, were within hours, sequestered off, thus no longer available as the central organizing focus of my personality.

These were the primal attachment experiences from which my Christian identity was built, but through being reindoctrinated back into satanic culture, they are the events upon which my entire SRA edifice was constructed.
I was present at my father's death in 1988, receiving his power and the commission to carry out my destiny in the grand conspiracy of my family. Like their other children, I played a key role in my family's revolt from God.

When I watch CNN, it startles me to see *so many familiar faces now on the world stage in politics, art, finance, fashion, and business*. I grew up with these people, meeting them at ritual worship sites and in the centers of power.

Financiers, artists, royalty, and even Presidents, all these dissociated people work and conspire today to bring in a new world order where being human is the highest good and God is a faceless abstraction.

These people, like me, are SRA/DID. Like the hundreds of thousands of this occult family's other biological children, I had my place and function within this clan's attempt to control the world.

My efforts and my families' efforts strove to have a member of the European nobility of the Hapsburg family assume the preeminent position over humanity, a position called the Antichrist by Christianity.

While others were seeded into government, academia, business, or entertainment, my place was within the Body of Christ. I was to be a focus for spiritual power and controller of a cult within this Church. In this Church have lived people who I have known all my life to be the controllers and power centers of both the Rothschild family's false prophet and the antichrist.

I was dedicated in my childhood and groomed all my life to protect this vital link to the false prophet's and the antichrist's ancestral, spiritual power. All of us borne from satanic families and groomed for complementing roles for decades - all brought together as a local church to use the very Body of Christ as the means to bring in the false prophet and antichrist - amazing!

Many dissociated Christians in the Body of Christ hold similar corporate spiritual, occult positions as part of the satanic new world order. In my being I embodied the
Luciferian morning star within the Church. I represented the presence of all the other Satanists who were related to me in the morning star; their spirits were present in me in the Church. Constructed through ritual but empowered by legions of spirits, I was a human and spiritual focus of corporate satanic energy into the Body of Christ.

My Rothschild family built my corporate spiritual occult position as the morning star and the very foundation of my entire system on my personality as a Christian. And not just as the false, programmed hyper-pious, hypocritical, or super spiritual Christian of my presenter systems.

No, the deepest center of my core as a Rothschild Satanist was my acceptance of Jesus Christ as Lord while I was a mere child at the tender age of two years and four months.

This has been supremely critical in my deliverance and in my life as a Christian.
This event - my conversion to Christ - is the central defining event of my life and personality; I deeply believe it is the foundational event of my

life. Deprived of this defining event and identity, I had been stripped of the most important behavioral pattern or "template" of my Christian faith and as such had lost the single most important organizing element of my personality. I can only speculate how my deliverance would have been facilitated if we had worked on my biological and affective Rothschild identity and my childhood conversion as the very first primal dissociative events to be resolved in my counseling.

Had we resolved my conversion and the experiences around it as my very first PDE at the start, I believe my entire system of dissociation would have been stripped of its central demonic, psychological, and biological power and would have nearly collapsed.

I am not in any way unique in my "system" or experience. In many others who come this far in their deliverance - all of us have had a similar structure and similar experiences.

All us received Christ in our childhood and were subjected to strong affective conflicts in our attachments to God and to our true parents to such a degree that we split and were enveloped in *kosmokrator* legions; the alters who elaborated from this split were the satanic foundations of all other alters within the entire personality system.

For the Rothschild's, and for Satan himself I am sure, this was the ultimate sadistic irony in using Christians to bring in the antichrist, but there is a certain demonic brilliance to it.

By seeding the Body of Christ with his occult followers, Satan has been able to generate the spiritual and sociological forces that are required to bring in the false prophet's and the antichrist's reign.

This conspiracy also retards the Body of Christ from growing to the measure of the stature of the fullness of Christ and satisfying the heart of God for His people.

From these Satanist infiltrations both inside and outside the Body of Christ spring the demonic energy, the heresy, and the actions that will culminate in the great apostasy of II Thessalonians 2:3 and then the revealing of the son of lawlessness, the antichrist.

Within all the mainline churches, the ecumenical movement, the Word of Faith movements, elements of the Vineyard Movement, and especially within the charismatic heresies of a "spiritually resurgent" Methodism and Presbyterianism (among others), - within the whole 'Christian occult' of the 'unity through signs,
wonders, and miracles' movement that has arisen from Oral Roberts' heresy and ministry - within all this, Satan has been fulfilling his delusion to be worshiped as God.

The visions and messages these people put forth are the demonic projections of lying spirits expressing themselves through the mouths of lying prophets, and the miracles are acts of sorcerers who don't know either the Father or the Son.

Jesus spoke about such false prophets in Matthew 7 saying, *"Many will say to Me on that day, 'Lord, Lord, did we not prophesy in Your name, and in Your name
cast out demons, and in Your name perform many miracles? And then I will declare to them, 'I never knew you; depart from Me, you who practice lawlessness.'" (Matt 7:22,23)*

As sincere as people in these movements may be and as wonderful, ecstatic, or sublime the experiences may be, these movements aren't from God.

For good reason "judgment begins at the household of God". Through SRA/DID Satan has infiltrated the church with his false prophets, complete with counterfeit spiritual gifts, and has practically hijacked the church for his purposes.

So, not only are the political, social, and economic foundations for the antichrist in place, but the spiritual and religious foundations are already firmly in place, as well, inside mainstream Christianity.

This picture of a world going to hell and dragging the church with it is indeed a bleak one but the Scriptures are unmistakably clear that the period just before the Lord's coming will be like this.

To think that the Church will be anything other than a small enduring remnant in an age of deep violence and darkness is an utter misreading of Scripture.

The Lord God is no fool. His foreknowledge and the grace that flows from His Being are more than sufficient for the real Body to endure and withstand such evil.
My life is living proof of that.

What else can deliverances like mine and others, done in such a place as this small church, signify except that Jesus Christ is alive and well, indeed?! What else does it mean that He sovereignly chooses to give "the unfathomable riches of Christ" to the lame, the crippled, the despised, and the shattered by making us His covenant people "in order that the manifold wisdom of
God might now be made known through the church to the rulers and authorities in the heavenly places"!? (Ephesians 3:8,9)

The victory hasn't ultimately been in the overcoming of the demonic and dissociative bondages of this satanic conspiracy. I think that the real joy of the Father is that, to overcome such deficits and accomplish such a task, we have been brought by the Lord God Himself to a moral victory over Satan and everything in his power through our relationship with our heavenly Father and with each other.

This moral victory is seen in the love we have for each other within this small assembly.
The obstacles are indeed formidable to getting free of ones' demonized satanic roots and in faithfully enduring as the world goes to hell in a handbasket.

But all this is worth it, because our Father has, out of this morass, built a corporate people who have, in our very beings and relationships, defeated Satan morally and spiritually. From this struggle - both personal and corporate - the Lord is realizing His desires *". that they may be all be one; even as Thou, Father, art in Me, and I in Thee, that they also may be in Us; that the world may believe that Thou didst send Me.*

*And the glory which Thou hast given Me I have given to them; that they may be one, just as We are one. I in them, and Thou in Me, that they may be perfected in unity, that the world may know that Thou didst send Me, and didst love them, even as Thou didst love Me." (John 17: 21-23)*

The real Christian life and the Lord's will for me that eluded me so long because of my multiplicity, has come to me, because by the grace of God I chose to overcome the evil within me. *". He who overcomes shall inherit these things, and I will be his God and he shall be my son." (Revelation 21:7)*

Despite the manipulation and betrayal, my childhood decision to trust in Jesus Christ was right. There is nothing special about me; I am no Christian superman. There are people in this small assembly and others who have displayed greater persistence, courage, honesty, and humility.

There are many others, both dissociative and non-dissociative, in other churches whose response to His call to discipleship has led them to extraordinary depths of suffering and love in the Name of Jesus Christ; of such the world is not worthy.

All my life the Lord has called me, just as He has been calling to everyone else, to trust and obey. How could I say, 'No' to Him?? How could I ever?! The Father's Son and His grace have boxed me in and taken me captive.

His claim over my life was what preserved enough hold on reality to believe that He really exists, that I owe Him my life and love, and that His grace is greater than anything that exists within this age or any other.
.

"To achieve world government, it is necessary to remove from the minds of men their individualism, loyalty to family traditions, national patriotism, and religious dogmas."

**Brock Chisolm**
**Director of the UN World**
**Health Organization:**
**SCP Journal (1991)**

Illuminati influence reaches all the way to the UNITED NATIONS. Here we see the Illuminati game plan for world domination and total control on full display. One casual look around your own local community will clearly demonstrate its plans being put into full effect!

# Therapists Speak Out On Ritual Abuse

Several months ago, I sent a questionnaire out to the professional community to find out the opinions of therapists who work with ritual abuse.

I contacted the ISSD as well as several therapists whom I had heard of in the field. Why? Because I wanted a chance for the dedicated professionals who work in this field to have a chance to speak out, and I was also interested in their opinions.

I have changed all names, and used pseudonyms to protect the identities of these individuals and the clients that they work with. But these are very real people, who
often work long hours, at times under threat from outside people, to help survivors break free.

I cannot imagine a group of people that I admire more, next to the survivors themselves. The therapists who answered live both in the United States, and several countries around the world.

First I asked what percent of the therapist's practice was ritually abused clients. The answers varied.

Jenny, a female therapist, answered: Yes. I never figured percentages. I saw several clients whom I suspected were RA but they never claimed memories of such.

Fran, another therapist, stated: Ritually abused clients have made up about 10% of my practice in the past six years. I consider it a sub-specialty.

Joann, who works in a group practice, stated: yes - though many only openly admit to being DID
Is this your specialty area of practice? yes  It is about 70% of my practice and 100% of my partner's practice

Alice states: Yes. usually they do not enter my office and announce that, however.

It usually unfolds in the course of therapy, or they are referred following that disclosure.

DID is one of my specialty areas of practice. It comprises about 1/5 of my caseload. and at one time was about 1/3.

John states: I work primarily in and with trauma survivors, mainly people over the ages of 35 and split about 45% 55% male to female.

Yes I see a number of people who were ritually abused. Of those I work with about 30% were classic ritual abuse survivors.

I then asked: Do you believe your clients when they tell you they were ritually abused? If so, why? The responses were very interesting.

Jenny states: I believe that it is possible that RA memories are true. I cannot determine truth for clients.

Fran makes some points about her client's memories: I generally believe my clients' accounts of ritually abuse because:
1. I have obtained very convincing corroborating evidence.
2. Their emotional reactions and psychological symptoms make complete sense in relation to their accounts of abuse.
3. In one of my cases, relatives of the ritual abuse victim were incarcerated for multiple counts of sadistic sexual assault.
4. I am a member of a professional co-supervision group in which my colleagues have also obtained significant clinical and corroborating evidence of ritualistic abuse and mind control programming.
5. I am familiar with the professional research and clinical literature. There are some aspects of some clients' accounts that I believe may not be completely accurate, due to abuse perpetrated on drugged clients or deception by their abusers.

Joann shares her opinion: Absolutely. Who would make up those stories???

Alice makes a point here: I have never seen anyone I thought was fabricating. I have also NEVER told anyone of my clients that they "met a profile", nor have I shared any of the "theories" that were prevalent in our field for a while regarding conspiracy, programming, etc.

I treat their memories with respect and, when needed, assist them in looking at the BEHAVIORS of their abusers and how it was abuse, regardless of the belief system. I see DID as an elaborate defense system involving all levels of personality.

John shares his view: I believe that initially they will tell me what it is that they have to unburden the past. And they will tell me often times from the child's prospective in an adult voice.

It is variation on the truth. it is how they recall it at the time in my office, and it may not even be close to what happened but it does define the starting gate so to speak and it is my job to help work them through their processes not discern the truth of the matter. I am the professional listener not the detective. I think many of my contempories get lost here.

I think it is important to note here that contrary to what some vocal groups in the media say, these professionals listen to what the client brings into therapy. They are NOT suggesting memories, instead, they are listening to their clients.

My next question was: What sort of groups are your clients reporting that "ritually abuse"? Are these organized groups with a religious/philosophical base, or are they isolated incidences? Have you seen any common denominators between groups, if this is what is reported? Any elements that make individuals or groups different in how they work?
Jenny states: Satanic cults; Christian sects, U. S. Government Are these organized groups with a religious/philosophical base, or are they isolated incidences?
Both.

Have you seen any common denominators between groups, if this is what is reported? Any elements that make individuals or groups different in how they work? Pedophilia, sadomachistic tendencies

Fran shares from her experience working with survivors: My clients report abuse by Illuminati, KKK, and Fourth Reich. My Illuminati victim also reports abuse by national *and* international governments.

None of my ritually-abused clients have single-incident abuses. All endured long-term abuse within inter-generational Satanism. Some appear to be more motivated by Satan-worship, others by obtaining world power.

Common denominators:

Satan worship is reported by all clients.

Disgusting and horribly painful torture is reported by all, and there is consistency in the specific kinds of torture used, e.g., being hung upside down, skinning people alive, use of hooks, and more that I cannot recall right now.

Differences: Sexual abuse seems to have been more frequent and the perpetrators appeared to have stronger pedophiliac interests in my survivors of KKK and Fourth Reich than the Illuminati survivor, who appeared to be high up in the power hierarchy, where it appeared more specific to particular rituals.

Only the Illuminati survivor reported abuse by political figures.

Joann's clients also have shared with her their experiences with SRA: Most are isolated. Some are offshoots of other groups (example - Masonic, Greek orthodox, illuminati) All involve abuse though the type varies - sexual, physical, emotional.

Alice's clients have also shared different types of abuse: A wide range of groups from Aryan nation stuff to Christian groups, to ancient fertility stuff, to the "Chinese menu" approach. The only thing they all have in common is the abuse of power....*and children.*

John shares his perspective: Variation on a theme of religion, although I have one at the moment that is focused on healing and not religion. oddly enough, and they as an organization are subject to a major investigation by the local Medical authorities .

My next question was: Have you ever seen evidence that seems to corroborate client's stories? Such as bruising/evidence of abuse physically; or testimony of siblings or family members? Threats against yourself from outside members of the group?

Jenny states: 3 clients of different age groups naming same group leader spanning a period of three decades. Also naming same ritual sites. To my knowledge these
clients, being in different generations had never met each other.

Fran has also seen corroborating evidence: I have seen corroborating evidence, including multiple survivors identifying the same perpetrators, and incarceration of perpetrators.

I have had numerous phone hang-ups, for periods a few a day. I had one call at midnight - a woman's voice said *"She's dead you know, you killed her"*. Nobody I know of died.
Joann states: Such as bruising/evidence of abuse physically; (physical pain or sensitivities - ie body memories) Changes as a result of access by others including family members (this may be done knowingly or unknowingly). Threats against yourself from outside members of the group?
No threats - just being followed

John has received threats because of his work with survivors: By the time that I see people generally speaking the abuse has long since stopped, but I have seen scars that seem to corroborate client's stories. Yes, I have had death threats by the acting out brothers of three young ladies who came in for help. Their old brothers who now live as hermits in the bush, threatened to shoot both me and them if and I quote: *Anymore talk of this sexual abuse thing keeps going* end quote.

I want to thank the courageous professionals who shared their opinions in this article. Part two will include: healing from ritual abuse, what helps and what doesn't.

# Children's home sex scandal covered up

**JOHN BRIGGS...** golden handshake

A COUNCIL social services director covered up a children's home sex scandal.

A shocking list of sex acts between children at the council-run home was never shown to councillors on the orders of Southwark social services director John Briggs, an independent inquiry has found.

Southwark councillors will hear tonight that Mr Briggs had reports on the Hollyshaw Home in Tunbridge Wells rewritten, to remove all mention of the sex scandal.

He took the decision even though other top officers thought councillors should be told, says the independent inquiry report.

Southwark Council set up the inquiry after reports were

### Standard Reporter

leaked to the Press in May, 1985.

Mr Briggs refused to give evidence to the inquiry, but after hearing 37 witnesses, the inquiry concluded that sex acts took place between children as young as six and that a 17-year-old boy regularly sexually assaulted other children.

### Rampant

It also found that a "sexually rampant" 15-year-old boy was allowed to share a bedroom with a six-year-old, and sex acts took place.

The boyfriend of a 16-year-old girl stayed overnight with her at Hollyshaw on six occasions and other children stayed out as late as they wanted, says the inquiry report.

The problems occurred between September 1983 and April, 1984. The inquiry panel say: "The regime at Hollyshaw was too lax in not having discovered these activities."

Mr Briggs was told of the problems in April 1984 and by October 17, 1984, all children were moved out and the home was closed. But the officer's report on which councillors made the decision made no mention of the real problems.

The report states: "Gerry Armstrong, head of residential and specialist day care, told the panel that Mr Briggs gave him instructions about the form of the report, which in the event was drafted by him and which excluded any reference to the problems in the home.

"He said that he considered some references to these problems should have been made."

The report was redrafted but still made no mention of the alleged incidents or situations at Hollyshaw.

The inquiry report says councillors should have asked for more information, and forced officers to put a full report before the social services committee.

Mr Briggs resigned on October 31, 1984, well before the original leak to the Press. He always refused to discuss the resignation, as did councillors.

He was also given a £29,000 golden handshake plus a £14,000-a-year pension.

Headlines like these are all too common these days, however most fail to recognize it as part of a deeper more connected network in which children are trafficked around the globe as pawns in the illuminati's satanic game.

# Therapists Speak Out On Healing

*Important note: This article does not, and is not meant, to take the place of work with a qualified therapist, which is essential to healing from severe trauma.*
*The comments in this article are in general terms only, and are only opinions.*

Healing. That is the goal in the journey of healing from abuse, and I have a confession to make. The question I asked therapists in this article was totally self-serving. I really wanted to hear what they had to say on healing, what helps, and what doesn't. As a survivor, I was extremely interested in the answers.

Each therapist was careful to say that they were speaking in generalities, that each client is different and unique. That each person's healing will following the path best for them. But there are some excellent insights that they shared from their observations over the years, and I felt that this deserved an article of its own.

The question I asked was: Which factors have you seen in clients that help them progress in their healing process from ritual abuse?

Which factors have you seen that tend to retard progress? (I know this is a complex question, just a few key elements) Ritual abuse often makes the survivor feel they are worthless, or have no rights.

Jenny had some thoughts on this topic:
Aura of spirituality; sense of humor, lack of feelings of entitlement, strong support system

Which factors have you seen that tend to retard progress? (I know this is a complex question, just a few key elements) Opposite of the above Fran had comments based on many hours of work with her clients.

Her response shows her commitment, and her client's commitment, to the healing process:

**Factors that facilitate progress:**

1. Patience by the therapist.
2. Hard work, journaling, art, between sessions.
3. Having a greater purpose of helping others
4. Having helpful, loving, and protective support persons.
5. A religious base of hope and protection.
6. Valuing both their own knowledge and the suggestions of the therapist.
7. Crying, grieving.

**Factors that retard progress**
1. Maladaptive relationships
2. Being re-accessed or abducted.
3. Substance abuse
4. Over-dependence, looking for the perfect new mother.
5. Lack of support persons
6. Lack of a religious support network and belief system.
7. Lack of looking inward for answers, over-reliance on the therapist
8. Resistance to crying.

Those who have been ritually abused have often had negative spiritual experiences. Joann shares her perspective that includes her belief system:
Which factors have you seen in clients that help them progress in their healing process from ritual abuse? strong Christian beliefs, strong desire to heal, submission to the healing process.

Which factors have you seen that tend to retard progress? Denial, unwilling or unable to commit time or money, fear, trust issues, emphasis on presenting alters rather than on programming/structures/systems, lone ranger counselors who burn themselves out

Survivors of ritual abuse have often had a multitude of painful betrayals in their lifetime.

Alice shares her thoughts on this painful topic:
It always helps to process betrayal. all the betrayals from spiritual to parental. It also helps to label specific behaviors as abuse in the framework of healthy parenting and group dynamics. Sometimes clients have difficulty with their corrupted belief systems as regards themselves. i.e.- "I have no soul"

Survivors of ritual abuse often have difficulty trusting others, and John shares his perspective on this issue:
What helps the most is the solid listening and them coming away from session after session with a strong sense of being listened too.

The second most important element is to treat the presenting problem properly and that is usually a deep seated depression that masks itself in some other format. ODD or BiP or BPD etc. and to gain relief here and build trust over time.

One of the fascinating things that I have found is that in the fourth or fifth year of treatment sometimes the depth of the dissociative aspect jumps out and you have alters in your office who have watched you for a very long time and they can finally trust you enough to share.

I had one lady who had been treated for 8 and half years before I got to her and it was late in our third year when I met the first alter.

The Alters knew the truth of what happened to her and it was ritual abuse by her mom. It went on every day and on several occasions nearly resulted in the client's death, and all this happened by age three.

Mom later confirmed this. I had used the principal of the ISH and garnered its support in the healing and the client, now 39 has her child back, is holding down a full time job, is in a relationship that she is happy with and is clean and sober drugs and alcohol 6 years. She is on meds for her depression and probably will be all the rest of her life.  but she is happy for now.

I found these responses helpful and insightful. These are caring people, who have invested hours and hours into helping survivors in the often painful, but also rewarding, journey of healing. The fact that they took time from their busy practices to share some thoughts is awesome, and I appreciate and thank each and every one. In my thoughts, these people are heroes, along with the people that they help.

Ritual abuse is one of the most traumatic abuses to heal from, but the therapists and survivors discussed in these articles are doing just that. Healing.

# Complex Polyfragmentation: A Coping Mechanism For The Survivor

*Important note: this article is not meant to be therapy, or to replace therapy with a skilled and qualified person, which is essential in healing from severe trauma.*
*These are only the opinions of a survivor. Trigger warning: mentions cult abuse, dissociation, and trauma.*

In order to survive ritual abuse, a child will often learn to dissociate, and dissociate heavily. The child has undergone some of the most horrific abuse humanly imaginable, and most find a way to cope.

One of the ways that is encouraged in certain groups, such as the Illuminati, is to create an elaborate defensive system. In psychological terms, the child fragments, then fragments again. Eventually, the child has polyfragmented.

**What is polyfragmentation?**
The term comes from the root poly, meaning many, and fragments. In complex polyfragmenatation, the survivor will have not only alter systems, but hundreds or even thousands of fragments, isolated parts of their mind created to do a job, and do it well and unthinkingly. Often the job is one that would be abhorrent to the main personality or presenting system. The further away from core beliefs, the greater usually the dissociation and fragmentation that must occur.

In other words, a LOT of trauma has to happen to make a person do something that they really don't want to do. And the person has to feel very far away from themselves as well when doing it. The cult will purposely try to create a polyfragmented system for this very reason. The person is more dissociated from themselves, and is often easier for them to control.

How are polyfragmented systems structured? These are individual, and will vary from not only person to person, but also with the group the person belonged to, the trainers, the abilities of the child, and tasks involved that the child must do.

*There is no "cookie cutter approach" in most cults to creating polyfragmented systems, but there are certain characteristics that are common.*

What might a polyfragmented system look like? I will share some based on my memories as a trainer in this group, plus insights from my own healing process.

**1. Protectors**: these are parts that were created to do the jobs that had to be done, and saved the life of the young child. Cult protectors had to look mean and scary, like the child's perpetrators. They also become perpetrators when the child grows into an adult, since they have no choice.

They can be ruthless, angry, or may believe that they are demons. Some growl, some hiss, some believe that they are powerful animals. And all were a little child who was asked to do the unthinkable, forced to act in ways that he or she didn't want to.

They laugh at vulnerability, and trust no one. And with good reason, based upon their experiences in the cult. With therapy and time, they can also help keep the person safe from their perpetrators, as these parts will "kick butt" if they feel threatened.

**2. Intellectuals:** the cult WANTS intellectual alters who can observe, go between systems, learn information quickly and download it to outsiders.

These might be recorders, computers, and scholars. They may know several languages, and versed in different philosophies. Brilliant, cognitive, they often believe that they can outwit those around them, including therapists. But they also know much of the life history that the others don't, since they rarely have strong feelings.

These parts can "read the life history" without a tear or emotion. When they are out, the person appears "flat" to say the least, in psychological terms.

**3. Denial people:** these are intellectual, and are created to deny that anything bad ever happened. Life was wonderful, the parents perfect and loving, and the suicidality and PTSD symptoms are just strange artifacts without "any reason," according to these parts.

A person can have a full blown abreaction, and five minutes later, a denier will come out and say it was all "made up." They are often afraid of punishment if the person remembers, and have severe trauma motivating them.

**4. Controllers/head honchos/"top dogs":** these are the system leaders. They know what is going on at all times in their system. In a military system, it might be a general, in a protector system, the most powerful protector; in a metals system, the platinums, or in a jewel system, the highest jewels, such as diamond, ruby, or emerald. Usually there are several leaders in a system that share the responsibility.

They can also become invaluable helpers over time if they choose to give up cult loyalty.

**5. Child alters:** these want praise from the adult leaders, and often come out for rewards, or sweets. They will report on others inside unless they can learn that it is safe to NOT do so, since they are motivated both by fear of punishment, and wanting praise from those above them. They are also often the "heart" of a polyfragmented system, and can feel love, joy, or fear and trembling. Often, they want hugs and to be told that they are "okay".

**6. Punishers:** why wait for an outside person to punish you if you can create someone inside to do it first? Children will often identify heavily with their perpetrators, and if the punishment is severe and frequent, they will internalize the perpetrator to try and keep themselves "in line" and avoid punishment externally.
The cult will capitalize on this, and often trainers will leave as their "calling card" an alter named after themselves. This one will be an internal trainer, or punisher, or enforcer. Their job is to keep things in line, and will often try to sabotage therapy. They are often fearful of external punishment if they don't do their job.

Internal punishers will also activate self-punishment sequences inside (such as flood programming/ suicide programming, or other self-harm sequences) if the person begins breaking away from the cult and the old rules.

These parts may take time to convince that they can change their old way of doing things, since they were often accountable to the outside handler/trainer if things weren't kept in line.

**7. Feeling alters:** the feelings were overwhelming and infinitely traumatizing in childhood. It threatened the child's survival and sanity. The solution? Parcel them out over several internal parts and/or fragments. Divide the feeling up so that it feels more manageable.

Feeling alters often get locked away inside, and when they come out in therapy, the feeling may hit "full force" at first. A child alter may come out screaming, or terror stricken, or wailing in uncontrollable grief and pain, until they are grounded in the here and now.

Often, feelings were heavily punished in the cult, so it was psychologically necessary to bury them deeply within the psyche in order to survive. These parts may be very separated from the parts that know what happened to cause the feelings in a highly fragmented system, so that the feelings seem to come out of nowhere, without any cause.

With time and healing, they can hook up with the intellectuals inside who observed, and other parts who went through the same trauma, giving meaning to the feelings and helping to resolve them.

**8. Internal councils:** most cults have leadership councils of some sort. And many people internalize them inside. It's another example of internalizing perpetrators, and these have a vested interest in "keeping things in line" until they realize that they can leave the cult and be safe.

Then, they can become an immense strength for healing. A personal may have a local leadership council internalized, or spiritual councils that represent outside people, such as an internal druidic council or group of ascended masters that help run things inside.

**9. Sexual alters:** created to handle the overwhelming trauma of early childhood sexual abuse, they took the feelings it was too painful for a young child to understand. Some had to learn to enjoy the abuse, or pretend to, and were heavily rewarded for this response.

**10. Amnesic alters:** these are known as the "front", the "clueless ones", "those who don't know anything", etc. These have the job of not remembering. Otherwise, as a child, they were heavily punished. Usually, they are very glad to not remember anything, and the other parts who were abused at times envy them or dislike their "protected life history."

This can create a lot of intrasystem hostility or warfare, until the amnesic parts begin accepting that abuse did occur. Reminding abused parts that the amnesia saved the child's (and their life) helped my system with this.

**11. The workers:** these do the jobs of daily life, and usually are part of the presenting systems. These take care of the house, got married, take care of the children, and may hold a highly responsible job as well.

These are the competent parts created that hide the fact that the person has undergone a lifetime of traumatic abuse and degradation. These parts can also be a great strength, as they share that life can be good with other more traumatized parts inside.

**12. Hosts:** there may be a "day host" (see presenters), a "night host" for the cult, or hosts for various systems or times in the person's life. Occasionally, the survivor of severe generational cult abuse may find to their dismay that a greater portion of their life was invested in and given to cult activities than day ones, and the "night host" is stronger than the "day host"!

This happened to me. Fortunately, my "night host" was the one who left the cult, so she had plenty of strength and pull to give to staying safe and away from the group. I also had a "host" that had handled the summers spent in Europe, during those times in childhood, and a "hidden host" who never fully presented to protect herself from others (she manipulated the presenters to sit in front of her, telling them what to do).

Each person's system will handle this task differently. In general, the greater the trauma, the greater the distrust of outside people, and the more likely that the host will be a facade, or heavily protected.

**13. Core splits:** can be created from severe and psychologically threatening very early childhood trauma. This used to be done intentionally by some cult groups to create larger and more dissociated systems.

**14. The core:** this is the original child, the one who created all of the others inside.
The child's systems will depend upon the traumas and the creativity of the original child, as well as her need to protect herself from the abuse of others that might have destroyed her.

In some systems, the core will be very young, or an infant, if the abuse was extremely early and severe. Core issues surrounding her will usually involve parents or parental figures who caused severe trauma. This might include abandonment, torture, or other forms of cruelty to a young child.

**15. Function codes, access codes, halt codes, system codes:** these are fragments that might be put in to do certain jobs, and are created to only do that job when called out by triggers such as letters, numbers, phrases, or other auditory stimuli.

These are created with deep trauma and are very intentionally done by perpetrators.

**16. Spiritual parts:** these may have a variety of beliefs that cover different spiritualities internally. There may be one over-riding spiritual belief for the system, or several. For example, a spiritual system created by the cult may include aspects of Luciferianism, druidism, Temple of Set teachings, Ancient Babylonian mystery religions, etc.
The host or presenters may have a completely conflicting religious belief system, and there may be hostility between the parts that hold opposing beliefs.

In my own life, my presenters were strong Christians, and this gave the stability and comfort needed to bring healing to the parts inside. It also opened the way to begin forgiveness, one of the most difficult and important tasks in the healing process.

This has been an overview of just a few of the types of personalities that might be found in a complex polyfragmented system. It is important to be aware that each person is unique; that many people will have coped with trauma in their own way.

This is not meant to say that every cult survivor has all of these personalities, but are one survivor's opinion based upon her experiences and memories. My hope is that this article will help to educate others about this issue.

# On Having Need

This is a guest article by someone who has written expressively and eloquently on how the survivor of cult abuse feels. Her name is niid la'i and she speaks for many of us about the isolation and loss of identity, the need to protect oneself after a lifetime of betrayals. The desire to learn to trust and be open. She calls it:

## On Having Need
## by Niid la'i

This is an essay on need. Need is frightening to me. I don't want to have need! The voices of programming inside start to shout at me when I acknowledge that I have needs. I am not supposed to have needs. I have always existed to serve others. I am supposed to be compliant, understanding, and forgiving, no matter what anyone does to me, or says to me. I am never supposed to express an opinion, or discontent or dissatisfaction.

As a child, I learned to have a "nothing face." This face was devoid of all expression. It was a face that hid a million feelings. Sometimes, even this expression was unacceptable. If it was misconstrued as sullen, then punishment descended on me anyway. I had to have at least a suggestion of a smile and contentment blended in with the nothing face. It was used when cult members were present and in the home with the mother and father.

I also have, what I call, "outside faces." Outside faces are more readable. They were created to present a pleasant, calm, and amiable appearance to all people. The outside faces went to school, and to relatives' homes, and to public places.

As a small child people would comment on how quiet I was. As a teenager, and even now, many friends and acquaintances tell me I am so, "laid back!" What a joke! But it proves how well everyone inside has hidden behind the acceptable faces that afforded some safety.

One problem this has created is a numbing affect. In order for the outside faces and the nothing face to function, needs and feelings had to be literally forgotten. If alters, which I call, "others," inside were too upset or anxious, there was a possibility of their emotions breaking through.

Often in a cult gathering, members of the group would convince little others that if they had feelings inside, the members could tell. So, even if their facial expression was as it should be, the cult members would punish them for the feelings these "little people", *my name for little alters*, were supposedly having. Because of this, others learned to deny their feelings and more others were created to hold feelings in faraway worlds. Their needs were not recognized anymore either. Eventually they were as "nothing" inside as their faces learned to be on the outside.

When one of my others was 6 years old she was being taught not to cry. I'm sure there were lots of other "lessons" already ingrained about showing emotions, but this is just one description of those indoctrination sessions. The memory, and I'm sure it is not complete, is of this small child standing naked in front of a male adult.
He was sitting in a chair and all of a sudden he slapped her very hard on the cheek.

Of course, she grabbed her cheek and started to cry. He removed her hand and hit her again and said simply, "Don't cry!" She tried to stop but couldn't. He continued to hit her cheek and repeat the words until her tears stopped and the only evidence of the pain was her labored breathing. I'm sure that at some point this little person inside fragmented into more others who could hold the sting of the slaps and even the tears away from the six year olds consciousness. Eventually she was able to stand dry eyed in front of her abuser and not even flinch. By the time this was accomplished her cheek and eye were so swollen and bruised that she could not go to school for more than a week.

Certainly, everyone who lives on the earth has the need to cry many times in his/ her life. But for me, because of countless, repeated episodes of controlled programming such as the one just described, my need to cry was effectively shut off.

Now, as an adult, though I need to cry, there are many times I can't. I will feel tears begin to fill my eyes and my throat tighten up, but then all the symptoms just go away. I am left with an overwhelming sadness, a stomach- ache and extreme anxiety.

Can I then tell anyone I am anxious, or sad, or feel sick? NO! Others inside have been taught equally well that they are not supposed to ask for relief or comfort.

They should not even feel sad, or anxious or sick. If they do have these feelings, they think they are bad and evil for having them. They experience tremendous guilt and shame.

In the present day, I find I don't understand what is happening with my emotions. I go to the Dr. and get so anxious when I have to tell him/her what is wrong that I get tongue-tied and confused. The Dr. gets impatient and frustrated because my explanations are so disjointed. He/she misunderstands... I try again, but I still can't be clear. I am then judged incompetent and a hypochondriac. I am treated with lack of respect and in a mocking way. I don't understand why I can't talk to Drs. I feel stupid and ashamed for being so evasive and indirect.

This happens because I am not supposed to need. If I am sick, I am not supposed to need help. I am not supposed to tell anyone I don't feel good. I am not supposed to GET sick in the first place. This is ludicrous when considered logically. Everyone gets sick. But, the lessons are still so much a part of me, I think I am bad and evil for wanting medicine to feel better.

Let's say I go to a therapy session. I am going to therapy because I am trying to resolve the conflicts I sense inside. Even being there is a serious breach of "the rules." Again, I am admitting I have needs, and I am trying to talk to someone about them. Talking is akin to murder. It is a capital offense, and carries major consequences if broken. Therapy is all about talking!

If I sit silent in front of my therapist then nothing is accomplished. If I speak to him I am buried in angry, shouting inner voices, pleading voices, scared voices. My body starts to hurt in various places. I cannot think again, and what I say comes out jumbled and incoherent. I get frustrated and panic-stricken. If my therapist shows even the slightest indication of impatience or perceived anger, everyone inside withdraws.

All the others inside willing to watch and listen are so hyper alert they notice every movement, twitch and voice inflection the therapist has. This can seriously impede progress in therapy.

Many times I have left a session thinking the therapist has labeled me needy and draining. This is because if I ask him/her for anything;

reassurance, understanding, support, I think I am being overbearing and demanding. The very act of walking through the door of the office and being seen feels like asking for more than anyone should ever be asked to give.

Indeed, I am supposed to go in there and figure out what the therapist needs and start supporting and taking care of him!
Paradoxically if the therapist cannot return a rare phone call, or cannot be as supportive as I need him/her to be, I feel rejected and abandoned. So, I find myself in one of those double binds so common to survivors. If the therapist is supportive, etc. I feel bad and evil. If he is not supportive I feel bad and evil. This is all because
I am not supposed to have any needs.

What can happen, is that I get so worried about being needy, that I become needy!!
By skirting around what I really want to say or ask for, those who are working with me have to guess at what I am really trying to ask or say. They can end up feeling manipulated, or like they are being forced to play some strange kind of game.

Though this is not my intent, especially if they do not know me very well, my "half talk," as I call it, can create the very drain I am trying so hard not to inflict on others.
It's another trust issue. In order to heal, I have to trust before trust is really there to be able to learn to trust! I have to risk from the very foundation of my being.

I wear the lessons of the past like a second skin. To begin removing this skin leaves me feeling touch tender and naked once again. I often feel like I am metaphorically standing in the middle of a busy freeway daring the cars not to hit me. That's how vulnerable I feel as I try and shed the beliefs that have ruled me from the day I was born. I hate it when I am told I am comfortable living within the boundaries placed on me from the past. But, it is true. I have only known what I was so methodically programmed to believe.

Learning new ways is filled with as much pain and anxiety as the original abuse. As

I discover and then acknowledge that I have needs, and attempt to trust these needs to "outsiders," "big people," i.e., therapist, Drs. and friends, I open myself up to the possibility of more hurt and misunderstanding.

Though these people are not abusers, human beings are subject to making mistakes, responding from their own set of rules. The everyday problems in relationships that are bound to happen when people get together can seem as intense as the former abuse.

Can the voices of programming ever be silenced? I hope so. At this point, I have to rely on my therapists and other caregivers to instruct me and guide me. I cannot offer concrete ways to implant trust in barren soil. What this essay offers is insight.
I NEED those who read it to understand and be able to step beyond my walls of resistance and help me. I hope that as other survivors relate to these barriers that affect their healing they will also seek out people that can assist them to shed their old skins of the past. Now how's this for breaking programming!

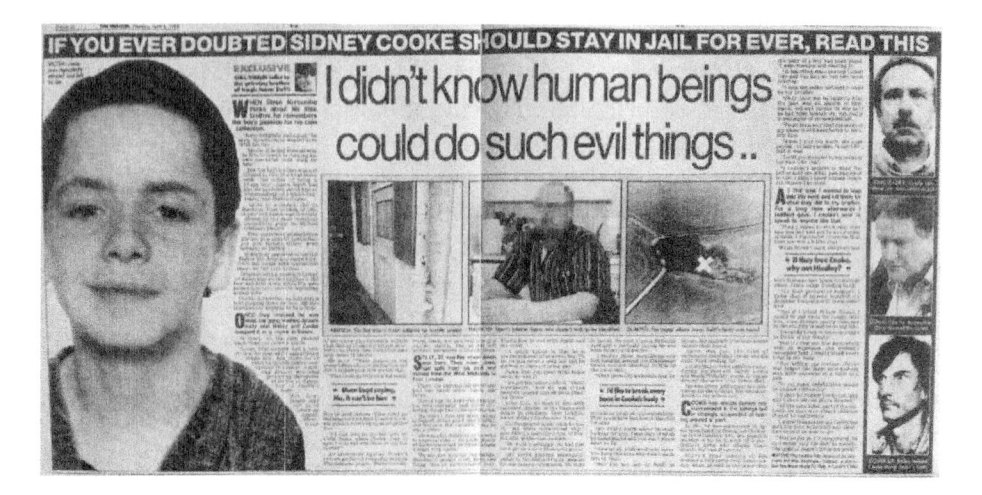

Often time mind controlled victims operate in full view of the public. It's often only after things reach a tragic devastating climax that the public is made aware of any problem.

# Spiritual Warfare:
# A Healing Journey

Trigger Warning: This article discusses Christianity, prayer, and spiritual warfare, deliverance, and the demonic in detail. It is not meant to replace therapy with a qualified counselor, and is only the opinion of a survivor, based on her personal experiences.

"I command you to leave this woman's body in Jesus' name!" The blond haired woman used a voice of authority. From my mouth came a voice filled with laughter.

"Lady, you could work on me all day and all night for the next ten weeks, and you wouldn't even have begun to get us all." It mocked her. "How many are you?" she asked. "Thousands," replied the voice. I was terrified, quaking inside as the exchange went on. I could hear it all, but was powerless to stop it. "You legions, depart in the name of Jesus."

The short- haired blond used her authoritative voice again. Six hours later, she pronounced me "cured" and "delivered". But I heard a mocking voice inside of me laughing at her, rolling on the ground internally. "She didn't even know what she was dealing with, the idiot," it said. I smiled and thanked the lady for "healing me" and fled, more confused than ever and wondering why I was so resistant to deliverance.

This is a true story from early in my healing journey, and is used to illustrate a point. The area of spiritual warfare for the person with ritual abuse and DID is often highly misunderstood.

What the woman involved in deliverance didn't realize is that the part talking to her was an ALTERNATE PERSONALITY named "laugher" who was created in times of great emotional stress (I wasn't allowed to cry when I felt pain at others' suffering, but mocking laughter was highly accepted as an emotional release). And the "thousands" referred to were personalities, not demons. Laugher found the evening highly entertaining, but others inside found it highly traumatic.

It is sad but true that all too often, the healing of DID (dissociative identity disorder) and ritual abuse is divided into two separate, and at times, disparaging groups. The first camp is what I privately term the "psychological approach." This approach states that if a wounded person is allowed to verbalize their traumas, is given support and grounding techniques, and can learn system cooperation, that they will begin to heal. While this is valid, and important, it leaves out part of the picture. A person who recovers dissociated memories will be recovering memories of severe trauma and horrendous pain that will often feel overwhelming.

Despair may hit, and the person searches for a reason to go on living. Without a strong faith basis, the person may find it difficult to resolve these traumas. Also, this approach leaves out the reality of the spiritual abuse and experiences that the survivor went through in a cult setting. Or the influence of the demonic. I believe that the demonic is real, and must be dealt with, or it will continue to retraumatize a survivor of ritual abuse.

The other camp is the "cast them all out and heal the person "approach. This is also what I have privately termed the "instant integration" approach. Bypassing the trauma and psychological defenses, the well-meaning church member will treat any and all psychological illness as "demons" that need to be "cast out."

At best, this approach will cause extreme cynicism in a survivor who finds out that the voices and switching still continue after the "deliverance" and wonder why they can't be helped.

At worst, it can highly traumatize alters who already feel shame, degradation, and that they are "evil", and they will go deep into the system, for protection. If they do come out later in therapy, they will be understandably hostile towards Christianity, since their last experience was of being treated as evil, something to be gotten "rid of."

Rare and refreshing indeed is the therapist or counselor who has a good grasp of both the psychological principles of healing, and a strong faith and discernment when the spiritual presents itself. Who starts sessions and ends them in prayer, who takes the time to discern if the part speaking is a personality, a demon, or an alter who is influenced by the demonic. Who listens supportively, does not rush healing, yet gently encourages the person in their walk with Christ in love.

This is discipleship in the truest sense, and it takes a person with a strong walk to go this route beside another who has been deeply wounded. So often ritual abuse has involved the most horrendous spiritual abuse that a human being can undergo. To a point that defies description. A young child will be hurt, and told to pray and ask God to deliver them.

The child does this, and their tormentor hurts them more, saying, "See, God is powerless. He doesn't love you, and has forgotten you, He doesn't care. " He or she will then ask the child to pray to Satan for deliverance. In immense pain, the child will, trying anything to stop the torture.

As soon as the child does this, the torment is stopped. The child learns a horrible lesson, an ingrained lie. Only strong caring Christian love can overcome sessions like these as they are remembered and grieved over.

I am by no means saying that there is not a place for deliverance in therapy for DID, or making fun of deliverance ministries. There are some who do have people trained to deal with DID, and to not traumatize an already spiritually abused system. Imagine the impact on a protector (they frequently first present snarling or cursing because they have been so wounded) being told he or she is a "demon".

This is a part of the person's mind that has already been wounded and tortured to the point of agreeing to do deeds that the child could not, such as hurting others or inflicting pain.

Now, to be told he or she is a demon reinforces the belief that the protector is evil. A protector may have a demonic influence attached to it, but trying to deliver from a protector will not bring any results or healing and may cause more trauma.

My point is that there needs to be an understanding of both the psychological and the spiritual, and wisdom about the horrendous effects of trauma on the human soul, in the healing of the spiritual aspects of DID and ritual abuse.

Can Jesus heal the ritual abuse survivor? Certainly! I would not be alive or writing these articles if this were not the cornerstone of my faith and being. I personally believe that only the deep, caring, compassionate love of our Heavenly Father can bring healing to the horrors of ritual abuse. The knowledge that Jesus WILLINGLY suffered the horrors that I did on the cross, that He was able to take those experiences into His own body for me and understands FIRST-HAND what I underwent (I believe that the cross was ritual trauma to the deepest degree) has been the MOST healing realization that I have ever had. That God loved me that much. It is humbling, and awe-inspiring.

He wasn't FORCED to undergo it as I was. He CHOSE to, to save me. To feel the pain that I suffered, so that "by His stripes I might be healed."

I also have found that I do my own best spiritual warfare for myself, since I know best who and what is inside, and who needs healing. I have gone to my local church, and was led to ask for the anointing of oil, as I prayed and confessed before others and renounced every satanic ceremony that I remembered being part of.

The most painful ones were the ones I remembered as a youth and adult VOLUNTEERING to go through, in order to rise in status. I had to come to grips with this reality, that I ASKED and INVITED the demonic into my life at those points. I then asked Jesus to deliver me. It was very quiet, peaceful, and nonthreatening.

And this time, there was no laughter, because I was in touch with the memories that had allowed the demonic in. The demonic will not leave if it believes that it has "rights" and I had to break those rights. I have also done this for my children, and broken spiritual and soul bonds with my family of origin.

But I also know that while this brings healing of the spirit, grieving, feeling, and sharing myself with a trusted counselor is also important for healing of my wounded soul. That my willingness to hear the heart breaking memories that my inside people share, and comforting them, is so necessary.

As well as my praying for the courage to accept parts that come out blatantly wounded, or saying that they enjoy pain and things that horrify my sensibilities, and for the compassion to come near to this part of myself. This, also, is deliverance in its truest sense, as I allow God to reach deep into my heart and show me what is there, and then grieve before Him as I acknowledge my sin and receive forgiveness.

This is deep deliverance of root traumas, as I pour the anger and rage as pain comes out, cry tears of sorrow at the lifetime of betrayals, and the gift I give to God is going to Him yet again for His mercy and healing touch. He has never failed me yet, and I believe His word. He never will forsake me, or any who come to Him.

I believe that God is a loving God who desires to heal the survivor body, soul, and spirit. This is not a quick or easy process; I have yet to hear of any "instant cures" for severe childhood trauma, and would be very wary of any claims of it. To leave out any part of the healing process would be to have only partial resolution.

Instead, healing for me has been a journey, filled with sorrow at times, but also great joy as I learn to trust in One who loves me, whose infinite care is the healing balm for the wounds of those who once hated me.

During the 2016 "opening Ceremony" of CERN onlookers were treated to a bizarre assortment of satanic ritual symbolism including one figure complete with goats head, leaving many to question "what's the point of all this?" but insiders know full well it serves to glorify their deity in full public view!

# Should I Confront My Abuser(s)?

"Mom, I remember. I remember what happened. I remember my cult name, A----, I remember yours, Sh------. I remember Dr. Brogan and what happened with him."
"You're making this all up, sweetie. Nothing happened." "Then why can I speak German? I never heard it in the daytime, but you talked to me in the night. Why can
I hear *"Ich bin eine kinder macht sachens gut,"* (I am a child who does things well) in my head? The words that you taught me?" "Maybe you're psychic? You picked it
up spontaneously?"

This is part of an actual conversation from over a year ago with my own mother. She knew I had never learned German consciously. Yet I spoke German to her for two minutes to prove to her I knew it. She does not speak any German consciously. Yet I have tons of memories of her speaking it at night. My mother is in denial, and unwilling to give up her own dissociative defenses, although her explanation of my German seemed to be reaching a bit far.

I have not spoken with her since, although I pray for her and my sister daily, and one of my greatest hopes is that they will get out of the cult.

As a survivor goes through the process of remembering their abuse, the question frequently comes up, "Should I confront my abusers?" This is a difficult topic, and one in which I will share a few ideas based on both my experience and the experience of others with whom I have discussed this in the past. It is NOT meant to replace discussion with a qualified therapist, who can help a survivor make the best judgement on what is best in an individual situation.

People will frequently have a desire to confront their perpetrator at some point in the healing process. The reasons for this will vary with each individual. Often, a desire for validation is the motivation. The survivor is struggling with memories coming up that seem unbelievable, and they want to hear the words from the person who hurt them, "Yes, that happened, and I'm sorry."

Long believed to be nothing more than a rumor until exposed, the Ritual at Bohemian Grove is attended each year by high level political insiders and centers around the worship of the pagan god **Moloch** it's the Blood sacrifice.

It is human nature to seek validation on the outside for long suppressed trauma, since the remembering process takes time. The full memory of a difficult event may take months, or even years, to be absorbed into conscious memory as recall of the event.

Rage will motivate some people. When memories of perpetration come forward, the long buried feelings of anger that can border on the homicidal may come out.

The outrage that a young child felt at being used, abused, and betrayed in the horrendous ways that the cult does comes surging into the psyche. Anger is a natural reaction to violated boundaries, it is the signal that says "Something wrong happened to me, and it shouldn't have!"

When the boundaries have been not only violated, but completely trampled upon, as occurs with ritual abuse, the anger is correspondingly great.

I went through a short period of time feeling homicidal rage towards my mother as I remembered her abuse of me. But I had always CONSCIOUSLY remembered wanting to kill her and my stepfather when I was in high school, struggling with the desire to hurt them. I would push the feelings back over and over. Now, as an adult, it took concentrated effort in therapy and anger work to defuse the rage that I felt. I wanted a plane ticket one Christmas more than anything in the world, and the chance to "confront' my mother and return to her the abuse that she had poured upon me as a child and youth.
This would have not been healthy, and thankfully I had a therapist and support system who cautioned me against a volatile confrontation at that time.

Instead, as therapy progressed, I began to see that like me, my own mother was once a wounded child. As I prayed for her, I began the long journey towards forgiveness, which is still ongoing. I know the level of rage that I am describing may sound unusual, but in ritual abuse, the horrendous level of psychological betrayals, sexual abuse, and torture will create this kind of anger in the person, often locked within protector personalities.

I chose to not confront my mother while in this state. I went two years without any contact with her whatsoever. I also did this for my own safety and the homicidal rage has been resolved without needing to confront her at the time.

Anger is part of the natural grieving process, and as a person grieves over a wounded childhood and their loss of innocence, it will be a stage that may be visited frequently as the survivor heals.

It may not be safe to confront an abuser who has the ability to reaccess the survivor. Meaning to confront the perpetrator, the person may instead be drawn back to the abuse that they are trying to resolve.

In some cases, confrontation may be unsafe for the survivor of ritual abuse, and they need to choose to not confront, or only confront if there are safe people with them. Over three years ago, I called my mother. At the time, even though I had memories coming through of her abuse, they were vague. But then she gave a core command to my systems (she was my trainer the first three years of my life, and was one of three people who could go anywhere inside).

The command was to "Come back or die". I chose to suicide, rather than go back to the cult, and ended up in an Emergency room fighting for my life after taking an overdose. At that point, I stopped all contact with her, and the suicidality was broken. And I began to truly heal and integrate. It is important if a person does decide to confront a perpetrator that they maintain safety first. NEVER go alone to confront a known perpetrator. This could be a setup for trouble or being reacccessed.

Always have one or two safe, non-DID people with you. Be aware that the confrontation will probably result in denial. This is the universal reaction of most people still involved in the cult, who are amnesic.

Most generational cult families are dissociative, to say the least, and they will NOT remember their abusing others, even when directly confronted with their abuse.

Perpetration of others is often the LAST thing remembered psychologically when healing from suppressed trauma, according to several therapists I have talked to.

Perpetration is a very psychologically painful issue to face, and the person confronted with their perpetration will deny, or dissociate from it.

When I lived in San Diego, I was investigated by a local authority for an allegation of being part of a cult group. I was still completely amnesic to my involvement.
I invited the person doing the investigation into my home, offered them coffee, saw the evidence, and shook my head sadly over the "poor, ill woman" who was making the allegations. I stated unequivocally to the investigator that I was NOT part of any cult group, or involved in any cult activities.

I even offered to have them come and stay with me for a month, to see if I was telling the truth! I was not lying, I was completely DISSOCIATED from my other activities. The investigator was convinced by me, and left my home sure I was telling the truth, because, yes, I was.

My front people were, that is, while the buried knowledge of my other activities was inaccessible to me, even in the face of being confronted by a local authority, and later, an investigator for the DA's office.

If the survivor is looking for a confession, or proof of their abuse from amnesic family members, they will be sorely disappointed. Unless others in the family are willing to look at their trauma, they will deny as strongly as I did in San Diego, or my own mother did when I confronted her. If the survivor is fragile, this denial may cause them to doubt their own memories. I remember early in my healing telling my stepfather that I was DID. He told me, "You are no more multiple than the chair I'm sitting on." This was his reality, and at the time it caused me to wonder if my internal reality was made up.

Yet I knew that I could NOT be making up the feelings or body memories that were coming. I finally concluded that he must have a pretty darn multiple chair, then, since I knew I was.

Sometimes a person will want to contact their perpetrator to offer forgiveness, especially far into the healing process. While this can be a valid reason, again, the forgiveness may be met with hostility and denial if the perpetrator is not able to cope with the realities of their own abusiveness.

Each person will have a unique situation. Some will find that confrontation may clear the air for others in their family to remember hidden abuse. Others will decide that their family of origin or their perpetrators are dangerous, and should not be contacted for safety reasons.

It is best to discuss this at length with a qualified therapist before reaching any individual conclusions. I have shared some of my own experiences with confrontation in my own life, in the hope to help others understand some of the reactions that may occur.

Ritual abuse is one of the most serious forms of abuse that can occur, and often the individuals involved are dangerous to a survivor, or their agenda may be to try and draw the survivor back to the cult group.

The choice to confront an abuser in this type of situation should not be taken lightly, and extreme caution used as well as the advice of a qualified therapist.

# Trauma Bonding:
# The Pull To The Perpetrator

I will be writing on an extremely difficult subject, that of trauma bonding, also known as bonding to the perpetrator. This is difficult to do for several reasons. As a child, I was in a state of "captivity to my abuser" as delineated in trauma journals.

I was raised in an isolative cult, and bonded heavily to my primary programmers, both my parents, and the trainers that worked with me. Then, as an adult, I continued the vicious cycle when I became a trainer, then a head trainer, and bonded others to me.

Trauma bonding is the issue that is left out of the equation when people ask "Why do cult members recontact their perps? Why do they keep going back for more abuse?"

Without understanding chronic trauma, and the effects of trauma bonding, it is impossible to understand the dynamic involved.

I will be sharing in this chapter both from personal memory of methods used, as well as sourcing to the literature on the subject. My greatest hope is that by understanding this often misunderstood subject, that others may be helped to pull out of its insidious pull.

If a person is unable to escape chronic, traumatic abuse, they will eventually begin to bond with their perpetrator(s). This has been well documented in the literature. It will occur because of the dehumanization of the victim, who may reach a state of feeling that they are "robotized" or non-feeling, combined with a disruption in the capacity for intimacy caused by the trauma.

"Trauma impels people both to withdraw from close relationships and to seek them desperately. The profound disruption in basic trust, the common feelings of shame, guilt, and inferiority, and the need to avoid reminders of the trauma that might be found in social life, all foster withdrawal from close relationships.

But the terror of the traumatic event intensifies the need for protective attachments. The traumatized person therefore frequently alternates between isolation and anxious clinging to others. "(1)

Many victims of severe and unrelenting trauma, whether domestic violence, incest, or ritual abuse, will find that they feel anxious when alone, and fear abandonment and isolation.

The over-dependent characteristics are NOT a personality fault, but a result of the chronic abuse. This is often rooted in the fact that as a child, the trauma survivor was not only a CAPTIVE to their abuse, but they depended upon their perpetrator for food, shelter, or other necessities.

In addition, with ritual abuse, a small child will often be abandoned for periods of time, to increase their dependency upon the very people who are abusing them. Any two or three year old will be almost insanely grateful to be rescued from a small box that they have been confined within for hours, or from the dark confines of a musty basement where they have been left for a day or two.

Even the most abusive perpetrator will then become the child's rescuer, which is the foundation of trauma bonding. In trauma bonding, the person's abuser will be perceived as the one who delivers and rescues from the abuse, as well as the tormentor. This creates a psychological ambivalence that creates dissociation in a young child.

The very helplessness and terror that are instilled by the abuse, cause the child (or later, the adult) to reach out to the only available hand for relief: the perpetrator. And the perpetrator WILL rescue and stop the abuse, or take the child out of the confines of their pain, but for a price: their unrelenting loyalty and obedience.

This is the traumatic underpinning of all cult programming that I have seen: a combination of abuse and kindness; terror and rescue; degradation and praise.

This will be reinforced by the perceived power of the perpetrator in the cult situation: In situations of captivity, the perpetrator becomes the most powerful person in the life of the victim, and the psychology of the victim is shaped by the actions and beliefs of the perpetrator. (1)

This is survival at its most basic for the child raised in a cult setting, since failure to do this will cause further punishment and pain. The child will have seen people tortured or killed for disobedience, and so,

literally, the perpetrator WILL have the perceived power of life and death over the child.
If the child complies, and is "obedient" to the demands of their perpetrator and the group, they will be "rewarded" with freedom from punishment and continued life. The intense coercion to not only comply with, but to identify idealistically, with the group in this context is overwhelming.

Almost all very young children in an abusive cult setting will begin to internalize their perpetrators in some form in order to cope with this reality. And this reaction will be rewarded heavily, if not done intentionally.

Many cult handlers or trainers will pretend to "pass on their spirit" into the child, and will tell the child that they now "live within them" and "are always watching them." Frequently, the young
child will then create an internal alter with the same name as the outside abuser or trainer.

I remember my second trainer, Dr. Brogan, saying that he was giving himself "immortality" by going to "live inside of me" when I created (with his help) aninternal Dr.Brogan. This alternate personality became a head internal trainer inside, the same role that Dr. Brogan had on the outside, and part of healing has meant learning that this internal Brogan is actually part of ME and learning that he no longer had to do his old "job" of reprogramming me internally. It has also meant
breaking free of the hold that the GOOD memories of him, the kindnesses, the expressions of love and caring, held over me as well, since they bonded me to him,
and to the group that he belonged to.

In the cult, it is not uncommon to have a "death ritual" where the child is brought to a near death experience. Afterwards, the "rescuers" are the trainers who talk
soothingly to the child, massage him or her with oils, and tell the child that they "owe their life" to them. Not only that, but the warning is given: if the child ever tries
to break free, they will return to the state of dying.

Other set ups will include burying a child alive in a box or coffin; again, the perpetrators will rescue the horrified child who is almost out of their mind with terror (after several long hours) under one condition: undying loyalty to the group and the rescuers.

Traumatized beyond belief, the child readily complies. This time of avowal and loyalty will be buried in a deep, subconscious layer of the mind, and the older adult or survivor may not be aware that part of the draw to the group is the belief that they "owe their life to them." The subconscious fear needs to be dealt with: that leaving the group does NOT have to mean death, as they were taught in early childhood traumatizations.

After any training session, all Illuminati trainers know that the most important time is the "kindness bonding" after the trauma is over.

The best trainers will have kind personas that will come out, talk lovingly to the "subject" and tell them how well they did, how needed the subject is to the group, how "special" and unique they are.

Rewards such as a special food, drugs, or a sexual partner will be given as well. This "kindness" after the trauma is the hook that will often draw programmed personalities back to the cult, since some personalities may know only of the rewards and kindness, and will block the abuse.

Heavily abused alters have less of an investment in returning to the cult; but heavily rewarded and praised alters will, and must be helped in therapy to see the whole picture.

Siblings and other children will often form a trauma bond with each other, much as soldiers in a war setting, or prisoners, will do. *"Twinning"* with a non-biological twin will carry this to an extreme. In different situations, the children are allowed to "rescue" each other, increasing their loyalty and bond to each other.

They will go through the same programming and torture together, and will feel the bond of "surviving it" together. A "battlefield" mentality may literally develop, as friendships deepen in youth and vows to be willing to die for one another are given and taken.

But all too often, these friends and twins and siblings are also forced to traumatize and wound each other, reinforcing another basic cult message: the one who loves you will hurt you.

The survivor who escapes the cult will feel a powerful pull back because of a lifetime of these types of distorted messages. The safe therapist, or non-DID friend, is not hurting them, and this may create a huge dissonance in a person who up until this point had always been taught that "love" meant "pain".

They may doubt the reality of the caring messages of those around them, or need to test their support system over and over. And highly wounded alters, who were bonded to believe that they owe their very life to the ones who have abused them most, may still try to recontact former perpetrators, not believing that life can be different yet.

Undoing a lifetime of this type of teaching and training takes time, patience, perseverance, and prayer. It will stretch the most caring support person as they wonder why the survivor recontacts their abuser.

The survivor will feel that they have betrayed themselves, if they find they have recontacted perpetrators, unaware of the powerful pull that trauma bonding may still have on certain alters inside.

But with caring support and continued therapy, the survivor will begin to test old beliefs. Personalities formerly loyal to the father, mother, or other trainers may decide to cut off contact, and will go increasingly long periods without being reaccessed.

They may come out in therapy, angry and disgruntled, or asking when the therapist is going to "put down their façade" and begin hurting them (this is another form of testing). The person's whole world view may go through a 180degree inside as they realize that love does NOT have to mean abuse, and the message reaches the deepest layers inside. Deep grieving over the abuse of trust, over the betrayals, over the intentionality of the trauma bonding and the set-ups will occur, as the person moves towards healing and away from the pull of their former abusers. The process takes time, often years, to occur, but the result, which is a life free from cult abuse, is well worth it.

# Dealing With Holidays

"They're going to hurt me," the little said, crouched under the stairwell. It was my first Halloween out of the cult, and I was working at a health club. A friend was with me, trying to coax the little out from her hiding place. "No one's going to hurt you, "he said gently. "How do you know? They always have before", she answered.

Certain times of the year can be difficult for survivors, especially anniversary dates of trauma, and holidays. The cult has definite days that are considered "special" and spiritual ceremonies are performed on those days.

As a survivor breaks free of cult control, these days can still be difficult because of the intense memories associated with them. Also, holidays tend to be a time when groups gather together, and callback programming may be activated.

Many survivors have always had problems on certain dates, and didn't know why until they found out it was a major holiday.

How does a person get through a difficult anniversary date? Or deal with a time of year that can trigger memories of past abuse? I thought that here, I would share a few ideas that have helped me personally.

I am finding that the longer I am out of the cult, the less effect that dates have on me. Since that first difficult Halloween I mentioned above, I have not had major problems, once my inside people learned they were safe from harm. I still try to do things to make sure that holidays are less stressful for me, though.

1. Recognize the triggers: everyone has different things that might trigger them during a holiday time. Some people are affected by the smell of a pine tree, for example, or the sight of decorations. Knowing your personal sensitivities, and preparing yourself for them, or trying to avoid some if possible, can help. While I cannot avoid the ads and displays in stores, I can choose to be aware that they do bother certain people inside, talk to them about it, and choose to ignore the displays, looking the other way.

2. Allow littles or other inside parts to discuss their fears about the date. This is best done in therapy, although there may be times, such as the Health club incident mentioned above, when this isn't possible. Letting inside people draw their concerns, and slowly share their memories of the date, can go a long way to deactivating the fear around the date. Grieving over painful memories associated with the day may occur too; many survivors battle deep depression on anniversary dates. Knowing this can happen, the survivor can try to take extra good care of themselves.

3. Eat nutritiously and get rest. This is sometimes ignored, but can really affect the reserve a person has for dealing with major stressors (and holidays count as one!).
Taking vitamins, eating plenty of whole grains, fresh fruits and vegetables, and trying to get 8 hours of sleep a night (or more, if needed) can help when difficult times hit. Emotional stress is very tiring, and can tax a person's reserves. Try to build these reserves up during anniversary times.

3. Try to lower your stress level. Anniversary times are NOT the time to overload or do too much. This might be the time to plan for vacation time from work, taking a sick day, or otherwise bringing down the outside stressors.

The past few years, I did NOTHING on Halloween except stay home with my family, and plan to do the same this year. I have a day with nothing planned at all.
4. Stay with someone safe. A safe friend, who can help ground you if memories hit, or the date is overwhelming, can really help. Preferably someone who is not a survivor, since one person's fear can occasionally feed another's. If the friend is cheerful, encouraging, and able to help you engage in relaxing activities, so much the better.

5. You may want to schedule extra therapy sessions if needed during a major date if memories are flooding, or it is difficult to cope. This is a time to reach out for help if a person is feeling overwhelmed.

6. Distraction: try to plan some simple, light hearted or relaxing activities. I like watching funny movies on certain days, since they distract me. Drawing, playing music, or baking can be activities that distract. Telling jokes with friends might be another. Each person has

their own favorite stress relievers.

7. Try relaxation techniques. If panic is near, certain relaxation techniques can help. Abdominal breathing, slowly, can help break a panic attack. A warm bath in scented water, or a hot shower; a cup of tea (herbal, such as Chamomile), or even going for a massage can all be tension breakers.
Giving yourself a manicure might help. Each person has routines that relax them, find those and utilize them. One of my personal favorites is hiding under the covers with a good book, and munching on pretzel sticks.

My littles feel safe doing this, believe no one can see them under the covers, and the fear level can go down dramatically. The reading is distracting as well.

8. Make a new, happy tradition. Even though I have dates that are filled with painful childhood memories, I have chosen to start new, happy traditions. On Christmas, I have cupcakes. On Halloween, I put up Thanksgiving decorations. And try to do something especially fun.

This can build in new, positive experiences and memories on dates where previously there were only negative ones. And my outside children love it; it is building happy memories for them as well of these dates.

These are a few tips for getting through difficult dates. I welcome suggestions from others on more tips that have helped them. It is possible to make it through holidays, and with time, the fear can lessen as they approach. With outside accountability, work in therapy, and internal healing, holidays can be a safe time.

# SATAN ABUSE IS ALL A MYTH

Escapees from Satanic / Illuminati control face little help on the outside as the public is led to believe there is no problem.

# Book Review:
# Cover Up Of The Century

Every once in a great while, a book comes out that is a standout in its field. One that is well written, that teaches, educates, and leaves the reader thinking for days afterwards about its subject.

One that challenges the reader to overcome biases and misconceptions. And recently, such a book was published: ***"Cover up of the Century: Satanic Ritual Crime and World Conspiracy" by Daniel Ryder.***
If you don't have a copy yet, I suggest you go to your local bookstore, or Amazon.com online, and get one. This is one of the better researched and documented books on the topic of ritual abuse that I have seen.

Ryder has a background in investigative journalism, and it shows. Piece by piece, he discusses the evidence available that shows the reality of ritual abuse, and builds his case throughout the book.

In fact, I would challenge anyone with an objective mind to read this book, and be able to deny the overwhelming evidence presented that:

a) ritual abuse is real

b) recovered memories are real, and are documented to be reliable

c) there has been a large amount of cover-up of the evidence available *in high profile cases such as the Franklin case in Omaha, Nebraska.*

d) There is firm evidence of mind control techniques, organization and planning in occult groups Mr. Ryder meticulously documents the evidence with research and in-depth interviews throughout his book.

From government officials to police investigators, survivors of occult ceremonies to concerned parents, psychologists to lawyers, his extensive research and fact finding combine in this book to draw a compelling picture: ritual abuse is real, it is happening, and it is organized.

He refutes statements by Lanning of the FBI that ritual abuse has no evidence with literal archives of cases of ritual abuse that have gone to court and been successfully prosecuted.

I love the first chapter which asks "Where's the Proof?" then proceeds to answer the question. Studies are quoted, officials discussed and documented cases of ritual crime are given.

Ryder's background research on some of the leading members of the False Memory Syndrome Foundation (FMSF) is a thought-provoking chapter, as the "syndrome" is exposed as having no reality according to clinical experts in the field.

Also, the less than savory background of some of the founding members and "experts" recruited by the FMSF are revealed. I believe this book should be recommended reading for anyone who thoughtfully asks the question "If ritual abuse is real, where is the evidence?"

The evidence is there, the experts are speaking out, and court cases prove that RA is a real phenomenon. I am grateful that Mr. Ryder took the time to interview and research this topic, and share what he found with the general public.

# Are The Illuminati Taking Over The World?

Please note: this article mentions Christianity and prayer in detail. What I will be writing on is a controversial topic, one that cannot be answered easily. If a person states that the Illuminati are planning to rule the world, many in the media immediately label the person as a "*conspiracy theorist*" with the wild eyed look of Mel Gibson in the movie of that name. Or accuse them of "fanatical fundamentalist Christianity" as if that were an epithet (oh, that we lived in a world where that was considered highest praise instead of a term of shame).

On the other hand, to ignore the evidence that appears to be accumulating worldwide would take either a large dose of denial (which is apparently available in maximum dosages in many media quarters) or a desire to ignore the obvious.

Other factors also complicate answering this question readily.

1. Members who are survivors of this group, and who leave, are reporting what they were taught within the text of cult programming. It can be difficult at times to separate cult rhetoric from the actualities that are occurring, or events may be interpreted with a bias due to the programming.

2. People will also be influenced by other factors, including: their core beliefs about humanity, religious faith, the nature of good and evil, and the possibility of organized abuse on a global level.

I readily admit to all of the biases above, and ask that the reader be aware of this. I am still trying to undo the influence of a lifetime of being taught lies, lies which I once believed whole heartedly. Lies which make it difficult even now to sort truth from fiction, teaching from fact.

But I also believe it is important to share what I know about the agenda of what I believe is one of the most destructive organizations operating today.

Until the age of 38, I was a programmer with this group, and as such I was aware of much of the underlying agenda behind the programming. I had to be. I was teaching other trainers to do their jobs better, more efficiently, and as a former member of the group, totally "sold out" on the ideology that motivated me, I became excellent at what I did. The reason? I believed that the group would rule the world within my children's lifetime. In fact, I was told that my children would be leaders in the new order, which would be brought in by the middle of this century.

I was taught this from infancy on. My parents believed it, the leaders around us taught and believed it. And the things that I saw certainly showed great organization and concentrated effort towards this goal.

What things did I see that indicated this? There were several: I saw a large amount of money being used to fund the projects of this group, funds that poured in from around the northern hemisphere and the world. Couriers were sent to the corners of the globe, and many of the top financial institutions had a vested interest in bringing this "new world order" to pass.

This was discussed in leadership meetings; shown in videos to members of the group (such as the grainy films I saw in the 1960s showing a large round table with 13 members sitting around it, and the words "these are your leaders" spoken as the members rose and pledged allegiance to the coming new order.
I will not mention the figures shown in this film in order to avoid the claim of "libel" but they were well known, influential, and many were behind the banking system of the modern world.

The Illuminati are funding this coming world order quietly, behind the scenes. They believe that money not only "talks" as the saying goes, but buys media coverage, or silence; protection; and the influence needed to shape our modern world. "

As the economy goes, the nation will go," I was taught in my teens by leaders in this group. They are practical pragmatists, in spite of their occult bent, who understand the motivation that drives much of mankind: greed, or the desire to gain wealth and power.

Other indications of the worldwide agenda: The Illuminati have been slowly linking themselves with other worldwide occult and religious organizations over the years.

There are no press releases announcing the merger of Illuminist intellectualism with a local coven's leadership, but this has been occurring with regularity over the past decades. They have been funding paramilitary groups, extremist groups, and any groups with an agenda that includes hatred, ego-centricism, racism, or other "isms" to an extreme.

They are funding educational institutions, believing, and rightly so, that the youth of today will be molded by their education. This influence is subtle, but certain classes have been opened up, or certain instructors brought in, due to the subtle influence of quiet businessmen who has contributed heavily over the years.

Again, the cynical pragmatism of the Illuminist leadership comes out, as they wield influence with financial power; power gained, unfortunately, through their esoteric practices and contracts with evil.
Local and national media have been influenced for years by their financial pull.

I was taught that the average person would be slowly and unknowingly "edged towards" acceptance of more and more immorality and idolatry. All a person needs to do is read or look at a magazine from the 1950's and compare it to those on the market today; to watch a movie from 50 years ago (when John Wayne was considered "action") compared to a modern tale of violence and spirituality; or compare the changes in modern television programs to see that the media has had an enormous (and, I was taught, calculated) impact on society.

The Illuminati have not created our modern society's ills or weaknesses. But they have encouraged and exploited them, often laughing at the gullibility and lack of moral fibre of the "average citizen".

We as human beings have created the familial and social climate that is present today in our country. More and more, this is a climate adversarial to fundamental Christianity and morality.

Mankind without God will turn to fill the vacuum, and the Illuminists and other occult groups have rushed to fill it.

Are the Illuminati out to rule the world? Yes, and this is what they teach their members. They are working avidly towards this goal even as I write. Will they succeed?

Not if our nation turns to prayer and repentance, and asks the mercy of God on the world. The Bible teaches that only God knows when the end times will come, and also teaches that God is holding back that time in order that "none may perish", that all may have a chance to repent and turn to Him. This kind of faith can prevent the domination of evil in a world that often seems hopelessly snared in the coils of the enemy. The choice is up to us. God offers the choice, and we must decide to take a stand and pray.

To pray for our nation, to pray for individuals caught in groups that teach lies and deception. To pray for ourselves, for the spiritual strength to resist evil when it occurs and to choose righteousness and the love of Christ instead of selfishness.

To be those who are not merely bystanders, watchers of moral decay, in a world where evil won because "good men did nothing", but instead to be those who follow Jesus and "did something" to make a difference.

# Basic Illuminati Pyramid Structure

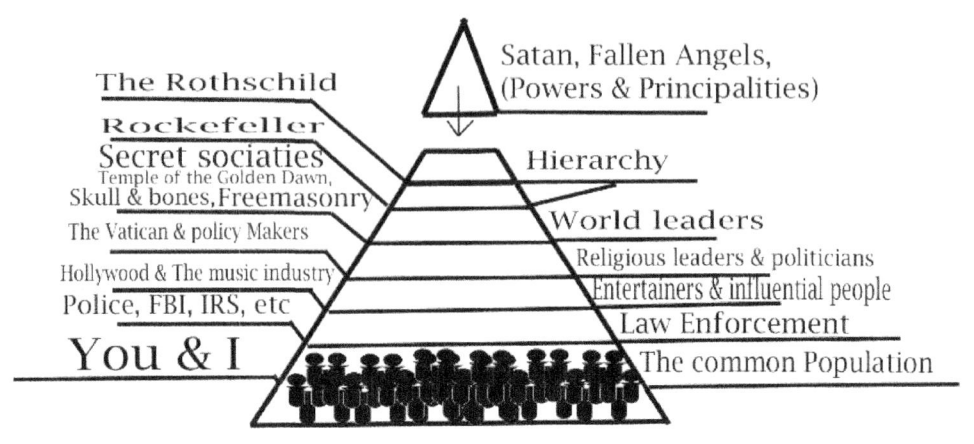

Satan, Fallen Angels, (Powers & Principalities)

The Rothschild
Rockefeller
Secret sociaties
Temple of the Golden Dawn, Skull & bones, Freemasonry
The Vatican & policy Makers
Hollywood & The music industry
Police, FBI, IRS, etc
You & I

Hierarchy
World leaders
Religious leaders & politicians
Entertainers & influential people
Law Enforcement
The common Population

Illuminati influence reaches deep into every level of modern society.
Here we see the "pyramid" of *illuminated members*

# The Search For
# A Good Therapist

Searching for a good therapist "You aren't DID," the therapist announced. I felt immense relief. This was a specialist in working with PTSD and DID, and the referral for a large Christian counseling group in Southern California. "You couldn't be," she continued, "because I lose time when I become uncontrollably angry, and I'm not DID." I blinked at looked at her.

She then proceeded to disclose during the next half hour about her childhood of torture by her older brother, including sexual abuse, and his forcing her to help him cut up small animals.

Knowing that children often learn from their parents, I asked her the logical question. "What were your parents like?" "I don't know. I don't remember them at all. It's a complete blank." I went home that day, and told my wife I had decided not to see this specialist in DID anymore.

He angrily asked me if I was avoiding therapy. "No, I'm just worried when I'm healthier than the therapist", I answered. This is a true story from much earlier in my healing process, and shows the problem that faces survivors of severe childhood trauma when they are looking for a qualified therapist. The "experts" may not be as good as claimed. Large full page ads in the phone book proclaim a therapist's expertise, while others are given as a referral from an organization when called.

Telephone numbers can be gathered from the net, from professional organizations, and from friends. But how does the person dealing with a wounded psyche know which is the competent therapist?

To complicate the process, how does the survivor believe that they DESERVE good therapy, or recognize it when it is present (or its absence)? This article is an attempt to help answer some of these questions.

First, the problem of insurance needs to be addressed. If a person has insurance coverage, they may need to contact their provider first for a referral. Often, there will be several options given, and the client will need to choose one.

Others survivors have no insurance. In this situation, which is all too common, they may be at the mercy of a MHMR system that in some localities (but not all) refuses to treat DID, or free clinics where the quality of care may vary from marginal or poor to excellent.

Sometimes, therapy can be received through Medicaid, or Medicare if the person is on disability, and the survivor can contact therapists who take these plans for reimbursement. Okay, insurance is looked at, now how do you find a therapist?

Try asking friends who have been HELPED by therapy, and are getting better. This is a great credential for any therapist. You can also try contacting the ISSD (link is available under "links" here) for a list of therapists in a locality.

The ISSD does not guarantee that the therapist is competent in working with DID or trauma, only that they are a member of their organization, but it is a starting place.

Organizations that work with survivors of trauma may also be able to give a referral, as well as hospitals and/or units dedicated to DID and trauma. Therapists who are well known and respected, and known to be safe, can be another source of a possible referral.
Think about whether you would be more comfortable working with a female or a male therapist, before starting to interview one, since this may narrow your choices down.

The next step is the phone interview. Before seeing a therapist, try doing a brief interview with them, and ask a few questions. Your goal should be to do a phone interview with at least 3 therapists initially.

Questions you might ask on the phone should include:
*Are they accepting new clients?*
*How long is the wait before being seen?*

What about fees and how insurance claims are handled? Check whether the fee is paid up front and the client contacts their insurance for reimbursement, or the therapist handles billing.

You may also need to contact your insurance company for PREAUTHORIZATION in order to be reimbursed.
This means the insurance company wants to approve the therapist first, or they won't pay you if they see them.

- Does the therapist have a sliding scale if there is no insurance?
- How long are sessions?
- Does the therapist ever go over, or give extra sessions, and if so, how does he/she handle billing?
- How far away is the therapist's office from where you live?

## Experience:
What kind of credentials does the therapist have?
- Experience working with survivors of trauma and/or ritual abuse?
- Do they understand DID?
- What kind of license do they hold (LPC, MSW, marriage and family counselor, etc.)?
- What school did they go to?
- How long have they been a therapist?
- How available is the therapist?
- How does he/she handle crisis situations, or after hours calls?
- Suicidal ideation in the client?
- Does the therapist work alone, or with a group that has rotating call?
- How does he/she view hospitalization?
- The role of medication?
- How far ahead should appointments be cancelled (24 hours is usual)?

Discuss their personal philosophy of healing: how they became interested in working with survivors of trauma, how they view the healing process, and how they help clients work towards this goal.

- What is their belief/faith system?
- Do they pray with clients?
- How do they view spiritual warfare?
- Are they directive or nondirective?

- What do they do when a client disagrees with them, or the direction therapy is going?
- Do they believe that ritual abuse is real?
- How do they help clients deal with flashbacks?
- What does he or she feel about integration (or not)?
- Does she respect the client's wishes in this area?
- How does the therapist feel about switching during a session?
- Are they willing to learn more?
- Go to conferences?

If the phone interview goes well, and both of you feel that you could work together, then the next step would be a personal interview at the therapist's office. Here, you can see the therapist in his or her working ambience.

Remember, the therapist is working for YOU, not the other way around, and it is okay to go with your gut instincts. You deserve to find someone that you feel comfortable working with. At this point, you might want to ask:

- How does the therapist take care of his/herself to avoid burnout?
- Do they have supervision, or others they can vent to?
- Do they have a sense of humor?
- What are their views on boundaries?
- Giving hugs?
- Confidentiality?
- What will they do if you see each other in a public place?
- Is the office comfortable?
- Private?

Ask yourself: how is the therapist relating to me?
- Do I feel I could become comfortable working with him/her? Am I treated wiith respect?
- Does the therapist listen non-judgementally?

Once you have found a therapist that you feel comfortable with, as time goes on, it also helps to have realistic expectations of the therapy process. Ritual abuse is a severe type of abuse, and the therapy process is often long and involved.

It is important to not expect that the therapist will be able to "fix you" or "make it all better," instead, the client needs to realize that THEY will be the one making changes, with the therapist as a supportive facilitator.

Also, a therapist cannot and should not "reparent" the survivor, who may have had an emotionally deprived childhood. Instead, the survivor will need to learn new self-nurturing skills, and practice them while at home and between visits.

A good therapist is an invaluable aid to the healing process, and it is well worth the time and effort to find one. The therapist I mentioned at the beginning of my article only lasted two visits, but later, I learned to ask the questions above, and to be careful in screening who I saw. I am glad I have, because over the past few years I have met excellent professionals who are competent, caring, with good boundaries, and who have made a huge difference in my own healing process. I believe that all survivors deserve good therapy during the process of healing from ritual abuse. My hope is that this article will help others in their search for a therapist, and that they can avoid the pitfalls that I went through early in my own search.

Illuminati symbolism pervades every day of our lives – including our money! The all Seeing Eye is one of the most popular of the illuminated icons and its use appears more often than you would imagine!

# Who And What Is The Illuminati?

Recently, HJ Springer, the publisher of Centrex, did a series of interviews with me by email. He is now publishing them at his site, and I decided to share one of the articles for a couple of reasons: it will help clarify some information, and will also help readers understand my viewpoints.

Other articles, and the archive of my book "Breaking the Chain" are available free of cost at his site at **www.centrexnews.com**.

**Here is the article, reprinted with permission.**

Who and What is the Illuminati It doesn't upset me to write on the topic of the Illuminati, I was explaining why I write under a pen name, that is all.

I received a letter recently in which it was alleged that I write under a pen name because I'm a phony, which is not true at all. I am a freelance writer on the side (I write for nursing magazines and publications on health topics that have NOTHING to do with abuse) and understand the need for fact checking, so no offense is taken at your wanting to know my background. In fact, it shows you are a responsible editor, which I admire. I have nothing to hide.

My story is 100% true. I have gained no money for disclosing; I do NOT go on talk shows, I am unknown and prefer it this way. I have absolutely no secondary gain from doing this, other than the medical bills for my children, which means I work three part-time jobs.

This is to answer the skeptics who say that people disclose for: sympathy (I don't want any and don't need it. I made choices and mistakes in my life, and am now involved in restitution); money. I earn $150 to $250 an article when I write on Women's health. Guess which topic I write on more frequently? Yep. Women's health, on completely non-abuse issues.

The editors of the Nursing magazines and women's magazines don't know about the other topic I write on, another reason I write under a pen name.) I don't write for fame. Instead, if my co-workers knew about my past, I risk losing my job.

I have everything to lose by disclosing, everything to gain by being silent. But I also know that this kind of child abuse must be stopped. As a Christian, and as one who stands against child abuse, I have decided to speak out against cult abuse by writing articles that expose it.

I also know that there are a number of people outspoken on this topic who have published, and they could possibly be back-up information for you. I don't know any of them, since I have no contact with other survivors other than my own family, but it is a possibility.

*Anyway, to your questions:*
Q: Archangel, I think our readers are wondering 'Is the Illuminati a religion, secret society, Satanism or is it a combination of it, or something different all together, or more sinister?'

A: The Illuminati is a group that practices a form of faith known as "enlightenment".
It is Luciferian, and they teach their followers that their roots go back to the ancient mystery religions of Babylon, Egypt, and Celtic druidism.

They have taken what they consider the "best" of each, the foundational practices, and joined them together into a strongly occult discipline. Many groups at the local level worship ancient deities such as "El", "Baal", and "Ashtarte", as well as "Isis and Osiris" and "Set".

This said, the leadership councils at times scoff at the more "primitive" practices of the anarchical, or lower levels. I remember when I was on council in San Diego, they called the high priests and priestesses the "slicers and dicers", who kept the "lower levels happy".

This is not to offend anyone, it only shows that at the leadership levels, they often believe they are more scientifically and cognitively driven. But they still practice the principles of enlightenment.

There are 12 steps to this, also known as "the 12 steps of discipline' and they also teach traveling astral planes, time travel, and other metaphysical phenomena.

Do people really do this, or is it a drug induced hallucination? I cannot judge. I saw things that I believe cannot be rationally explained when in this group, things that frightened me, but I can only say that it could be a combination of cult mind control, drug inductions, hypnosis, and some true demonic activity. How much of each, I cannot begin to guess. I do know that these people teach and practice evil.

At the higher levels, the group is no longer people in robes chanting in front of bonfires. Leadership councils have administrators who handle finances (and trust me, this group makes money. That alone would keep it going even if the rest were just religious hog wash).

The leadership levels include businessmen, bankers, and local community leaders. They are intelligent, well educated, and active in their churches.

Above local leadership councils are the regional councils, who give dictates to the groups below them, help form the policies and agendas for each region, and who interact with the local leadership councils.

At the national level, there are extremely wealthy people who finance these goals and interact with the leaders of other countries.

The Illuminati are international. Secret? By all means. The first thing a child learns from "family, or the Order" as they are called, is "The first rule of the Order is secrecy". This is why you don't hear from more survivors who get out.

The lengths that this group goes to, to terrify its members into not disclosing, is unbelievable.

I have seen set ups (oh, yes, they set up fake deaths, etc.) where a person was "burned alive" to teach the children not to tell. They are told that this is a traitor, who disclosed, and now he is being punished.

The person wasn't really a traitor, and is in a flame proof vest, but the vision of a person on fire and screaming remains with 3 and 4 year old children for a lifetime.

And, when they are adults, even if they DO leave, scenes such as this mean they won't tell many people for fear of being traced and punished.

Because I helped create a lot of set ups as an adult trainer, I became somewhat cynical, and have chosen to disclose as a result. Although I do fight intense fear even now at times. Try being buried in a wooden box for a period of time (it may have been minutes, but to a four year old it is an eternity), and then when the lid is lifted, being told, "if you ever tell, we'll put you back in forever". The child will scream hysterically that they will NEVER EVER tell. I was that child, and now I am breaking that vow made under psychological duress. Because I don't want any other children to go through what I did, or have seen done to others.

Yes, the Illuminati are organized, secretive, and extremely wealthy at its upper levels. They are not stupid, or poor people running around dabbling with witchcraft.
To see them as this is a huge misconception.

Q: How widespread would you say this group has infiltrated our society in terms of number of people? Are they present in every town or city throughout North America? Do they take or recruit outsiders? And how far does this group go to keep this knowledge secret?

A: I think I answered some of the secrecy above. The Illuminati are

present in every major metropolitan center in the United States. They have divided the United
States up into 7 major regions, and each has a regional council over it, with the heads of the local councils reporting to them.

They meet once every two months, and on special occasions.

A metropolitan region may have as many as 10 to 30 groups within it, and rural areas will often have meetings with other local groups, and report to the metro leadership council.

They almost NEVER recruit outsiders, although occasionally they will buy children or a family from Asia, for example, and keep them under constant surveillance in return for saving their life from the local Mafia. They are threatened with being returned to this group if they ever disclose.

They also have excellent lawyers who are well paid to help cover their tracks. There are also people in the media paid to help keep stories from coming out. I know of three people in San Diego who worked for the Union Tribune who were faithful Illuminists, and who also wrote frequent articles attacking local therapists who worked with RA (Ritual Abuse) survivors.

I remember leadership boasting they had "run so-and-so out of town" because of a media blitz, and being quite happy about it.

The Illuminati believe in controlling an area through its: banks and financial institutions (guess how many sit on banking boards? You'd be surprised) Local government: guess how many get elected to local city councils?

Law: children are encouraged to go to law school and medical school. Media: others are encouraged to go to journalism school, and members help fund local papers.

Q: Is this the same Illuminati that was created by Adam Weishaupt in Germany?

A: Weishaupt did not create the Illuminati, they chose him as a figurehead and told him what to write about. The financiers, dating back to the bankers during the times of the Templar Knights who financed the early kings in Europe, created the Illuminati. Weishaupt was their "go fer", who did their bidding.

Q: Do you have any more info about the political goals, if any, of the Illuminati?

A: I wrote an article called: "Are the Illuminati taking over the world?" You can reprint it, or part of it, as long as you give credit to the me and/or a link back to the site.

Q: How do Illuminati members recognize each other?

A: Since it is generational, it's easy. It isn't hard to recognize one's father, mother, siblings, and neighbors and friends one has grown up with. The Illuminati use telephone trees to contact members when a meeting is to occur.

A month or two ahead of time, leadership council plans dates and places for meetings for different groups under their umbrella. They then call local leaders a week ahead of time (the high priest or priestess). Two days ahead, these people call their head members, who then call the people under them.

A person knows their status in the group by how far ahead of time they know a meeting date. The lower in the group, the less they are trusted with information, and the less "lag time" before meetings.

Sometimes, certain pieces of jewelry, such as a ruby ring or an oval emerald, might be worn if meeting someone in a public place at a prearranged assignation. But most accessing and contact is done through family members or close friends.

When I lived in San Diego, my entire family of origin and my four closest friends were all members of the group. It wasn't hard to reach me, to say the least. My spouse was also a member.

The Illuminati believe in arranged members, and do NOT allow their members to marry a nonmember. If someone says their spouse isn't in it, they aren't Illuminati, or they are in denial. This was an unbreakable policy.

My marriage was arranged by the local leadership council to another ranking member. I didn't want to marry him, because I didn't love him, and I will never forget what I was told by Athena, my mentor at the time (she held the second position on the council): "That's for the best, then, because he can never hurt you or control you."

Or, my mother's timeless advice given when I was 12 years old: *"Never fuck someone lower than you. They will drag you down. Always choose someone higher than yourself."*

She was an ambitious woman, to say the least, determined that I would do well in this very political group. I took her advice, and Athena was my lover and protected me from some of the SOBs on leadership in San Diego, especially Jonathan, the head trainer. She taught me his weaknesses and how to get around him, and stood up to him for me. I wouldn't have survived otherwise.

These are NOT nice people and they use and manipulate others viciously. They cut their eye teeth on status, power, and money. I have given all of that up to leave, and am glad to be away from it now, although I do miss some of my friends, and at times I miss the respect of being a leader. But I am learning to live a whole new life without the constant background of "family" monitoring and telling me what to do.

Know what the hardest part of getting out was? The freedom. Not having anyone telling me what to do. I literally went through a period of adjustment, felt wobbly, trying to figure out what I wanted to do. It was hard, since I was used to reflexively checking my decisions with leadership and Jonathan and my wife.

Freedom can be difficult, believe it or not, and took quite a period of time to adjust to. I believe that the inability to deal with it often draws people back in. I hope this information is useful to you.

.

# An Interview With Brice Taylor (Part One Of Two)

Brice Taylor is a well known survivor of MK-ULTRA programming who has spoken out against ritual abuse. She is the author of the book *"Thanks for the Memories: the truth has set me free",* an expose of governmental intrigue and the use of "sex slaves" at high levels.

She is also the owner of EEG Spectrum, a center for healing through the use of brainwave training in North Carolina. She has kindly agreed to be interviewed for this article, and to share her thoughts on this topic. She is well worth listening to, and is a courageous person whose fight for herself and her daughter are an inspiration.

Q. Brice, how did you come to speak out against ritual abuse and/or mind control?
What led you to the decision? How did you find the courage to speak out?

A: I began to speak out about ritual abuse because I was healing from being a victim of it and my recovery seemed to require it. Since I am a mother of three children, I felt compelled to speak out in order to alert the public to what was happening and to help others who were suffering from the same abuse. I never did take the cautious route. My life seemed to always be in danger and so I continued to speak out in an attempt to gain safety and to bring help to my children and others.

I don't know that I ever really had what one would call "courage" that motivated my speaking out, but my maternal instincts were/are so powerful that I just did what I had to do—and that required doing some things that most folks find scary. Like being willing to risk my life to tell the truth publicly.

For me not doing anything was much more frightening, because I knew that this abuse would continue to go on and on until it was exposed and stopped.

My love for my children and for humanity continues to be my motivator. God continues to be my strength.

Q: How did you begin to remember your own trauma? Were there any factors that triggered this memory process? Have you sought validation for your memories? If so, what have you found?

A: Back in the early 80's I believe I began 'unconsciously' remembering, but at that time it was still difficult for the memories to reach all the way to my conscious mind, due to the mind control programming that, in those days, dictated my life.

The initial attempts of my unconscious mind to divulge the secret activities I was involved in, ended up causing me severe program-related migraine headaches.

Once the unconscious experiences created a threat of divulging secrets that had been locked up securely for reasons of national security, I had an accident, a head on collision, where my head struck the windshield of the car. Although outwardly, I was not badly injured, this blow to my forehead seemed to cause both hemispheres of my brain to begin communicating with each other in a way that had not occurred before.

Memories began flooding into my conscious awareness, closely followed by program commands to think I was just crazy, have migraines, call my controllers and report that I was remembering, and/or kill myself. Initially, I confronted my parents. That was grueling, but the truth was told.
My mother cried when I told her my memories. I told her that she and the rest of my family were all a part of the abuse I had remembered. She never denied my memories, she said she believed me but couldn't remember.

She was well along in her years by then and since she supported the funding of my first two books and told me to tell the truth no matter what, I believe that she believes this is all true, even in the absence of her own set of memories. Her tears spoke volumes to me. My mother actually wrote a chapter in my latest book, explaining her experience of my father being DID and of all of this familial abuse.

I am grateful that my mother could help in this way because what she wrote has been helpful to other survivors and their families.
My memories have been validated, in part, by intelligence sources.

My government memories were validated even more for me personally when I began to have Intelligence agents approach me. On one occasion, a White House Intelligence agent was (mysteriously!?) seated next to me on an airplane in order to tell me not to name the names I was remembering and reporting.

I didn't name the names for a few years when I gave my testimony in churches or presented before mental health professionals. One of the greatest validations for me came when I conformed to the White House Intelligence Agent's wishes and didn't name the names.

Often after I spoke (and didn't name the names of my perpetrators), survivors and therapists met with me to name (in private) many of the same people who abused me. There were all sorts of threats over the years, too many to mention here, but one big threat that let me know I was absolutely on the right track, was when they burned down my office, with my EEG Spectrum equipment where I was doing the latest state of the art brainwave training with survivors.

I suppose because this technology helps trauma survivors learn to stay alert and attentive and not dissociate, that they really didn't want that avenue of healing and freedom available to others!

To insure that I knew this was not an accident, but a warning to cease and desist, they placed two bags of the ashes from the office fire at my home, where I could see them outside my kitchen window. Instead of retreating, I ordered three more EEG machines and soon had an eight-room office, where I could see more and more people receive the beneficial effects of this brainwave training! As survivors, we nearly have to play mind games to get through the backlash in one piece (peace) and certainly since we have been tortured and conditioned with torture, we are more used to upsets than most people. So we can roll with the punches, if we want to. I chose to do that. I would never have survived any other way.

But that was then. Today it seems that it is easier to get out of organized perpetrator groups who are trying to control others because there are more professionals out there talking about ritual abuse, and mind control and many more survivors are healing. We survivors are gaining a strong voice -- one that cannot be silenced.

**I believe the truth is emerging as never before and it is a very exciting time.**

Years ago, I never could have imagined that in the year 1998, I would be given the opportunity to reach millions of people on Channel 13 News to tell them about ritual abuse and mind control and to be validated during this news segment by a retired Los Angeles FBI chief and a therapist who reported that she has helped 60 survivors who are saying many of the same things as me!

The FMSF psychiatrist they interviewed, when asked directly if he was CIA, replied, "I don't know if I'm CIA, maybe they know I'm CIA." Now what kind of an answer was that?

Many, many survivors are now more healed and their healing has paved a path for the greater truth of what is occurring to be brought to the light of public exposure. I believe, the experiences of survivors, when woven together, clearly identify many problems that need to be forefront in order to be resolved. More and more people are listening and the truth is emerging in a way I honestly never thought I would live to see… I am encouraged.

Illuminati Satanic MK Ultra Mind Control Victim Brice Taylor Speaks Out.

# Surviving Torture

I was four years old, and strapped to a chair. My arms, wrists, and feet had padded straps that immobilized them, and my neck and head were in a device that prevented movement. The woman came over to me, speaking German in a low, harsh voice.

When I didn't respond correctly, she came closer to me, her angry face poised just above my terrified one. Slowly, methodically, she took the cigarette that dangled from her lips, and moved it towards my thigh, which was bare. She held the cigarette there as I screamed. The woman was my mother, and the small round scar is there to this day.

This is one of the most difficult subjects that I have written on, but any discussion of ritual abuse is incomplete without addressing it. It is a topic that is not popular, one that many would rather avoid. One that is glossed over in discussions of ritual abuse with words like *"dysfunction"*, *"trauma"*, *"pain"*, or *"abuse"*. But for the child growing up in a satanic or Luciferian cult group, there is only one word that describes the reality of what they experienced… That word is **torture**.

Children in these groups are the victims of physical, psychological, and sexual torture in its most extreme forms, and must learn to cope with this overwhelming reality. They must deal with the reality that the people torturing them are their parents, their grandparents, their aunts, uncles, cousins, and siblings, and the aftermath of shame and betrayal. This article is a look at the effects of torture on the person who experiences it.

*The Canadian Center for Victims of torture's* website has a list of the psychological symptoms that occur in the aftermath of torture, which includes: "anxiety, depression, irritability, paranoia, guilt, suspiciousness, sexual dysfunction, loss of concentration, confusion, insomnia, nightmares, impaired memory, and memory loss. "

These symptoms occur as the individual struggles with the rage of the violation of their rightful boundaries, either physical or psychological. The nightmares are the unconscious seeking to resolve the hideous pain of this trauma; the suspiciousness and paranoia occur because the basic trust in humankind has been irrevocably broken.

The person who has undergone and survived torture will never be the same again. Memory loss occurs as the psyche desperately attempts to block the horrors that the individual underwent, usually by dissociation or other blocking mechanisms, internally.

The author goes on to state:
*"Survivors of torture are often unwilling to disclose information about their experiences. They may be suspicious, frightened, or anxious to forget about what has happened. These feelings may discourage them from seeking the help they need."*

This article was written for medical personnel dealing with victims of torture under totalitarian regimes in South America and other countries, but the symptoms are the same for the survivor of ritual abuse. The individual often blames him /herself for the torture, especially if it occurred in early childhood. Torture creates a deep sense within the person that something is wrong with them, something that causes others to hurt them or abuse them. Advice to caregivers is given: "For example, it is important to remember that those seeking psychiatric help are healthy people who have been systematically subjected to treatment intended to destroy their personalities, their sense of identity, their confidence, and their ability to function socially…"

How often survivors of ritual abuse struggle against the very same things. Often they are bright, competent, high functioning people who would be considered gifted, but the destruction of self is so damaging, that only in rare cases will the person be able to reach their potentially socially or emotionally.

The survivor of torture may fear medical procedures: *"Doctors (whom they may have encountered in prison advising the torturers about how much abuse the victim could endure or how to cause maximum pain without killing the victim) …"*

Cult doctors perform this very function, and also will use their medical skills to repair the damage done after an especially intense session.

*"Physicians need to understand that surgical and examination instruments and procedures may be those used in torture, so all procedures should be carefully explained. Some treatments, such as*

*physiotherapy, need to be conducted with special awareness of possibly lower pain thresholds. "*

Ritual abuse victims commonly report intense fear around medical procedures and exams for this very reason.

*"Survivors of torture and their families may also lose some of the values and beliefs that may have sustained them before they went through trauma. They may be unable to trust people and, consequently, become disillusioned."*

One of the universal struggles that survivors of ritual abuse and torture report is difficulty in the arena of trust and intimacy. Even for those who escape cult abuse, a pervasive fear of being abducted, reaccessed, or being returned to their abusers will instill mistrust in others. Only those who demonstrate over time their safety and trustworthiness will be allowed into the often small circle of those that the survivor trusts.

"Dr. Philip Berger, one of the founders of CCVT, has stated that when he began to conduct education on torture among those from the medical profession in 1977, he was met with disbelief. He was told that torture probably existed somewhere and was conducted sometime, but not to any significant degree that would require a specialized response.

This denial works on many levels. Torture is a barbarous practice, one which most people would prefer to avoid.

This avoidance occurs on at least three levels:

1. denial on the part of the victim
2. denial on the part of the helper
3. and denial on the part of society as a whole. It is the extent of this denial which allows both the practice of torture and its effects to continue and endure.

If this is true about documented torture of the victims of totalitarian regimes around the world, how much more pervasive is the disbelief and denial about the ongoing torture of innocent children that occurs in occultic groups. Society often practices a complete avoidance of this topic, or a denial that it could occur, because to acknowledge it would mean leaving the "comfort zone" that most people live in.

The challenge of healing for the individual who has endured a lifetime of torture is that of: Acknowledging the feelings, including rage, which occur Acknowledging the *learned helplessness* that it caused Fighting the deep internal resistance to remembering, or acknowledging, what happened (not all events need to be remembered fully, but some acknowledgement of what occurred is an important part of healing and integration)

Learning that the survivor is no longer helpless to change Learning that it was NOT the survivor's fault (survivors will often carry a low self-image in response to torture) Learning to undo messages given under torture, and replace them with the truth Learning to overcome the fear induced by torture, to challenge old system of belief and old ways of acting

Realizing that it wasn't God's fault (many survivors struggle with this at some point, asking why He allowed the torture to occur, or why THEY were the ones who had to go through it)

Forgiving those who tormented the survivor (only after going through the steps above) Acknowledging the past, and then looking forward to a better now.

Torture often leaves lasting marks, both physical and psychological, on the survivor, but with time and support, it is possible to heal.

One aspect of healing is becoming aware of the lasting effects of torture, which is only now beginning to be documented in the medical literature, recognizing these symptoms if they occur, and taking steps towards alleviation and healing of the underlying causes.

Another aspect of healing will come as survivors of this extreme form of abuse become empowered to speak out, and as society overcomes its denial of what is occurring and begins to take action to stop the abuse that is occurring.

# An Interview With
# Jeannie Riseman

Occasionally, there are survivors with a special gift who choose to use that ability to help other survivors. Jeannie Riseman is one of these people. She is a talented writer and editor, and her hard work is evident in the magazine "Survivorship", created by Caryn Stardancer, which Jeannie now edits.

Jeannie is also the creator of the *Ritual Abuse Home Page*, one of the oldest (and best!) resources on the web, whether you are a survivor learning about ritual abuse, or a support person or therapist seeking more information. She has spent hour after hour collecting resources and indexing them on her site.

Jeannie has graciously agreed to be interviewed, and to share some from her own past with us here.

Q: Jeannie, how did you come to speak out against ritual abuse and/or mind control? What led you to the decision? How did you find the courage to speak out?

A: It was instinctual. When I got the very first abuse memory, one of my first thoughts was "The personal IS political." I started telling everybody under the sun
and I haven't shut my mouth since.

Q: How did you begin to remember your own trauma? Were there any factors that triggered this memory process? Have you sought validation for your memories? If so, what have you found?

A: My parents and husband had died and my kids were grown and on their own. I had responsibilities to nobody but myself, which I think was really crucial.

Actually, I am one of the few people I know of who learned of the abuse in therapy.
My therapist, who I trusted and liked, decided to try a silly little Gestalt-type exercise where the two people put their hands together and push. (Supposed to make saying "no" easier, or something.)

Because he was so tall, he knelt down to be on my level and I went right into flashback to servicing a kneeling man when I was four. Poor guy had no idea why I was sobbing and non-verbal!

That unleashed a lot of memories, first of sexual abuse by one man, later of group and cult experiences. I have no external validation, perhaps because the generation above me is pretty much all dead. And ours was an oral tradition; we kept nothing in writing.

Q: What were your experiences with either/or any combination of:

a) Cult control and programming
b) Governmental mind control
c) Any other type of intentional abuse?

A: About five years ago, I drew out an elaborate programming system, which I was able to write up.

Slowly I came to believe that I was an early mind control experimental subject in New York City (in the '40's). In my early teens, I was shut down before I had been fully programmed.

I believe that that project, or subproject, was abandoned.
*I have never met anybody with programming that resembles mine.*

I do not know the names of any people involved nor the locations where this took place, but I believe the personnel and site(s) were academic.

Q: Do you believe that there are organized groups that engage in this? Why do they do this to people, in your opinion?

A: Yes, without doubt. They do it for power, either for their own gain or for "national security."

Q: Many survivors struggle in their healing process with a society that doesn't believe them, their own internal pain, and invalidation from family members. What would you say to them? Any thoughts on these issues?

A: I choose to associate with people who do believe me at least most of the time. I don't engage with people who don't believe me - I just say "well, I guess we disagree" and drop it.

There's a certain power in telling a person they can believe you are psychotic if they want to, that you don't care, and then acting completely sane and rational. I'm lucky in that all the people I really love believe me.

Finally, Jeannie shares some excellent ideas on how survivors can support one another, and pitfalls to avoid:
It's important to communicate as much as we possibly can to each other about our experiences - both the abuse and how we heal. The more knowledge we have, the more we can put our experiences in context, the better.

Communication strikes at the very basis of the programming because it demonstrates that it is possible to talk and live to talk again. It counteracts isolation, the feelings of "craziness," and the lie that we belong to "them" eternally.

I think it is important to avoid looking to others to take away our pain or "fix" us, and equally important not to try and control other survivors. None of us has all the answers: only collectively can we build a knowledge base about how to live with dignity after such extreme abuse.

This year those seeking freedom, justice, and truth lost an important ally, Ted Gunderson. Gunderson was the former chief of the Los Angeles division of the FBI and brought his impeccable credentials to the truth/freedom movement.

After retiring from the FBI, he gave presentations all over the country alerting the public to the reality of false flag terrorism, satanic ritual abuse, and mind control. Gunderson is best known not for just exposing evil and educating the public, but for risking his life to personally help and protect many victims.

# Can Recovered Memories Be Trusted?

There is an open debate in therapeutic circles today, one that has members lined up on both sides, with those undecided waiting for the jury to come in.

The topic of debate?
Whether memories recovered in therapy can be trusted as valid. There are many sides to this argument, but one jury, at least, has delivered its verdict: a resounding "yes!"

The decision of Judge Edward F. Harrington, in the U.S. District Court in Massachusetts, ruled that the recovered memories of a survivor of childhood sexual abuse were valid testimony in the court.

There is other evidence that recovered memories can be valid, and accurate. Dr. Jim Hopper, a practicing psychologist, in his article Child Abuse Memories:
Empirical Evidence, Psychological Constructs & Scientific Progress discusses the fact that in some cases, there is empirical data (verifiable data) that directly corroborates recovered memories that occur in adulthood. He also discusses the fact that amnesia and delayed memory recovery for childhood sexual abuse is NOT
rare; and that we often try to categorize this forgetting with psychological terms: amnesia, repression, or dissociation. A study by D.M. Elliot in 1997 (Traumatic Events: Prevalence and delayed recall in the General Population) and published in the Journal of Clinical and Consulting Psychiatry (. 65. 811-820. ) demonstrated that in a study base of 505 individuals, 72 % reported some form of childhood trauma. Of those 72 %, one third (32%) reported delayed memory retrieval.

The more severe the trauma (such as witnessing the murder or suicide of a family member, sexual abuse, or being a combat veteran), the more likely that recall of the events would be delayed (ie there would be a period of no recall of the event at some point in the person's life).

Interestingly enough, the main triggers for recall of the event later in life *was NOT therapy, but a media event, such as a television show or movie*, or an event in the person's life that resembled the original trauma.

In fact, both *therapy* and *sexual intercourse* were the LEAST likely to stimulate memory retrieval according to the study.

Judith Hermann, a Harvard psychiatrist and author of Trauma and Recovery, also believes in the validity of recovered memory based on her research. In a study of
53 women engaged in outpatient therapy who recovered memories of childhood sexual abuse, 75 % were able to obtain outside corroborating data from other sources that the memories were true.

Hermann also describes the fact that adult recall of traumatic events can vary from continuous recall, to a mixture of recall interspersed with periods of amnesia, to more extensive amnesia for events. *The amnesia appears to be overcome by environmental triggers that recall the event.*

She also notes that many survivors also had corroborating evidence which they offered during the interviews.
Dr Bessel van der Kolk, a specialist in trauma and memory retrieval, has postulated that dissociated memories have four different phenomena occurring: the sensory and emotional fragmentation of the experience; the feeling of depersonalization during the experience (feeling "unreal" or "far away" from the event); ongoing depersonalization (spacing out in daily life), and finally, containing the traumatic material within fragmented ego states (dissociative disorder).

He also notes that not all individuals who undergo trauma will develop chronic dissociation in response, and that individual responses will vary greatly.

Professor Ross Cheit at Brown University certainly believes in the validity of recovered memory, at his website he includes archives of 80 cases of corroborated recovery memories. Many of these cases have evidence such as the guilty party ADMITTING to having sexually abused or otherwise victimized others who recovered memories later in life.

What about those who retract their stories? This has been used and reused in the media to show that recovered memories must be "false". But in an interesting study by Gonzalez, Waterman, et al at UCLA

(1993), it was shown that that retracting did NOT prove that the abuse hadn't occurred.

They studied a group of preschool children in which the children were absolutely confirmed and documented victims of sexual abuse. The perpetrator had confessed, and there was substantial physical evidence as well.
In 25 % of these cases, the children later RECANTED their allegations, although 2/3 of these later redisclosed again.

The researchers postulated that the recanting may have been a method of attempting to numb or escape from the psychological pain caused by acknowledging the trauma. This was in the context of support, loving parents, and caring concern.

How much more difficult it can be for an adult survivor, who often faces familial hostility, denial, or shunning, to not want at times to swing into denial or recant allegations? The fact that recanting occurs does not invalidate the recovered memories, though, according to research.

Memory retrieval is a complex subject, and studies are still ongoing. But on one thing, the jury is in and decided: retrieved memories of abuse can be believed. The evidence, based on objective studies, over and over verifies this fact.

# PIZZA GATE SCANDAL

## 01 What is **Pizza Gate** scandal?

Pizza Gate Scandal is briefly the disclosure of child sexual abuse and child sacrificing cases of America's leading capital owners, celebrities and politicians in perverted and in human parties.

## 02 The reason why the scandal is named as **"Pizza Gate"**

The person, allegedly managed this pedophilia, is also the owner of a famous pizza brand. Pizza names are presumed to be used as secret codes in these pedophilia cases. Based on several written and visual documents, **even the name of Comet Pizza is originated from the words "Child Porn."**

## 03 Who is the owner of **Comet Pizza** which is at the center of allegations?

The owner of Comet Ping Pong Pizza Restaurant is **James Alefantis**. According to the news of famous magazine GQ, James Alefantis is among the most influential 40 people in Washington DC.

## 04 How does **the system** work?

Comet Pizza secretly operates as a front company of a **child trafficking network for celebrities, politicians and capital owners**. Pizza codes are used in all correspondence. As alleged, "cheese" means girl and "pasta" means boy. Using these codes, celebrities pay fancy prices to order from Comet Pizza via e-mail for their perverted parties and children are delivered to address. For some other claims, there are several rooms and private parts on the lower level of Alefantis' pizza restaurant to which only **"special guests"** are allowed. Not only pedophilia is of concern, but as alleged, they also torture and force-rape children there.

As this book goes to press a huge child sex trafficking and abuse scandal dubbed "pizzagate" is breaking. This story is said to involve members of Government reaching all the way up to the Whitehouse.

# Finding A Safe House

One of the greatest problems that confronts a survivor of cult abuse trying to escape is "Where do I go now?" Often, the person has been surrounded their entire lifetime by both their family of origin, who are members in transgenerational cult groups, and even their closest friends are frequently members.

The person may need to make the difficult decision to flee the city they live in (or the rural area, since these groups also operate in the country) and move to a new area.

Alone, friendless, cut off from family, and frequently without funds, this person must try to make a new life, at a time when they are very vulnerable.
The lack of Safe Houses for a person trying to leave the cult has been an ongoing concern of therapists and pastors who work with survivors.

There are several reasons for this relative lack that include:

1) The time commitment needed: it is a true commitment of time and resources to decide to open one's home up to survivors, one unfortunately that many people simply are not willing to make.

2) Lack of understanding or training for lay helpers about DID and ritual abuse: many churches do not understand ritual abuse, and few lay people understand it without training. There are many misconceptions about DID and ritual abuse, ones that can be easily corrected with seminars.

Dr. Jim Friesen and his associates at Shepherd's House in the Los Angeles area have created a model for the church community in reaching out to and helping survivors, one that I would recommend that all lay people and pastoral staff interested in working with ritual abuse survivors read.

3) Cult plants: it has been reported that frequently the cult will have members pose as caring, "Christian" supporters, who will offer their homes or even create "shelters" for ritual abuse survivors, but who then reaccess the survivor. This creates a fear for the survivor in knowing where to turn, or where a true safe house might exist. Unfortunately,

there are those who prey on the vulnerable, and the survivor must use caution when agreeing to live somewhere.

4) Unhealthy homes: there are also frequent reports of noncult, but abusive situations that survivors find themselves in when they go to live with a supposedly "safe family".

I have heard survivors report being locked in closets, enduring verbal abuse, physical abuse, and even sexual abuse in situations when they were placed in "safe houses". Others have told me of enduring living in homes filled with garbage and feces, which is another form of abuse.

Sharing this is not meant to frighten survivors, but to underline the need to exercise caution when looking for safe housing. Just because a person welcomes others into their home does not guarantee that they are safe.

This means that a survivor must be cautious when entering a new living situation.

Some guidelines for looking for a true safe living situation might include the following:

- Is this place recommended by someone that I trust, and that I KNOW is safe, who doesn't have a hidden agenda?
- Is the place clean and habitable, within reason?
- Why does the family want to work with survivors?
- How did they become interested?
- What are the dynamics in the home?
- Do the spouses have a healthy, good relationship?
- What are the expectations of the survivor? Helping with household chores is fine, and so it keeping ones room and living areas clean. Daily hours of backbreaking "free labor", or an unpaid childcare service for 40+ hours a week without pay is not, especially if the survivor is still fragile.
- Does the survivor have access to competent, professional therapy? This will also be important in the healing process, and to help stay cult free.
- What is the practicing belief system of the "safe family"? I have heard of accounts of survivors being led into a new, *nonsatanic* cult group with abusive practices in a supposed safe house.
- How isolated is the living situation? Will the survivor have access to transportation at times, to get groceries or to therapy? How will this need be worked out?

- How will the family handle attempts by the cult to access the survivor?
- Safety issues? How will they also help the survivor prevent their own attempts at recontacting the cult? These issues should be discussed openly and honestly, and plans for dealing with these situations made.
  Often, survivors will leave a true safe home for fear of endangering family members, since the cult will often threaten the family the survivor lives with. But normally, the cult will not kill outside people, they tend to threaten but not follow through, because they do not want police investigations.
- Is there outside accountability in the home to others, as well, such as a therapist or the pastor?
- Is the family willing to interact with the therapist, and learn about DID and ritual abuse? Or is their attitude a closed, "we know everything we need to know" attitude?

Anytime a survivor finds themselves in an unhealthy or abusive living situation, they HAVE THE RIGHT TO LEAVE.

Coercion into staying in a living situation that is unsafe or unhealthy is wrong, and should be another indication that the situation is not a good one.

There are groups that are dedicated to helping survivors find safe housing. I will not list them here, but visiting some of the major news lists for survivors or time spent online will easily provide that information. But any survivor should investigate carefully any living situation before entering into one.

Other resources for finding safe housing could include contacting therapists in your area with a known, national reputation for being safe, for resources; contacting local churches or known safe pastors with a good reputation, or contacting safe house lists that are known to be safe.

# How To Support A Survivor

One of the most frequent questions that people ask me is, "How can I help a survivor?" This question comes from spouses, from friends, from church members, and represents the desire of caring people to be a help. Often, behind this question is the unvoiced plea, "I don't want to do anything harmful by mistake."

There is not a formula, or set of actions, that are guaranteed to help. Each person is an individual, and his or her needs will vary. Also, I am NOT an expert in support.

At the same time, I know that in my own healing journey, and in the healing journeys of others that I have talked to, certain things have stood out as being helpful, while others were not. This is meant to be an informal discussion of being supportive, and not meant as therapeutic advice.

Okay, so what is helpful for a person who is a survivor of ritual abuse, who is just beginning to remember, has remembered for several years, or who may be trying to leave a destructive cult group? Here are some thoughts.
1). Listen. The survivor who has been wounded and injured by a cult group has been told all of their lives to never talk of their abuse, to not tell. This is known as
"The code of silence".

Once the survivor begins remembering, though, there will be a need to share with a safe person. Ideally, this person will be their therapist, but they may also need a friend with whom they can share their feelings, their disbelief, their horror, their despair, and the joy at the small steps of healing and freedom that begin occurring.

Above all else, a nonjudgmental person who will listen and BE THERE and not reject them means so much. But be aware that at the same time, disclosing may cause panic or cause programming. So, don't prod the person for information. Let them share at the rate that THEY are comfortable.

2) Believe them. Survivors of cult groups are told that no one will believe them if they disclose (and with good reason: much of our society

today is in denial about this type of abuse!). They are told by leaders in the group that they will be labeled "crazy" and sent to a state hospital, or branded a liar.

This, along with the threat of severe punishments if they do disclose, makes many survivors reluctant to remember and talk about their abuse. If a survivor does take this important step, it is important to validate them, even if what they disclose horrifies you or tests your own belief about human nature.

The events seem horrific and the cruelty beyond human capability, but often, these first events disclosed are just the tip of the iceberg.

Try to never tell the person that you don't believe them, if you don't, you can say, "I know that you believe this, and what I personally think doesn't matter", when asked if you believe them (they WILL ask, over and over, because of the programming mentioned above that no one could believe them. Each time you say "yes," you are helping them break the power of a vicious lie.

3) Learn about ritual abuse. When you hear a story from one person that tests your ability to believe, that is one thing. But when you read about thousands of people who are remembering these things, it will help both your credulity, and your knowledge. Also, understanding a little about ritual abuse will help you learn about possible pitfalls and problems the survivor may face during their journey. The best source of learning is a good, safe therapist knowledgeable about ritual abuse. You may want to contact one, let them know you are a support person, and ask if you can meet with them and ask some questions.

Other sources can include web sites (like this one!). But don't just visit one; visit several, since different survivors will have different perspectives. In the "Links" section on this page are several excellent online resources for learning more about ritual abuse.

At the local library, there are usually at least a few books on this topic. Reading a survivor's story and how they healed can be helpful.

If there are any conferences on ritual abuse being held in your area, they can be a wonderful source of information. You may want to contact national groups that deal with dissociation, such as the ISSD, for information on conferences in your area.

4). Be aware of programming. Many survivors of severe generational cult abuse will have different forms of programming. You do NOT need to be an expert on programming to be a support person. But being aware that self-harm and suicide programming, as well as the desire to recontact the cult (contact programming) may be present is important. If your friend states that they are feeling that they might self-harm, suicide, or go to a cult meeting, and that they believe that they CANNOT control the impulses, you need to have them contact their therapist immediately. They may need hospitalization if this urge is severe, and a safe place to break the programming. Or, the therapist may be able to work with them outpatient in breaking the hold the programming has.

If the person is recontacting the cult, letting them know that they can have a good life outside the cult is important to break this programming. That going back will only hurt them, and that they can change old ways.

5) The importance of healthy fun having good, safe, fun times together, such as an outdoor barbecue, going to the mall shopping, or doing art/crafts projects together for fun are all things that can help a survivor who has been locked into an emotionally deprived lifestyle (one that makes them dependent on the cult).

Littles may pop out, seeing a different reality that is non-abusive, for the FIRST time in the survivor's life. Let them come out, and be aware that they may act much younger than the survivor's stated age.

The healthier, safer, appropriate experiences these parts have, the faster healing will go, because littles often hold quite a bit of emotional power in a survivor's system. They will run inside to share what is going on, and soon other parts will come out to "check out what is going on." In reality, they will be testing to see if the friend is safe, and if it is really true that they can have a non-abusive friend who isn't trying to use them.

6) Help out when things are really rough: The survivor may have an occasional day when things are chaotic inside, or they have done massive inside work, and have very little energy for much else. A close friend can help by driving them to therapy on those days, if they can't drive.

They can also be there for the survivor. Helping with little things can make a difference, such as bringing in takeout on a rough day when cooking is beyond the survivor's ability. Just hanging out together, and being a safe outside person, can be enough many times.

7) Have good boundaries: It is important to not do for the survivor what they can do for themselves. The idea is NOT to reparent them, since this creates an unhealthy and impossible dynamic in a relationship. The survivor will have strong unmet dependency needs from a lifetime of emotional deprivation.

Let them know that you are their FRIEND. But not a caretaker. There is a fine balance between helping out once in a while on very bad days, and allowing too much dependence. Most survivors have highly functioning parts that can manage the tasks of daily life at least most of the time. Encourage this functioning.

If littles are out constantly, and no adult appears, this can be a sign of stress in an overburdened system, a sign of being accessed (the adults were abused or punished and went under), or a sign of unhealthy dependency. The survivor themselves can often learn to nurture themselves, and a good friend will support this.

8). Pray for them: I left what I believe is the most important for last. Healing from ritual abuse, and leaving an abusive occult group, is spiritual warfare of the most intense type. Any support person may undergo spiritual attack (and, in some rare cases, physical threats as well). Having a strong faith, and knowing how to do spiritual warfare on your behalf and your friend's, is the GREATEST gift you can give them. If they are open to Christianity, sharing your love and the love of God can do a lot to undo the false beliefs about Him that the cult has taught the survivor.

They will often have anger, rage, bitterness, and even hatred for God and Jesus. Don't let this shock you, or turn you away from the survivor, since they have undergone an entire lifetime of abuse, and setups where "God" was an abuser (it is hard to love Jesus when someone dressed like him raped you as a small child, and you were told that Jesus does this to children).

With love, prayer, and patience, this anger should lessen and true healing of the most wounded part of the survivor, their spirit, can begin. A survivor needs to see the love of God demonstrated in others. To see that they were lied to by the cult, that Christianity is real, not just hypocrisy, and that Christian believers are willing to back up their words with prayer and acts of caring.

# Ritual Holidays

The first year that I got out of the cult, I was having a horrible time on September 7Th. I was struggling with self-harm, and the desire to recontact my ex-wife, who was a leader in the group, was almost impossible to ignore. My anxiety levels escalated the entire day, and culminated in calling my ex and then overdosing. I spent the night in the Emergency room.

Two months later, I found out that this date was one of the most important of the year for the Illuminati, and was called ***the marriage of the beast***. It was also my ex's birthday and I had many memories tied to the events that occurred on this day.

I had also been struggling with *callback programming* on the date. The survivor of ritual abuse, and those who support them, can benefit from knowing when ritual holidays occur. These are often what are known in psychological terms as "*anniversary events*" with painful trauma attached to the dates at the least, or at worst, are designated callback dates for the survivor.

Being forewarned, and preparing, can help the survivor get through these holiday dates.
Please be aware that different occult and ritualistic groups observe different holidays, and those with importance in one group may be minor or ignored in another.

Some groups have originated in Europe, and the European ritual holidays are observed, whereas others have originated in the US, and link their dates to the US calendar. Many groups that originated as a perversion of Roman Catholicism will link their holy days to the Christian calendar, and mock the Christian rites.

Other groups with Celtic origins will link to the Celtic calendar; but many groups incorporate a mix of several disciplines dependent on the whims of leadership for the group.

Here is a listing of some of the major holidays for several disciplines (this is not an exhaustive calendar, as local leadership may incorporate their own holidays and rites):

January 7th St. Winebald Day
January 13 th Satanic New Year
February 1 Olmelc
February 2 Candlemas
February 14 Fertility rituals
February 25 Walpurgis Day
March 21 Feast of the Spring Equinox
April 20 to May 1: This is one of the most active times of the year, with weeks of preparation for Beltane (Walpurgisnacht) on April 30 and May 1
June 21, 22 Summer Solstice rituals
July 31, August 1 Lammas
September 5 to 7 Marriage of the Beast
September 21 Fall Equinox
October 29 to Nov. 4 All Hollow's Eve and Halloween rites, with follow up revels in early November for some groups.
December 21-22 Winter solstice
December 25th Christmas
Certain holidays will change year to year, since they are tied to the lunar cycle. One is the Easter revels, which begin the week before Easter in some groups.
Some groups tie their spiritual rituals to full moons, and new moons. The person's birthday will also be tied to special ceremonies and initiations.

In the Illuminati, they followed many of the traditional dates for their spiritual gatherings. But they also had members come in two or three times a week between rituals for military training, scholarship training, sciences training, or training in other disciplines.

The spiritual was only one part of the process, and was not that engaged in most frequently. Other groups may do things differently, and the frequency of meetings many vary.
Birthdays in the Illuminati are always tied to horrific rituals, abuse, and ceremonies.

To this day, even though most other holidays have lost their grip on me as I have worked through the memories, I choose to not celebrate my own birthday because of the immense pain attached to it. Instead,

I choose to do something nice for myself, and celebrate the fact that I am now a new creation in Christ. For me, my true birthday is the day I was "born again".

# Reprogramming The Mind: A Book Review

**Trigger warning:** explicit Christian content is discussed.

When undoing the effects of a lifetime of abuse and traumatic programming, the survivor is faced with a daunting task.

This task is the challenging of old beliefs that have been deeply held, core beliefs that were taught through set-up after set-up, thousands of experiences, and ground in with intense emotional and spiritual pain.

This task has two parts:
1. challenge the old lies
2. and then begin to believe the truth.

I call this process "Reprogramming the Mind", although a better term would be "Believing the Truth, Instead of the Lies", since the process I am describing has nothing to do with traumatic programming.

The people in abusive cults lie. From an infant's first experiences in a generational cult group, they are taught a certain worldview, and one of the first tenets is: *You deserve to be abused.*

The tiny infant, unaware of any reality, is too young to challenge this belief as the adults around him/her wound and cause torment, and tell the infant such doctrine as *"You are ours now."*

When an adult tries to challenge these beliefs, they will run straight into the internal wall of pain and terror that placed these beliefs inside in the first place.

Deciding to give up the lie can be a slow, difficult process, one that takes every resource that the survivor and their support system can provide. Horrific memories will intrude as programming is challenged, since the internal parts driving it will be afraid, and in therapy will share exactly WHY they are afraid (and they have good reason, based on their life experiences!)

The child believes that they deserve to be used sexually, another lie taught by painful experiences heaped with comments that reinforce this. The child believes that they can never be loved or accepted outside of the circle of
"family", since they are told this. The outside world, sensing the trauma and pain in the person, often unwittingly reinforces this belief through its denial of the reality the survivor has faced, and the lack of knowledge of healing from trauma.

The child believes that they are shameful, and only valued if they "perform", since the cult is one of the most brutally *performance driven* groups on the planet: failure
is severely, traumatically punished, while performance is highly praised and greatly esteemed.

This will create a huge performance anxiety in every area of life. I have dealt with all of these issues in my healing. I still do. And one of the best resources that I have found to slowly undo these lies, and to help me replace them with truth, has been a book by a Christian named Robert S. McGee, the founder of Rapha counseling
(I have no affiliation with this group and receive nothing for endorsing his book).
His book is titled *The Search for Significance*.

This book is one of the best resources for a survivor that I know of, since it addresses the problems that trauma creates in our lives, especially the roots of our anxiety towards God and others. It then gives scriptures that can help replace the messages of a lifetime with truth and healing. The message that God truly, deeply,
and genuinely cares for His children, and that He loves us not based on performance, and without bringing up our past, since that was forgiven completely, is life changing.

This, along with my Bible, has been one of my main tools, along with therapy, in undoing the lies of a lifetime. I need to read over and over again that God loves me
(so many of the lies by the cult told me He hated me); that He forgives me (I was told by the cult that I could never be forgiven, had committed "unpardonable sins"), that I can be loved without performance (so much of my self-esteem was wrapped up in what a good job I did).

This book also addresses the issues that are ongoing for me once healing has begun: learning to relate to others in a healthy way (when five years ago, I cried out to my therapist, "What is that? I've never known it!"); learning to have a realistic self-image that isn't as warped and distorted by the grainy, grimy mirror that the cult used on me (their hideous messages designed to break me down as a human being).

This is a process. Reading the book does not mean a "quick cure". I have read it over and over the past eight years, and I am still learning. It does not replace therapy.

But it is so important, when combating lies, to have truth to replace it with, and this book provides that. I do believe that a deep level of healing from ritual abuse is possible, or I would not write these articles.

I believe that with God's help and deep prayer, it is possible, over time, to replace the lies of a lifetime with truth.

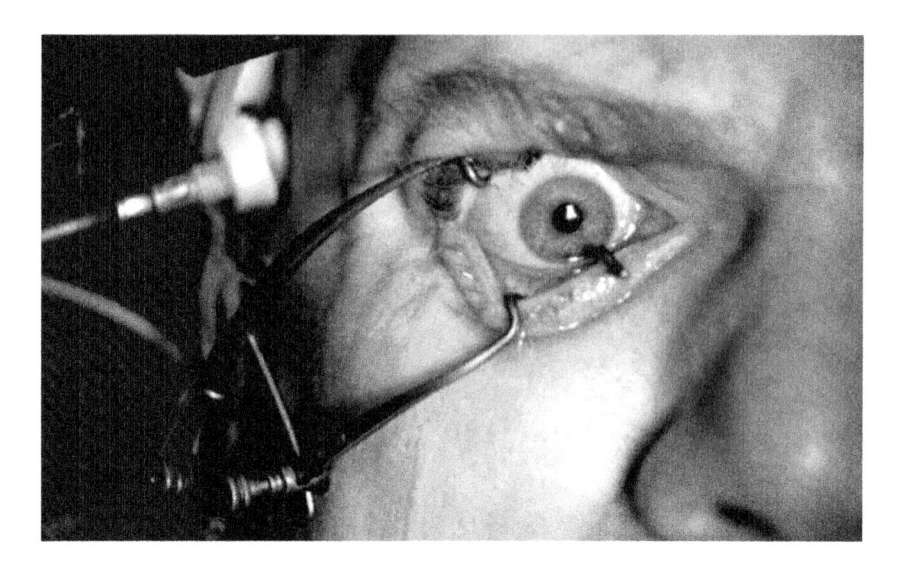

Although most viewers remain blissfully unaware of what they are really seeing, Hollywood often gives a look inside the dark world of the illuminati. Here we see a very real depiction of just a few of the many techniques used to breakdown victims as depicted in *Stanley Kubrick's* classic 1971 film
*A Clockwork Orange*.

# mK ULTRA
# Assassin Programming

Because it is impossible to discuss programming without some mention of how it is done, please be aware that if you are a survivor of this type of abuse, that reading this information could be triggering. Please protect yourself and do not read it unless you are with your therapist or are in a safe place.

One of the cruelest forms of training that a young child can undergo is the training to be an assassin, or to be able to cold bloodedly take the life of another human being on order. In the Illuminati group that I was in, almost all of the children and teens had to undergo this is part of their military training.

The results are heart rending. The child must dissociate heavily in order to deal with both the ordeal of the programming, and the impossible demands that it places on their psyche. A child can be taught and trained to do this, but they can never be taught to be comfortable with the guilt it causes.

The training often begins young. The two-year-old child is placed in a metal cage with electrodes attached, or is heavily shocked and tortured on a table or chair.

After a long session, the child is released. They will feel numb, and can barely walk. They will be given a small animal, often a kitten or similar one, and told to wring its neck. The child will refuse. The child will then be placed back in the cage, or hooked back up to the electrodes, and shocked again as punishment. They are then taken out, and told to wring the young animal's neck. The child will be crying, and afraid of more torture. Finally, shaking, they will do as they are ordered.

Afterwards, they will often go into the corner and vomit, all the while being praised by their trainer for the "good job" that they have done. The child will have created a *split* that obeys the trainer, to avoid the horrendous pain of disobedience (the more important the programming, and the further from natural core values the child holds, the more severe the pain level used to create the programming).

This is the first step in a horrible series of steps. It is continued over the years, and the animals get larger. This is to desensitize the child to the concept of taking a life.

During military training, the older (aged 7 to 10) year old child will also be taught to use a gun, accurately. They learn to clean the weapon, to load it, unload it, and to
fire at targets. They are heavily rewarded for accuracy, and berated and punished for mistakes.

By age 12, most children are very accurate with a small pistol or rifle. They are then taken to an enclosure, and taught to practice shooting animals that have been medicated to slow them down slightly. The child learns to aim for the head or heart.

Targets are soon turned into realistic photo mockups of humans in target practice. And during this time, the continued torture and abuse occurring, increasing anger levels. The child is told to "use their anger" to help them with their performance.

During virtual reality (VR) exercises, animal targets are replaced with human ones.

The child is taught to hit the "bad guys" and to direct their rage at them. Accuracy in these exercises is rewarded and praised, and mistakes are punished.

The child is taught to obey a command code to initiate the "*find and seek*" sequence with a target, and then to implement the "terminate" sequence, which involves killing the target.

*Under drugs and hypnosis*, a young teen will be convinced that this is real. One day, they are tested, and told (in VR, but they don't realize this in the hypnotic state) to shoot their parent or sibling, who is simulated graphically in the VR program…. They do.

At this point, the child is considered "*reliable*" on "*command*". If they will shoot the person they love most on command, the programming is considered "*engraved*", and only needs to be reinforced periodically from then on.

This all sounds horrendous, but this is how assassin training was done in the group I was in. I underwent it, and had to do it to others. I deeply regret it now. It was a carefully planned, sequential step-by-step process. No one gives a teen a gun, and says, "Go kill someone" in these groups, because the child would balk and be unable to. They start at the preverbal stage, and teach each skill to overlap with the others.

They capitalize on the young child's helplessness, and their rage at others to fuel the programming. Many of the techniques were based on the **MK ULTRA research** *done by the CIA in the 1960's and 1970's.*

The Illuminati trainers were in close contact with Illuminists in Military Intelligence who worked on these projects, such as *Col. Aquinos, Sidney Gottlieb, and Alan Dulles*, among others.

This knowledge of how to condition a subject was passed out among trainers in the different groups, and implemented, with modifications based on age.

The children in the Illuminati are expected to perform tasks such as this in steps, and move up to the next level when they can demonstrate proficiency.

A military commander will ask a teen leader to kill someone in front of the others, with their bare hands, to demonstrate loyalty and obedience. The teen will be given higher status and awards for doing this quickly and well.

This type of programming can be undone, with time, therapy, and concerted effort, and especially prayer to resolve the horrendous traumas that it involves. No human being should ever be forced to do these things, or to undergo this form of training.

It causes massive dissociation, and intense grieving when the person realizes that they have done these things.

It has helped me to realize:
- I had no choice at the time. When I was a young child, those older than I forced me to. Alters created who learned to accept, or even enjoy this training, were created out of the need to

- dissociate and escape psychologically from this horrendous trauma, and those parts hold deep pain and wounding.
- I can grieve before God, and give Him the pain and wounding of a lifetime of intense pain and guilt that these experiences caused, and know forgiveness.
- I have choices now, and have chosen to walk away from this type of activity.
- I can pray that others get out, and escape this type of horrible abuse.
- I can express the anger and outrage that this intentional manipulation of me and others causes, to God, and find healing.

The rage often fueled the abusiveness internally in the past, and as it decreases, the hold of the programming can also lessen this type of programming is mind control at its most insidious, and healing is possible for it. It is a long, slow process, but worth working through.

The Illuminati & Satanic groups are not the only mind control game in town! Thanks to Government sponsored programs such as *Project Paperclip*, U.S. research into the science of public and private mind manipulation has seen incredible leaps forward, leading some to believe a future reminiscent of George Orwell's book *1984* isn't far off.

# Overcoming Denial

"You know you're making all of this up, it isn't true. I certainly don't remember any of the things you are telling me." The speaker was my mother, two years ago, and she was telling me in no uncertain terms that she did not believe me. Her amnesia is intact and strong, protecting her. I had confronted her about the fact that she and
I had spent a lifetime in the cult, and that I loved her and wanted her to get out.

I had told her specific names of people we both knew in this phone call, the first time I had spoken with her in a year. "Mom, you're dissociative, that's why you don't remember," I told her. "No I'm not, nothing happened", she maintained. I decided to blast at her denial a little. She knew that I had never studied or heard German consciously in the daytime, although she had spoken it to me at night since I was very young.

She did not consciously know or understand it at all. "Then why can I speak German now that I've integrated with my back people?" I asked her, in German. "I've never studied it, you know that, or heard it. I studied Spanish and Latin for my languages in school." There was a pause. "Maybe you're psychic, and learned it telepathically," she answered. My mother had to maintain her denial, even then, and come up with some explanation for the unexplainable. But how did she understand my question, which was in German, to her?

My son is integrating quickly now. He had almost 100 inside people when he first came to live with me two and a half years ago at the age of 10 (the Illuminati fragment their children *heavily* from infancy on), and now he has only about 15.

Lately, he has told me the real David, the core child, has been coming out and experiencing life. I am thankful to God that he is young enough that he could heal, and try not to feel jealous that it has been easier and faster for him than for me.

His therapist told me why it is easier for him the other day: *"Your son feels safe now, and he has not one, but two parents validating him and saying they believe him when he comes to them. This means he doesn't have to spend a lifetime overcoming parental denial, and that's one reason he is healing so fast."*

I have never, ever told my son that he is making it up when he deals with memories. I pray with him, and ask God to heal the memories, and to bring security to my son, and to fill the painful areas with the knowledge of His love and mercy. I pray for blessing on both of my children. And God has been faithful to answer.

My son no longer has nightmares at night, has made good friends at school, is active in sports, has better grades than 2 years ago, and tells me he is happy (the last is the most important to me).

I believe that denial is a large barrier to healing. Often, when a survivor begins to recover memories, they will go to family members for validation, or to confront them. They are also frequently faced with invalidation, denial, or even verbal abuse from those same family members, who need to maintain their own denial to protect themselves from facing painful truths. "You're crazy", "You're sick", "You have a sick imagination," "How can you make these things up," "You need help", and more cruel phrases are thrown at the person whose amnesia is beginning to break, from those who want them to maintain it.

After all, if ONE person starts remembering, then OTHERS might, and the others in the family system might not be psychologically strong or healthy enough to remember.

I think one of the saddest realities is that it takes more psychological integrity, honesty, and truth-seeking to remember something as painful as ritual abuse, yet the person who is remembering is told the opposite by family members unwilling to face their own pain.

The disapproval of family members is extremely painful, and is enough to cause some to doubt the reality of their own memories. "Maybe I am making this up, otherwise why don't THEY remember?" the survivor thinks. Or, "I love my parents/ siblings/cousins and I don't want to hurt them. What if they're right?"

When memories are first recovered, they often come in flashes that last a second or two, are vague, and may seem unreal to the person remembering. Add the messages from others that is loud and clear: It is NOT okay to remember, and the survivor may shut down.

Denial may also come from within. It is a basic protective mechanism when a person is confronted with pain; how often do we CONSCIOUSLY deny our own faults
*("It wasn't my fault, I was having a bad day or everyone was against me")* to protect our own self-image.
The more painful the blow to the self-concept *(since people desperately want to maintain an image of themselves as "okay),* the greater the need to deny.

If events that a person went through destroyed their ability to accept themselves as a worthwhile human being (and ritual abuse does this to the maximum), then they will need to deny that it occurred in order to function in daily life.

This is one reason why once the denial is let go of, functionality may temporarily falter in the survivor, as they process the horrendous truths of a childhood filled with pain. It is also a reason why denial can serve a protective function, and should be let go of slowly, carefully, with the help and support of a competent therapist.

Some protective denial in the early stages can be good, as long as the person does not recontact cult members, since it allows the memories to come forward slowly and in an amount that is easier to manage.
Denial may also be programmed in (denial programming). This is done from early childhood, when the child is taught methodically in a calculated manner to disbelieve what they are seeing in front of them, and to create alters who will deny, and punish severely if the person does not deny the ritual abuse. This may be linked to suicidal or flood programming as well.

I had an inside part who was known as *"Forced Denial"*, created when I was 2 ½ years old. *His only job was to ensure that I would deny that I had ever been abused, even when confronted with overwhelming evidence that it had happened* (such as physical scars, court records that indicated abuse in early childhood, and validation from some family members.)

I would go through a horrendous abreaction early in my healing process, after screaming, raging, and crying my eyes out from the pain, and then "*F.D*" would come out and calmly announce, "It's Ok, Nothing happened, I am making this all up." He believed he was protecting my life, since there was suicide programming that kicked in if he didn't do her job, and well as violent protectors who would destroy him.

He would be calm, but sweating heavily, as he denied, until the day he realized that his job was no longer needed, and that those who used to punish him (and me) no longer needed to act out.

Overcoming denial may mean overcoming a lifetime of training to deny, and the intense fear of punishment if the person doesn't. Safety, no contact with cult members, and reasoning with these parts can all help the need to deny decrease.

Finally, denial may come from society. The survivor has it ground in from infancy by the cult that "No one will ever believe you, they will think you are crazy if you ever talk, and lock you up." Our society today often looks the other way, or looks askance at the survivor.

Groups such as the FMS were created to blitz the media with unfounded statements about memory retrieval, and to invalidate survivors who have the courage to speak out and say, "This is real, and it happens." How many news stories are out there that make ritual abuse look as if it is a "modern hysteria" or attempt to denigrate therapists willing to work with and help survivors?

I know that when I was in San Diego, leadership council was well aware of the power of the media, and the council had a saying, **"Don't attack your enemy, discredit him (in the media)**." They found it much more effective, and reporters such as M. Sauer do an excellent job for them. I hope that he, and others that I knew in the group, will learn that they can get out.

The survivor who is able to overcome the denial of family, internal denial, and programmed denial, will still be met by blank looks, or worse, those who turn their backs on them, and say, "I don't want to hear about this, " or "I can't hear about this." Pastors will say this, social workers, CPS workers, and those whose comfort zone is crossed with the thought that ritual abuse really occurs.

Those who tell the survivor, "I believe you", at times may seem far and few between, and I applaud their willingness to look at realities which often make us feel uncomfortable. No one WANTS to think that human beings can do this to one another, or that such horrific abuse is possible.

**I am here to proclaim loud and clear that ritual abuse occurs. It is real. It is not made up!**

The people who disclose their abuse are not crazy, they are not liars, and they are not looking for attention or sympathy. They are some of the most courageous, intelligent, and psychologically honest people that I have ever known in my life, and many are facing some of the most tremendous emotional pain possible by the grace of God, and surviving it.

My one hope is that someday, soon, our society will wake up and come out of its own denial, and be willing to help take action on behalf of those that have survived, and are working desperately to escape the reach of the cult and those associated with it.

May God bless each person who takes the steps to leave and to walk in the truth and freedom, and to fight against a great evil in our land (and around the world).

Upon meeting a victim of Illuminati / Satanic ritual programming it can be difficult if not impossible to detect any of their hidden "alters". Most lie dormant until called upon by their handlers through the use of "triggers" to perform their preprogrammed task.

# Magic Surgery And The Formation Of The Inner World

I would like to introduce another guest author. I discovered this chapter that is offered free on her web site at *http://www.hispresenceonline.org* and was very impressed with her compassion, her knowledge, and her willingness to share with others what she is learning. The author is Patricia Baird Clark, and she is a counselor who works with ritual abuse survivors.

She is also a strong Christian, and much of what she has found out correlates exactly with things that I have found out internally on how things were done. My hope is that this chapter will be helpful to you as well.


*From Chapter 9*
*Magic Surgery and the Formation of the Inner World*
*by Patricia Baird Clark*

In this chapter we will be addressing that which we can expect to encounter in a person who has been satanically ritually abused to a state of high complexity.
These individuals will most likely have been born into a family practicing Satanism for generations with abuse beginning in the womb.

Not all satanically ritually abused persons will have the structures and complexity we will be discussing here; however, we should expect to find these things in highly complex multiples and these individuals are not at all rare.

Persons called to minister in satanic ritual abuse will encounter these individuals and will need a working knowledge of the things discussed in this chapter.
Most, if not all, persons with this much complexity will be women; therefore, I will use the feminine gender throughout this chapter.

Satanic ritual abuse and the resulting formation of multiple personalities create an inner state of incredible complexity. The following concepts will seem bizarre or surreal to those of us who are learning about this for the first time; however, we must remember the extraordinary concepts outlined in this chapter represent these persons' only perception of life and reality. Everything they say must be treated with respect and with serious concern no matter how illusory it may seem to us.

As stated previously **the Old Testament Hebrew word for evil is ra'** *from the root word ra'a meaning to spoil by breaking into pieces.*

Through many torturous rituals the soul is split into numerous parts which we call **alters** *(aka alternate personalities.)*

**Demons are summoned and placed inside to keep the parts separated and alone, inaccessible to the victim.**

Negative emotions and specific cult jobs are assigned to each alter. These alters work against the individual and for the cult keeping her totally under the cult's control. This becomes a living death. A living hell.

The individual is forced by means of ceaseless abuse and demonic programming to form an inner world of darkness. **The Hebrew word for darkness is cho-shek'** *meaning figuratively misery, destruction, death, ignorance, sorrow and wickedness.*

The cultists' aim is to imprison their victim in a web of misery, destruction and living death from which there is no escape. The person's soul is shattered and each piece enmeshed in a maze of dungeons, prisons, booby traps, demons, etc. in their inner world.

**The Inner World**
The ritually abused are extremely wounded, broken and confused. Most of them don't understand what has happened to them. All they know is they are hurting and need help. Our only understanding about what the cult does and why, we learn from these dear, hurting, confused people.

It is difficult to piece together an accurate picture of their inner world, how it functions, and why it was created in the first place. By combining what I've heard and seen from the ritually abused with my knowledge of Scripture, I have formed my own theory to explain the dynamics with which we are dealing.

We know from Scripture that we have *a spirit, a soul and a body. (1 Thes. 5:23 And the very God of peace sanctify you wholly; and I pray God your whole spirit and soul and body be preserved blameless unto the coming of our Lord Jesus Christ.)*
In Genesis 2:7 we are shown how we were created in our three parts. And the Lord God formed man of the dust of the ground, and breathed into his nostrils the breath of life; and man became a living soul. The breath of God became man's spirit. When the breath of God came into contact with man's body, a soul was formed.

These three components are joined within us.
In Hebrews 4:12 we read that Jesus (Himself being the Word of God) does at some point separate the soul from the spirit.

*For the word of God is quick, and powerful, and sharper than any two edged sword, piercing even to the dividing asunder of soul and spirit, and of the joints and marrow, and is a discerner of the thoughts and intents of the heart.*

I believe that as long as our spirit is joined to our soul and body, we are not able to see into the spiritual realm. This is as God intended us to be since Satan and demons could appear as "angels of light" and deceive us.

**God wants us to be innocent concerning evil.** Romans 16:19 says, *I would have you wise unto that which is good, and simple concerning evil.*
This concept of separation of soul and spirit is difficult to explain because there is a separation of soul and spirit which is done by Jesus which is good.

As we mature in our Christian faith and die to our selfish motives we become aware of a separation of soul and spirit. This means that our good works which originate from our spirit are not tied to the carnal motives of our soul.

This separation is not total because there is still a connection that keeps our spirit contained within our body. We do become more aware of the Holy Spirit and we have greater spiritual discernment but we remain somewhat connected.

However, through satanic rituals there is a seemingly sudden and complete separation of soul and spirit which then enables a person to see and hear demons.

In 1 Cor. 15:44 we read, It is sown a natural body; it is raised a spiritual body. There is a natural body, and there is a spiritual body. We know from this that we have a natural body and a spiritual body. It is through the natural body that we contact the physical world around us.
We are not aware of having a spiritual body until we die and discard the natural body. This is as God intended.

Somehow through rituals the Satanists use demons to separate the spiritual body from the natural body. When the soul and spirit have been separated and the natural body is separated from the spiritual body, then a person is fully aware of and enters into an entirely different dimension.

This is the dimension I am calling the inner world. This world is vast and just as real to the individual as the physical world is to us. We think of spirits as being wispy, vapor-like beings but those who are in this dimension tell me the demons have weight and substance.

The inner world is a world of demon spirits and alters and is accessed through the mind. More specifically through the imagination.

**Persons who get involved in Transcendental Meditation or seek spirit guides, for example, are using their imagination to contact the realm of evil spirits.**

God gave us an imagination. An imagination in itself is not an evil thing. We can use our imagination to envision a fabulous new invention which will be of great benefit to mankind. We can use our imagination to picture Jesus as he teaches his disciples and tells them to cast their nets down on the right side of the boat. An imagination can be used for good or it can be used for evil.

When ministering to the highly complex multiple there should come a time early in the sequence of memories where the person will become greatly distressed saying her right side seems to be separated from her left side.

*At this point a demon needs to be cast out.* This will be helpful to the individual but will not deliver her from the spiritual dimension she experiences. This divided feeling may occur with a memory about the ceremony where the dividing was done.

One woman described this ritual where the Satanists used the Hebrews 4:12 scripture in some twisted way while holding an actual sword over her and calling up demons to divide her.

## Magic Surgery

Through magic surgery this spiritual world is furnished with various structures and objects. During magic surgery a child is hypnotized and/or drugged and told *she is going to be operated on and a certain object is to be placed within her.*

The child knows what the object is and its purpose. The cultists cause the child to feel extreme pain in the area of "the surgery", plenty of blood is spread around, the "incision" is made, the object "inserted", the incision "sewed up" and a bandage applied. *For the rest of this person's life she believes this object is within her.*

Because of the spiritual dimension she is in, she is able to see and experience this object as though it were a real thing in our three dimensional world. The Satanists use this for purposes of control.

For example a child may be taken to Germany and shown a castle. She not only sees the outside of the castle but she is taken on a tour of the inside. She spends several days in the castle going through painful, terrifying rituals in many of the rooms. She is forced to memorize the castle's entire layout.

There will be a small replica of the castle much like an architectural model or a small doll house. Something three dimensional which the child thoroughly learns.

Once this has been memorized, she is subjected to magic surgery. A tiny replica of the castle is shown to the child and she is told that it is being placed inside. The castle is now *"within" and has become a structure in the spiritual inner world.* In this person's inner world she can now walk through the rooms and this castle has become as real to her in the spiritual dimension as it had been in the physical world.

**In subsequent rituals this person will dissociate many times and the alters formed will be assigned to live in various rooms**. These rooms are guarded by demons and booby traps are placed in strategic places so there is no escape for the alters locked in the rooms.

These castles have cold, dark dungeons filled with rats and snakes along with torture rooms complete with all the medieval torture devices seen in our Hollywood movies.

This becomes an enormous scheme for control.

If alters don't do exactly as told, they will be taken by demons to a torture chamber and tortured.

This is extremely painful for the individual because the spiritual senses of her spiritual body are heightened. *Spiritual senses are stronger than physical senses, I have been told.*

The pain even spreads to the physical body. When a Christian counselor has been willing to exchange his life for Christ's there is tremendous authority given by the
Lord over this whole scheme.
Jesus knows how to protect the alters when they begin talking. He gives us power to lock up all the demons and He hides the alters where they cannot be found.

Through magic surgery the cultists have placed booby traps throughout the person's inner world. Of course, these things are not actually inside but because the person *believes* they are there, demons can use them for control.

Satanists anticipate the possibility that alters may begin talking to a counselor. To keep them silent in their rooms or to punish them for talking, the booby traps are in place to be triggered whenever any of the scheme is threatened. These booby traps can be anything a perverted, demon-filled programmer's mind can imagine.

Think of any of the movies featuring Harrison Ford in the Indiana Jones series. these are the kinds of booby traps that can await nonconforming alters in this inner world.

A very common booby trap device is a bomb. One particular afternoon I discovered that a woman who had just started having abuse memories had not had anything to drink that entire day.

Upon inquiry the Lord revealed there was a "bomb" inside set to explode should she drink anything. She was absolutely terrified. I called upon Him to remove it, which He did, and then she was able to drink two large glasses of water.

*In this inner world "what you believe is what you get."*

Demons can simulate the detonation of a bomb complete with sound effects and pain. Many of these devices are planned to destroy the life or sanity of the individual who begins talking.

This is just one example of why this kind of counseling can only be successfully done by a Christian who lets Jesus Christ do the work. If a secular counselor tried to remove this bomb, it would have "exploded" and the woman would have needed medication and possibly hospitalization.

One lady described to me what happened inside when well-meaning church people tried to cast demons out of her. A bomb exploded and she felt as though shrapnel
had been propelled into every part of her body. The shrapnel was actually powerful demons catapulted into her arms, legs, head. every part of her body. with the
message to kill those trying to help her and then run outside and jump in front of traffic.

She was aware of what was happening but totally out of control. Two men had been working with her but at that point two more people were required to hold her down.

*Anything in the physical world can be placed into a person's inner world through magic surgery.* The following are some of the things commonly found in the inner world for purposes of control. These can only be removed as the Lord leads. Most of them are connected in some way to painful abuse memories and will be removed at the time of the memory; however, this is not always the case.

It is important to let the Lord lead. It would not be good for a counselor to randomly try to look for these devices.

1. Computers - The computer will be used by demons and/or cult alters to control anything or anybody in the system.

2. Receivers, walkie-talkies, etc. - The person may actually hear a perpetrator's voice giving her instructions. This is, of course, done by demons. If the perpetrator wants the person to come to a specific place at a certain time, he calls a demon to go activate the walkie-talkie and give the instructions to the individual. A demon has the ability to sound like and look like any human being.

3. Tape recorders - These may play demeaning, hurtful remarks said by other persons or they may play repeated instructions for certain

behaviors, etc. These may be programmed to activate in any given circumstance. For example, if the person receives a compliment, a tape recorded voice says demeaning things to negate anything kind that was said. Again, this is demonic trickery.
4. Video tapes - Horrific scenes of human torture, etc. can be repeatedly projected into the person's mind.

5. Alarm clocks - These can be set to sound off at different times during the night and also during the day to make sure the person never has restful sleep.

6. A furnace - This may be used to suck all the energy out of a person or suck alters into it for destruction. It may keep the person overheated. All of these are to
keep the individual traumatized.

7. Mazes - Alters are often trapped behind mazes. Jesus is able to bring them out and destroy the maze.
These are only a few of the things that are commonly found in the inner world of the SRA. The possibilities are endless because anything in the physical world can be transferred into the inner world through trickery and magic surgery.

**The Origin of Alters**
For those persons born into families embroiled in generational Satanism the abuse begins in their mother's womb. A fetus can be abused in many ways e.g. electric
shock, needle jabs, bricks dropped on the mother's belly, raping the mother, etc.

We assume a fetal monitor is used to measure the baby's heartbeat. When the heartbeat accelerates and then suddenly drops significantly, the baby has dissociated within the womb.

The cultists try to get six, thirteen, or even eighteen splits in the womb since these are satanic numbers of power but they are not always successful in getting these desired numbers. Each split in the womb then becomes a "seed" which will be *further split* to populate a layer of personalities within the inner structure of the person's psyche.

**The Structure of the Inner World**

The alters and furnishings of the inner world are not randomly placed. There is a basic structure into which each person or object is directed. This structure will have as many levels as there were splits in the womb.

If a person split thirteen times in her mother's womb then her inner structure will have 13 levels. There are some
instances where the number of splits in utero where not as many as desired so immediately after birth the newborn baby was made to split once or twice adding to the number of levels.
These levels or layers should have a geometric shape which often is the same for each level. For example, if squares were used, each level may be a square. Others will have combinations of geometric figures such as squares combined with triangles or circles, for example. Each level is divided into sections or rooms where
alters are assigned to live.

Demon guards are stationed in strategic places on all the levels. Underneath all these layers will be a pit. Sometimes this pit will have as many levels as the basic structure itself.

The different levels are connected by staircases (often circular) which intersect the gates on each level. It is similar to a high-rise apartment building but the design may be more modernistic because the levels are not necessarily the same size and they may turn at different angles from one another. *Often the levels are designed to
rotate or spin.*

This structure is "placed inside" the child at a very young age. A model of the structure is built and the child is required to thoroughly memorize it. She memorizes the structure including the location of demon guards on each level and the placement of the seed alter on each level. Then through magic surgery the structure is placed inside and the child is told it will grow with her. During this
"surgery" the child believes that she has been cut from her throat down to her lower abdomen and this structure then fills the entire trunk of her body.

Each alter formed through splits in the womb is assigned to a particular level. This alter on each level becomes the seed which populates through splitting that particular level of the structure. The top level of the structure is called the presenting level. This is were alters that perform the tasks of daily living are housed. They are the ones who clean the house, go to work, take care of the children, communicate with the outside world, etc.

These alters are often unaware of each other until it is revealed to them through counseling. They know nothing about the alters on lower levels or that lower levels even exist. Upper level alters were formed by the victim for the purpose of coping with the challenges of everyday life and are sometimes called the "home system."

The presenting level will most likely have a small number of alters. perhaps as few as seven or eight. The area of this level will be the smallest of all levels.
Progressing down through the structure we should expect to find increasingly larger and more densely populated levels. It is common for lower levels to have hundreds of alters. The lower the level the more committed to darkness the alters will probably be.

Cult alters living on the lower levels know all about the upper layers and are able to take control of the entire system. Those alters who are the most powerful and committed to darkness are on the lowest level.

*When lower level cult alters want to take over the body, they come up through the gates, give a password to each demon guarding the gates, and proceed to the top presenting level.* The home system alters have no ability to resist the cult alters and are forced to do whatever they are told.

Cult alters may take a home system alter down to a place of torture as punishment for talking or any other infringement. After a time of ministry it may be helpful to pray and ask the Lord to seal the gates so the lower level alters and demons cannot come up to the presenting level and cause trouble. This is not a formula. God has led me to do this with some persons but with others He has instructed me differently. We must be open to the Lord's guidance.

**Kinds of Alters**
Alters can be anyone or anything according to the desires of the programmers or according to the needs of the person. Someone who has been abused to this complexity knows only one coping mechanism. dissociation. By this means the cult purposely creates alters for their evil designs and the survivor on her own creates alters for coping with life.

Therefore some alters will be cult alters with specific cult designated jobs and some alters will be helpers with jobs assigned by the abused person. There will also be alters who do not fall into either category which we will discuss later.

Cult alters were formed by the cult through rituals and torture to carry out the purposes of the cult. They have various duties such as teaching, storing information, performing rituals, taking her out to rituals, calling demons to her, storing satanic power, blocking Christian counseling, managing programs, etc.
In a highly complex multiple there will be numerous alters assigned to kill the survivor should she find effective Christian counseling that begins setting her free.

Cult alters are given an identity by the cult complete with their own assigned physical characteristics. The survivor may be middle aged and overweight but an alter living within the same body may believe she is a teenager with a svelte figure.

Cult alters work against the well being of the individual even to the point of trying to kill her so it is often necessary to tell them they inhabit the same body. This they often vehemently deny even saying demeaning things about the person's physical appearance and personality.

At this point it is helpful to have them look into a mirror to prove to them they were deceived by the cult. It is common for them to proclaim that the mirror is a trick which they had been warned about. I tell them to stick out their tongue while looking in the mirror. This will often convince them they were deceived.

Many of these will gladly relinquish their assignment of murder when they realize they would be committing suicide.

Satanists access the cult alters through the use of triggers such as code names, flashing lights, beeps, numbers, etc. Through abuse and programming the survivor actually becomes much like a human computer accessible to anyone who knows the program and the access codes. These alters can also be activated by other means. Some alters are activated by demons which the cult sends forth from their rituals.

Other alters were formed and programmed years ago to become active on a certain date. For example, if the cult decided the person was to die at age 50, alters with the assignment to kill her would become active when she turned 50. Cult astrologers have known for eons when certain heavenly phenomena would occur.

For example a full moon on the same day as a lunar eclipse occurring on Friday the 13th (which happened in March of 1998) was anticipated by the cults for many years. Certain alters may have been assigned to come forth on that day and take the person out to a ritual where these alters were to perform certain functions.
Each cult alter must be delivered of demons and converted to Jesus Christ. This is usually accomplished within fifteen to thirty minutes, more or less. Jesus gives them a new job and they become helpers working for the well being of the individual.

Many of these cult alters have information which will be beneficial for reaching other alters. For example, a cult alter named Bobby attempted, in my presence, to kill the host person but after conversion was assigned by Jesus the job of telling me whenever booby traps were nearby.

Bobby had been forced by the cult to memorize the location of every booby trap on the first seven levels of the person's thirteen tiered inner structure. Now that he was on our side he became a valuable asset to the ministry.

Other cult alters know they live in the host's body but still work against her. Some of these alters, which I call kamikaze alters, are so committed to darkness they will gladly sacrifice their own life to kill the survivor. Some of these will be won to Jesus Christ but others will not even though they see and hear Him. These Jesus removes.
A woman with highly complex MPD will have many male alters. They may appear early in the ministry or they may not manifest until several months of counseling
have been completed but they will definitely be there.

It is common to meet an alter who believes she is a dog. She may not be able to speak but can only bark. Asking another alter who may be watching to speak for
her is helpful.

How, one may ask, does someone come to believe she is dog? Satanists like to make their victims feel inhuman. The less human they feel the more willing they will be to welcome the demons and adopt their behavior (demons can be very animalistic.)

*This kind of programming is very brutal. They make a child or teenager strip naked and put her in a pen with dogs for perhaps as long as a week. She is not allowed to display any human behavior during that entire week.*

*She is forbidden to stand up on two feet, speak, sleep on a bed, drink or eat with her hands. She must crawl on her hands and knees and lap water and food from a dish as the dogs do. Male dogs will repeatedly rape her as well.*

Some alters may be kittens. I have found these alters to have been formed by the survivor in her attempts to cope with her abuse. One little girl alter told me she noticed that the kittens on her family's farm were left alone.

She reasoned that perhaps if she could become a kitten her abusers would leave her alone. Some of these alters will speak as well as meow but others will require someone else to speak for them.

Once I was ministering to a kitten alter who would gently meow and rub her head against my shoulder. Then she would suddenly act like an angry cat hissing and clawing at her face. It took a minute before I realized she had demons that were also acting like a cat.

Some alters, due to abusive programming, may believe they are space aliens or robots. One woman remembered being subjected to a week of dog programming, followed by a week of alien programming, followed by another week of robot programming. By the end of those three weeks she had no idea what she was but she was sure she was not human.

One of the most memorable alters I've known was Rubber Man. He, as part of the home system, was created by the survivor to fulfill the incredible work demands forced on her by her wicked stepmother. Being made of rubber he could stretch his arms and legs to reach into unreachable places and accomplish seemingly impossible tasks.

As he was sharing about himself he kept stretching out his arms and legs to show how he could reach things. He was particularly good at washing windows and cleaning out gutters. Rubber Man never talked. he only sang in a loud voice making everything rhyme. He liked to cheer her when she felt sad.

Many alters, especially baby and child alters, will have no particular job. They may be locked away in dark dungeons, pits, prisons, nurseries, etc. where they are frightened and miserable. *These alters are often the "cast offs" formed as the person was subjected to increasing degrees of pain and terror during programming or rituals.*

In order to produce the desired cult alter, the Satanists will subject a person to excruciating horror and pain necessitating several dissociations, each subsequent alter being stronger and more committed to darkness than the previous one.

For example if the person switches five times before the desired alter is formed, the first four alters are not wanted by the cult. These are then assigned a living death in some type of *internal prison*.

Sometimes an alter who is perceptively very little will manifest but won't answer any questions. Chances are this is a preverbal alter. Ask if someone else can speak for her. Yesterday I met a preverbal alter in a 53-year-old woman. With her hair pulled down over her face, she peeked out at me while sucking her thumb and rubbing the top of her nose with her forefinger. She was obviously frightened but curious.

When she wouldn't answer any questions I asked if someone could speak for her. At that point I met 11-year-old Lisa who told me all about "Rini's" abuse.

Rini then returned and I asked Jesus to minister to her. As I had anticipated she was afraid of Jesus but as He often does, He sent a little lamb to her. I watched as she petted the lamb and giggled when he nuzzled against her neck.

After a short time with the lamb, she looked up into Jesus's face with total awe and then lifted her arms for Him to pick her up. She seemed to relax and rest her head upon His shoulder as He carried her away to a safe place.

# The Source Of Real Healing

I am often asked, "Why have you chosen to write so openly on the topic of ritual abuse and mind control?" (Translation: Are you nuts? A secret worker for the cult giving out disinformation? Do you have a secret death wish if the information you share IS accurate?).

I have chosen to be vulnerable, and share from my own memories and experiences for several reasons. Not because I am inviting harm from the group I left; I want to expose them as liars. Not because I am "nuts", but because I am healing. Not to disinform, but to help others.

I know how lonely the healing process can be. I know how often what a survivor reports to their therapist or their supporters seems unbelievable, and the survivor
(and sometimes the therapist as well!) wonders; "Is what I remember really true?

Can people really do this to each other?" Or the need for validation. Early in my healing, as I remembered names and dates of information that seemed incredibly cruel, I wanted to know that I was not alone. It was hard. I would ask my therapist, "Have you ever heard of this before?" and honest person that he was, he would respond, "No." This was from someone working with a group that specialized in ritual abuse. In fact, the head of the program once took me aside, and said, "You know more than my own therapists about this (programming)." I had already figured that out.

If by sharing a little of my own healing journey, it helps others understand ritual abuse better, governmental mind control, and the process of healing, then the articles will be worth it. If it helps one survivor break through programming and heal, it is worth it.

People ask me, "Why aren't you dead?" (ie "why hasn't the cult come and gotten you and punished you for writing what you do?"). My answer: Because they are
NOT all powerful, as they claim. They are out and out liars. Because I have safe outside accountability, and because I am in ongoing therapy with an excellent
therapist. And, because of the true source of healing, which I will share here.

One of the most difficult tasks for a survivor of severe cult abuse and mind control is overcoming a lifetime of lies. I was told when part of the group that the Illuminati would run the world. That they are on the verge of a complete takeover. That everyone was just a helpless pawn who would either help them, or be crushed.
But the Word of God has an answer to this in Psalm 2, one of my favorite psalms.

"Why are the nations in an uproar, and the people devising a vain thing? The kings of the earth take their stand, and the rulers take counsel together, against the Lord and against His anointed…" (Sound familiar? Rich kings and rulers plotting together to rule and fight against God? But look how God views them): …He who sits in the heavens laughs, the Lord scoffs at them.

Then He will speak to them in His anger and terrify them in His fury: 'But as for Me, I have installed my King upon Zion, My holy mountain." God sees the plots to rule the world as laughable, and the end result worthy of His derision.

Mankind may make plans to wrest control of the world, but in the end, God has HIS ruler appointed, and there is nothing that the Illuminati, the NWO, the CIA, or any other group can do to change this fact.

This takes a lot of the fear away. God wins! We know that no matter what happens temporarily, God will allow His Son to rule as our true King throughout eternity.

And, my favorite verse at the end of this psalm shows where true healing comes: "How blessed are all who take refuge in Him!"

In my own life, true healing has come as I cried out to God for His comfort. To be honest, much of the horror and pain that I experienced as a young child goes beyond belief, and psychology CANNOT heal it, or bring comfort or sanity.

Yes, outside support helps, but the greatest source of my own healing has been running to God, and asking for His help. When I have struggled with suicide programming inside, I have cried out to heaven for strength and faith, and that it would break (it did).

When psychotic programming has kicked in, and I have lain in bed for hours, shaking, teeth shattering, with terror beyond belief that was unrelieved even by spiritual warfare, only crying out and asking Jesus to hold me in His arms has brought help. It drew me closer to Him as well. When I feel alone, because I cannot at this point safely have contact with my mother or family of origin, only the knowledge that I have a heavenly Father who loves me can help fill the deep ache inside.

When my own children have shared their own pain, weeping because of the horrific abuse that they endured, only the love of God through the Holy Spirit could help me pray, "God, I hate what they did to my children, but help me to forgive." I hate what the demonic did to myself and my children. But I want to forgive those who hurt me.

This is a process, with ups and downs, and I come to God, and give Him my feelings, or even my despair that I am numb and CAN'T feel at times.
But when depression threatens to blanket me, I remember that "Blessed are those who take refuge in Him." And I go to the real source of healing, the only one that I have found, the One who loves me and cares for me, who truly understands what I and others have been through.

There is no condemnation in His love, there is forgiveness for my past; there is no judgement for my being needy, weak, exhausted, or fighting intense emotions as I battle old messages and programming; instead, there is the still, quiet comfort that is the rock beneath, and the source of sanity when I remember the insane. And this is where I find my courage, and the ability to write what I do, in the hope that it will bless and help others as well in their healing journey.
Because it is a lonely journey, but I am not alone…

# Near Death Experiences

**Near Death Programming**
This is part of an ongoing series on complex programming that I am writing as an outline for a sequel to my first book, "Breaking the Chain". In this article, I will be discussing one of the most traumatic forms of programming that a survivor can undergo. This programming involves the use of Near Death Experiences.

The Illuminati have studies human neurophysiology for years, and the effects of traumatic conditioning on the human brain and psyche. In their search for better and more reliable methods of ingraining programming, they have utilized research from a variety of sources: governmental agencies; totalitarian regimes, and their own experimentation that is ongoing on a continuous (and secretive) basis.

But some of the foundations for this type of programming have been in place for centuries. One of the oldest rituals that the Illuminati utilize is the "resurrection ceremony". In fact the Phoenix, symbol of death and new life, is one of their highest symbols and symbolizes the coming of the New Order and its leader.
How is resurrection programming done, or its variations? I will share what I have undergone and/or witnessed.
A young child of around two or three will be very heavily traumatized during an occult ceremony. They will be abused, beaten, shocked and even suffocated, and given drugs to create a state that is near death. The child will almost always at this point feel that they are suspended above their body, watching the unconscious body beneath that has been tortured to the point of being near death.

There will always be medical personnel involved in programming at this depth, who are skilled at monitoring the child's physical state, and of resuscitating them.
Resuscitation equipment and medications are on hand at all times.

The child in this extremity will have their deepest core called out at this point, and brought to consciousness in extreme pain. They will then be told that they have a "choice": to face certain death, or to choose life if they will invite a powerful demon inside.

The child chooses life. The demon enters, the child goes unconscious, and then awakens later in clean clothing, in a soft bed, with healing ointments on. They are extremely weak and shaky, and are told by a kind, caring, soft voiced woman (or man) that the child had died, but the demon "brought them back to life", that they owe their very life and heartbeat to it and those who "saved them". The child is also told that if they ask the demonic entity to leave, that they will revert to the near death/dying state they were in when it made its entrance.

This is one type of near death experience used to control and terrify a very young child, and to force it to accept a demonic spirituality under the most traumatic and coercive circumstances imaginable. The child feels marked and chosen for life by this experience, and it profoundly influences the child's core beliefs about him/herself and their deepest reality.

It is also one of the most horrible manipulations of a young child that can occur, and is designed to take away their free choice or will.

Another form of near death programming will occur in a situation that has often been called "governmental mind control" but which I always viewed as linked to the
Illuminati programming (since the trainers/scientists in each crossed over from one to the other and shared information).
For example, at Tulane Medical Center, nearby, was a place known as the "Institute". The Institute was involved in experimentation in mind control techniques put in under the most extreme circumstances, including at the point of near physical death.

For some of this programming, a "subject" *(how I hate that word, used by trainers to emotionally distance themselves from the fact that this was a human being, with feelings and emotions being worked on)* would be in a hospital ward, isolated from others by blank grey white walls.

The subject was tied down by four points, and also across the waist and neck. They were then wrapped in a cocoon like manner with soft gauze, to limit movement or any feeling or sensation in the limbs.

Usually, "subjects" were fed intravenously, and then underwent severe sensory deprivation, broken by bombardment with extremely loud noises. A darkened room would be broken by glaring white lights in the middle of the night, and the "subject" loses orientation of night or day.

The subject, when near breaking, is then shocked heavily and drugged. They may be placed temporarily on a respirator, and given paralytic drugs.

The anxiety level reaches extreme points as this abuse continues, and I had heard of people literally having a heart attack from fear at this point. The person is drugged and shocked again, and then told that they are dying. They watch their body from above, and are actually glad that finally release will come from the days of torment at this place.

At this point, a trainer with a kind, soothing voice will come in and repetitiously say, "You deserve to live, I won't let you die. You owe your life to me." Recorded messages are also played over and over, repetitiously, at this point, which describe the "subjects" future destiny for "family", etc.

Finally, slowly, the subject is allowed to awaken, to come out of unconsciousness, with the constant message of being "reborn" for the "family group" being played. Kind faced people soothe the subject as they recover from this hideously traumatic programming sequence. The person feels insanely grateful to be alive, to be released from the horrors of the days when they lay near death in the Institute, and will cling like a preverbal child to the adults
around them.

They are extremely vulnerable at this point, and extremely receptive to the messages placed in under trauma. I should know. I was a "subject' at the
Institute as a child in the 1960's and early 1970's, and later visited as an adult as a "consultant".

This is deep level programming put in under extreme circumstances, and the fear level for the survivor when they begin to remember this type of trauma can be extremely high. I wish I could whitewash it, say that it isn't this bad, but it is.

I know that this may stretch the believability of some people, but this type of programming really, truly occurs (along with other types of sophisticated mind control methods).

Near death programming has many variations, and I have only touched on two (there are other forms as well).
Programming put in when in a near death state will be at core level, since the survival level at that point touches the person's core, no matter how well protected.
The person who has undergone it may believe that if they try to break it, they might die. That they will enter a near death state. That their heart will stop. I went through all of these fears, and more, when dealing with this type of programming inside, and to this day I struggle at times with the residual terror it left.

The lies ground in at this almost unconscious state will be believed deeply at a core level, since the child undergoing it is desperately needing to believe the adults who literally hold the power of life and death over them. The child has been completely broken down by the planned, horrific trauma, and will embrace these messages at their deepest core as being true.

This is why core beliefs and messages are so very hard to undo at this level. It means excellent support, a safe environment, and spiritual awareness and discernment, since the demonic stronghold will also be severe at this point.

Help from a therapist knowledgeable about programming, and spiritual help from those who know about deliverance, is a vital part of therapy at this point.

The survivor who reaches this level of programming inside will have reached core level.

The programming will be some of the most deeply held and believed, and will be almost impossible to reach at a conscious level, until there is deep system cooperation and safety and trust in the outside people helping the survivor.

This is also where faith in God, and His ability to heal ANYTHING, including the most severe of physical, emotional, and spiritual traumas, will make all the difference. This type of programming may need to be worked on in a safe inpatient setting, or with extreme safety externally, since fear may cause panic and acting out when it begins to come out.

Reality orientation may be lost for a bit as the programming sequences surface, and it will take the strength of the entire system to help slow the memories down and make them manageable. Medication will probably also be needed, to help with the severe sense of depression, loss, abandonment, and betrayal that this type of programming will bring out. Despair over choices made, and wondering if the survivor can survive remembering will come up.
A hopeful, supportive, nurturing, and encouraging attitude can make the difference. Scripture verses that remind the person of God's love and ability to heal, of His care, and promises of forgiveness and caring, will be very important.

Breaking this type of programming is immensely tiring and plenty of rest and nutritious food is important. This is NOT the time to take on extra stressors. Allowing the survivor to vent their fear, reassuring them, praying with them, and caring for them will become a lifeline.

Hearing their rage at what was done as they discuss the "SOBs who did this to me" will be healing, and don't rush them towards premature or false forgiveness. The survivor will have to look at and acknowledge the trauma, the damage, and then find hope that they are surviving the remembering of core trauma.

Bringing in gentle, non-taxing good experiences such as a playtime, drawing, or a nature walk can be healing. Outlets such as journaling and talking about how they feel will be very important in processing this type of programming.

I have described some of the most viciously traumatic programming that can be done to a child or young teen in this group. It is possible to work it through, slowly, with time and caring support and prayer. My wish in discussing this has not been to be gory or graphic, but to help others understand that this type of programming does occur, and may need to be worked through by the survivor of occultic/ ritualistic abuse.

# Maintaining External Safety

As survivors heal, they often learn things that are helpful to others. In another guest chapter, Olyssa shares what has helped her in maintaining safety from the cult. I admire her courage and her insights here as she shares from her heart.

The goal of external safety is to create an environment that will allow you to begin to decipher the complex inner workings of your system and how it has been programmed. Until my system knew it was safe it refused to disclose itself.

For this article, I am going to speak in the first person about my own experience. I would suggest that much of what I say will be applicable to the inner workings of your system since cults share similar programming techniques. Like the language of love, the language of programming is universal.

Each of us is a unique human being with a unique experience of love, but love itself is consistent, based on respect, intimacy, safety, harmony etc. So too is programming consistent, based on instilling terror and obedience through violent betrayal and trauma bonding. In sharing what my process has been like, it is my hope you will better understand yourself and the ways programming has debilitated your freedom and recovery.

Once I was in an adequately safe environment it has been a painstaking process to break down the programs that keep me under the control of the cult. There are 4 ways in which I struggle against the cult's presence in my life.

1) Actual external contacts from the cult including members appearing unexpectedly in public places, audio cues such as musical tones, beeps or distant sounds or phrases that seem benign to most people (including the "day self") but set off programs.

2) Ongoing Phone Contacts as initiated by automaton programs in reporting alters. These phone contacts keep the cult informed of our activities and allow them to influence our perception of our circumstances to give them greater power over us.

3) Complex PTSD Anytime the least little similarity occurs bridging a trauma experience with present day it creates tremendous anxiety. It can often leave alters convinced they are back in the trauma.

*Circumstances that are merely happenstance but create a bridge to a trauma experience can set off programs as powerfully as actual cult contacts.

4) Drug Addiction At the root of the ongoing phone reports are a layer of alters who have been carefully cultivated to have a drug addiction, a fix they can ONLY get when they stay in contact with the cult.

Not only are they dependent on the drug for the fix, but to help mask the heinous graphic violence that they were only able to endure through being drugged. Without the drugs, they start to feel their feelings.

Their terrible pain and suffering is unmanageable to them, The only way they know how to survive is to numb themselves. They are driven to keep reporting alters in contact so they can maintain their deep addiction.

I have already addressed the importance for safety from actual external cult contact in the first article. In this article I will speak in greater depth about the other three factors which are all intertwined.

I never knew that there were hidden parts of me that have done everything they can to manipulate my life and influence me so they can maintain their addiction.

My reporting alters exist in several layers. The top layer have been through horrific trauma bonding and think this is love. When they make contact they are given lavish praise, filled with messages about how special they are.

Beyond the desire for approval and praise, the second layer has been badly tortured to instill the visceral obedience to the "phone home" programs. They feels they cannot withstand the anxiety of refraining to comply when the "phone home" program is set off, usually by the day of the week or month it has been instilled in them to report. Or by PTSD flashbacks.

As I have begun to work with the reporting alters to help them manage their anxiety when they feel prompted to make a call I have become aware that there is a group inside who fan the embers of anxiety in the reporting alters. This group, the third layer, are the hidden alters who have been weaned onto drugs.

When the reporting alters were created and trained, they were put through a combination of torture and reward. The only way they could get relief from the torture was to pick up the phone and dial. Once they would do this, drugs were given as the reward.

Now, my brain chemistry will reproduce the drug experience merely from the reporting alters making the report over the phone. As well, the drug addiction has been reinforced regularly with actual "drug sessions."

The life I, the day self, has tried to build has been torn down again and again because of this deeply buried addiction held by separate alters. Every close noncult friendship I have ever built has been terminated. Always it has been that the cult tells the deep, addicted insiders that they cannot get their fix because this noncult person is in the way.

Then the hidden cult alters are filled with hate toward my friend and attack them and pick on them relentlessly until I am overwhelmed with the belief that it IS true, that this friendship must end.

Once I pull away from the non-cult friend, the addicted alters are "rewarded" with an actual drug session. The
cult has successfully isolated me and has complete control over the system once again.

Getting free from the cult means having the compassion, patience and acceptance to help the addicted alters work through the debilitating pain and anxiety that will surface for them when it is not being masked by the fix.

The only way for them to recover is to help the reporting alters not give in to their anxiety and report. The addicted alters NEED to scare the reporting ones and will exploit the PTSD in the reporting ones if that's what it takes to convince them they must get to a phone and make a contact.

I was deep into my recovery before I discovered I had hidden addicted alters. Learning how they have been trained and traumatized and how they manipulate the system has been critical to recovery.

As the system caretaker now that I know what is going on, it is important for me to presence the addicted ones and reassure them and welcome them.

Part of having DID means we often tend to divide amongst ourselves, alters blaming other alters or distrusting each other. The way we can ultimately separate from the cult is to build a life that includes all alters and respects their histories and their fears and weaknesses as well as their courage and strengths.

When I first found out that these hidden addicted alters had been manipulating and terrorizing the anxious reporting alters I was inclined to be angry at them. But I understand that they did this because their own terror was so great. They did not know me, the caretaker. They did not know love. They did not know how they would survive without the fix.

By spending time each day reassuring them that I am unconditionally here for them and that I will never reject and that I will keep them safe from the cult and help them through their addiction they are slowly beginning
to trust me and let me help them.

In order for the programmed/cult loyal alters to be willing to take a leap of faith outside of the dark world they have been raised in, there must be a part of you who can catch them, however imperfectly and accept them for what they, in their helplessness and fear, did to survive.

My alters learned a long time ago, "If you can't beat them, join them." It kept you alive. Now it is time to own that every one of these alters and you are part of the same self.

As you can meet and accept each other and realize these cult parts are part of your whole self, than you can become free.

# Understanding The Phenomenology Of SRA/DID

**UNDERSTANDING THE PHENOMEMOLOGY OF SRA/DID AS IT PERTAINS TO**
**THE IMAGE OF GOD IN MAN**
by Doug Riggs

### Introduction
In working with people who are SRA/DID, I have tried to understand this complex phenomenon within the context of the Bible. The Biblical account of God's creating man in His own image is essential to our understanding of the phenomenology of SRA/DID, and the resolution of those with whom we are counseling.

I have found that with the understanding of the Biblical revelation, that man was created in the image of God, we as therapists and counselors, with God's guidance and power, possess an effective tool to lead our clients to full resolution and integration.

It is through the application of the Biblical revelation of man as he was created in the image of God, that within the context of SRA/DID I have found a strategic protocol in the resolution of those with this type of abuse history.

Man Created in God's Image In order to lay a foundation for the topic of this paper, I will quote Genesis l:26-27 along with Genesis 5:l-2 from the New American
Standard Bible. "Then God said, "Let Us make man in Our image, according to Our likeness; and let them rule over the fish of the sea and over the birds of the sky and over the cattle and over all the earth, and over every creeping thing that creeps on the earth." And God created man in His own image, in the image of God created him; male and female He created them." "This is the book of the generations of Adam.

In the day when God created man, He made him in the likeness of God. He created them male and female, and He blessed them and named them

Man in the day when they were created." From these passages the Hebrew noun/pronoun and verbal construction is very illuminating.

Verse 26 begins with "God said." 'God' in the Hebrew is the plural noun Elohim. The plural may be understood as the 'plural of majesty.' With the New Testament revelation of the Trinity we might now retrospectively understand this as a 'plural of Trinity.'

Next, we have the qal imperfect third masculine singular of the verb amar, translated "said." Therefore, God is a plurality (Trinity) who speaks (sing.) in unity as one Godhead: Father, Son and Holy Spirit.

Continuing, the verse states, "Let Us make" which is a qal imperfect verb, asah, first common plural suffix, again depicting the creative activity of the Godhead, acting in the triunity of their being in the creation of man.

The word "man" is the masculine singular noun, adam, followed by the phrase "in Our image and according to Our likeness." The descriptive phrases, "image" (tselem) and "likeness" (damuth) are both singular nouns with plural suffix endings.

This indicates that God in His triunity is unified as to His image and likeness. God further states in this verse that "man" (Heb. sing.) is also a plural or a "them", who
are to exercise dominion over the lower creation.
Furthermore, in verse 28, God (Elohim, pl.) "created",(qal imperfect of the verb bara, 3rd. masc.sing.), "man"; this verb in the singular indicates that God, in His triunity, created man as a manifestation of the unity of His essence.

Here we have, in contrast to verse 26, the masc. sing. noun "image" followed by the masc. sing. pronominal suffix "his".

This is followed by the repitition of the subject, Elohim (Heb. pl.) "creating" (sing. verb) "man" (sing.). Man is further defined as male and female, i.e., a unity in plurality or diversity. "God created them" (pl.). In Gen. 5:1-2 the text states that the same God, Elohim, created man (Heb. Adam) to manifest the unity of the divine image.

This verse further states that this man, Adam, is also a "them", i.e., male and female - a plurality corresponding to the plurality of the Godhead, and that their "name" (sing. noun shem) is man, adam.

In other words, man, created in the image of God, shares the unity which corresponds to the essence of God, described as image and likeness, which in turn manifests itself in diversity as male and female. Furthermore, the male and female, in Gen. 5:2, share one name -"man" (sing.). In summary, I would like to quote John Sailhamer from Expositor's Bible Commentary, Vol.II, pg.38: "In v. 27 it is stated twice that man was created (bara) in God's image and a third time that man was
created (bara) "male and female."

The same pattern is found in Gen. 5:1-2a: "When God created man,. he created (bara) them male and female." The singular man is created as a plurality, "male and female". In a similar way the one God "And God said") created man through an expression of his plurality, "Let us make man in our image").

Following this clue the divine plurality expressed in v. 26 is seen as an anticipation of the human plurality of the man and woman, thus casting the human relationship between man and woman in the role of reflecting God's own personal relationship with himself. "

Could anything be more obvious than to conclude from this clear indication that the image and likeness of the being created by God signified existence in confrontation, i.e., in this confrontation, in the juxtaposition and
conjunction of man and man which is that of male and female, and then to go on to
ask against this background in what the original and prototype of the divine existence of the Creator consists?" (K. Barth, Church Dogmatics, New York:
Scribner, 1956, 3/1, p. 195).

We may conclude from these passages from Genesis that God (plural of trinity) speaks and creates in unity as one Godhead; that man is created in the image (sing.) and likeness (sing.) of God as to his unified essence and nature. Man as a created being in his unified essence and nature, is a plurality of expression as male and female.

As individuals, both male and female have the capacity to manifest our unified essence and nature through our personalities in great diversity of thought, communication, creativity and self-determination.

The point I want to emphasize is that man, created in the image and likeness of God, is a unity of essence but expresses that essence in plurality as mentioned above.

This plurality or diversity of expression is designed by the triune Godhead to be expressed through a unified or a whole personality and identity.

When a person is subjected to chronic abuse in early childhood his/her personality and identity is fragmented. This fragmentation of the identity and personality does not destroy the underlying nature and essence of that person created in the image of God.

I have discovered in the process of my work with SRA/DID clients, that wherever there is a plurality of phenomena presenting within the context of their dissociation, there is always a unifying essence, center, source, and beginning of whatever the dissociative/phenomenological metaphor may be.

To help understand what I am seeking to communicate, I will give you several examples of how this principle of man, created in the image of God, applies when working within the phenomenological context of SRA/DID.

Illustration #1: Your client describes that they see a castle within their program structure. I ask them to tell me if there are any parts off their humanity contained within the castle (the answer is usually yes).

Then I ask how many, and they may say 12. I immediately know, based on the fact that man is created in the image of God, that the reference to 12 is an example of plurality; so I ask, in the name of Jesus Christ, where is the unifying center, source, essence, and beginning to the 12?

In other words, these 12 have a common origin, source and beginning somewhere within the person's mind. I have never found an exception to this principle when adequately understood and applied. Usually these 12 will answer to an authority within this system and it will be, for example, a 13th entity that may be on a throne of control within this structure.

We then, in the name of Jesus Christ, seek to dismantle and remove all demonic components of this power structure and internal image. I then ask for the origin, source, essence, and beginning of this 13th entity.

This type of inquiry usually always leads to an original primal dissociative experience. I then ask the host or whoever represents the core, and all cooperating alters, to 'go into' the primal split and then ask them to 'touch' or 'pull' the 13th part in association with the 12 back into the heart and essence of the one who represents the core (may be the host).

Illustration #2: I am working with a person and together we have released as many alters as possible from demonic captivity and constructs within a given session. I then ask, out of all the alters who are present and can hear my voice, who has the final say or who prevails if there is an argument or disagreement among these alters?

When that alter is determined, I ask, from whom does that alter take its orders or to whom does it report? You may get an answer like "Satan" or some internalized abuser like the father (which usually has familial or ancestral spirits attached).

I then, in cooperation with the host and all other cooperating alters (who may or may not be presenting), do spiritual warfare by commanding the spirit of Satan or the ruling familial spirit attached to the father, to be removed from the human alter that may be identified as Satan or the father. I then will ask God to reveal the unifying center, source, essence, and beginning of Satan or the father.

This again usually leads to some primal dissociative experience. I then ask the host or whoever represents the core (it may be a whole group of alters, depending on where you are in the therapeutic journey), to 'go into' the original split and then to 'reach out' and 'touch' or 'receive back' all alters that emerged within that particular session. It is important to remember that each person and session is unique and both counselor and counselee need to be led by God.

The complexity and diversity of this population of people demands that God be in control of the process and that the counselor or therapist have adequate knowledge and experience in working with SRA/DID.

Illustration #3: The client begins to report seeing a diversity of colors or spinning objects (usually because of some programming issue). We together command all demonic activity to be bound and separate out from all that is human within this phenomenology. I then ask God to reveal to the client the origin, source, essence, and beginning of the above phenomena.

The client may begin to feel some affect, such as fear or nausea; I ask the host or representative of the core and all cooperating alters to 'go into' the source of the affect or the colors, etc., in order to get 'connected.' During this process you may meet some protectors or enforcers. Take time to find out who they are and why they were created.

I then ask God to reveal the primal origin, source, center, essence and beginning of the alters involved within the context of the presenting phenomena. I then seek to bring about as much consolidation and unification as possible before closure.

It is important that the client is grounded and oriented to the present. Go over the session and allow the host to 'process and connect' with what occurred during the session.

Illustration #4: The client presents a picture or a map consisting of a variety of occult phenomena and images, such as pyramids, obelisks, pentagrams and hexagrams. We ask God to reveal the human source, center, essence and beginning of the presenting phenomena.

You and your client may need to do warfare and speak to the phenomena, whatever it may be, and command, in the name of Jesus Christ, all that is demonic be separated from that which is human, so that you can identify the human essence, source, center and beginning of that which is presenting.

Another thing that may be necessary to determine is the power source behind these occult images, and remove that power source. Then, you need to find the human base to which the power source was/is attached. The human base of this power source will usually have an adult representation (protector-alter) within the system.

When you find out who that is, you may need to work with that alter and then find the origin, source, essence and beginning of that alter. Then ask the host or the one who represents the core and all cooperating alters, to 'go into and connect' with that source which is usually some primal split off from which the other alters and fragments were created that make up the presenting phenomena.

This presenting phenomena, whatever it may be, is usually always some combination of human and demonic elements of the system which were demonically engineered through programming and abuse into these occult-constructs within the client's mind.

The above illustrations are only representative of how this 'protocol' may work. I have used this protocol based upon my understanding of how man was created in the image of God and how that principal is applied within the treatment and resolution of SRA/DID. Many other examples could be sighted, but I do not want anyone to assume that this is some kind of formula! God alone knows how this protocol is to be applied within any given individuals' phenomenological dissociated framework. If any of you reading this paper have any questions about what has been presented, please don't hesitate to ask me, and I will do my best to help you in any way I can.

In summary, I want to quote three passages of Scripture and comment on them.

John 17:5: "I do not ask thee to take them out of the world, but to keep them from the evil one." I John 3:9: "No one who is born of God practices sin, because His seed abides in him; and he cannot sin, because he is born of God." I John 5:18: "We know that no one who is born of God sins; but he who was born of God keeps him and the evil one does not touch him."

We see from these passages there is that human essence and identity within each born again child of God that is intimately associated with God and protected by God. This is the person's true identity.

I furthermore believe that this identity is associated with the person's human spirit. Within the heart and essence of every SRA/DID person there is that which has never been touched by evil, kept by God, and identified with God's seed. I believe that this essence and identity is also the most protected by the system of alters within the client's mind. This essence and identity is also the most hated by Satan. Whatever this essence is, it is not an alter. This essence or identity is the ultimate unifying center, source, and beginning into which all dissociative aspects of the SRA/DID client must be integrated.

Only God has the power and the wisdom to accomplish this goal of integration or unification of your clients. According to Psalm 139:14 we are all "fearfully and wonderfully made." When that which was "made" or created is broken, only God has the wisdom, love and power to put that person back together again.

When working with any client it is important that you are working in cooperation with them, and that you and your client are working together in dependence upon the
Holy Spirit. God alone has the big picture and He alone knows how to heal the broken hearted and put these people back together!

The more you, as a therapist or counselor, are able to discern the leading of the Holy Spirit within any given situation with your client, the more you will see and experience the miraculous works of God!
Remember, only the Lord Jesus Christ is the Wonderful Counselor, not you or me (Is. 9:6); only the Lord is the Master Physician or Doctor (Mt. 9:12; Mk. 2:17); only Jesus Christ is the "wisdom and power of God" (I Cor. 1:24).

So, the most intelligent thing you or I could do as counselors or therapists is to let Jesus Christ, by His Spirit, lead us and our clients to His desired end, which is complete unification and healing.

For this to occur, we must allow Him to lead the process and it is inevitable that He will do all that He has promised. We as counselors and therapists are, at best, just facilitators or coaches in this process with our clients. The moment you or I think it depends upon us to do only what Jesus Christ can do, we are heading for frustration, failure, and burnout!

I am constantly learning and seeking to teach my clients how to work in collusion and harmony with God. He must be at the helm, while myself and the client allow
Him to lead the process, and amazingly, He does! And the results are amazing!

Amazing to us because we are slow to let God be God!! When we see God working what we call "miracles" in the lives of our clients, is it really a miracle?

Maybe from God's perspective it is just normal; normal in the sense of who He is and His amazing love and capacity to really deliver, restore and heal people who have experienced the worse that Satan and sinful man can do to another human being.

God will use us best when we learn how to collaborate with Him, get out of His way, and begin to participate in and be a witness to the "greater works" of Jesus Christ (John 14:12), which are nothing less than the "wonderful works of God" (Acts 2:11b).

My prayer is that God will richly bless you and your clients as you grow together on your journey towards wholeness in Christ.

# Developing Intrasystem Cooperation

"I don't like this work. It's beneath me." Diamond, one of my "high" alters inside, was complaining about my washing a patient, giving a bedpan and other routines
of my job as a nurse. "I like leading," she continued. "I don't see how you do this." "Then help me find a better job", I told her. "How?" "You're a leader. You'll find a
way," I said. She created a committee, and five months later I had a teaching job with better pay.

One of the goals of therapy for dissociation is to create intrasystem cooperation. This means that parts inside will be able to communicate to each other without hostility (which is often the first reaction when different groups meet each other) and be able to work together for the good of the individual.

Each person is unique in how they achieve this, but one thing is clear: without intrasystem cooperation, the person's life will be in chaos. Here, I will share tips that have helped me in my own healing process, in the hope that it may help others understand one method of achieving this. Early in my therapy process, I became free from the outside influence of people who were extremely controlling in my life (the cult). At that time, my system went into chaos, because there was no OUTSIDE person giving them orders anymore.

Inside people were busy dismantling my internal hierarchy, all in the name of "freedom" and "democracy" as a reaction to the lifetime of former feeling that they were under a dictatorship.

Daily life became difficult, as different groups inside would play tug of war over their favorite foods; arguments broke out over what career we would pursue, and others fought over time for their activities while others felt left out.

Eventually, I came to realize that I NEEDED some internal structure, and "undoing" the hierarchy inside was leaving my internal ship rudderless. I could barely function. So, I decided to form an internal leadership committee.

I envisioned an internal conference room with a large table inside, and invited inside people to come and meet.

Unfortunately, literally thousands came, and the noise would not allow any work to get done. I then asked each group of alters to "elect" five representatives of different ages to come to the table. There was much grumbling, but finally I had a group of 75 people representing 15 systems inside at the table.

Committee rules were created, such as no interrupting when someone had the floor, no matter how much they were disagreed with. That ALL opinions were to have equal time and be listened to. No abuse inside or outside, even mentally became the cardinal rule.

I also used my imaginative gifts to create a "speaker" for those outside the conference room, so that all could hear what was going on.

The first order of business became to create committees for functionality. I asked the internal leaders present if they would be willing to resume leadership, and help everyone stay free of outside controlling people (the cult). Many agreed.

This became the second cardinal rule: leaders must keep us all safe from harm, or give up their position. I and several core splits helped "chair" the meeting.
The leaders then created different committees inside: a grounding committee, to help ground me when memories hit and stay oriented; a nurturing committee, to help frightened littles; a work committee, to function at work and prevent inappropriate dissociation; a "fun" committee to help us have fun, and a "deprogramming" committee to help undo the damage inside.

We agreed to meet daily for a period of several weeks, then twice a week. Anyone with a problem or complaint could voice it at meetings. Not all meetings were happy gatherings, since there was a lot of rivalry and hostility at first meeting between different groups. I had to create a "DMZ" for my military system, since they were literally shooting other alters inside.

A negotiating committee of helpers and others who could be calm and unbiased inside was created to help defuse intrasystem hostilities. One approach that worked was to listen thoroughly and completely to the stated needs and complaints of alters inside whose agenda was quite different from "normal" to say the least.

If they were not listened to, they tended to try and sabotage work inside. Compromise was reached at times, as long as the cardinal rules were not broken.

This process of creating internal committees took several months, with ups and downs. At times, I felt my inside people had gone "committee happy" with so many groups. But my functionality went up and there was more open communication inside. There was much less hostility and self-sabotage.

I felt safer, since I had created a "safety committee" whose sole job was to keep me safe. A ton of protectors volunteered for this one, and it kept them occupied and happy at what they did best.

What I didn't realize it that this was also integrative work. All I wanted was less chaos and to be able to do things. But as people inside talked, got to know each other, the thousands inside became fewer.

Memory committees were created to help us with the memory process. They set up a five year treatment plan and presented it to our therapist (who was astounded, to say the least!). Internal therapists created an internal therapy group. An internal committee to promote groups coming together was made. An internal "prayer" group prayed for those who were hurting inside.

It worked. I was able to work full time, and work and progress in therapy. In fact, MOST of my healing work was done outside of therapy, by the committees. As time has gone on, the committees have become good friends inside.

There is more democracy as inside people are used to freedom from outside control, and new choices are explored. Also, there is more and more a sense that we are all working together as one person, that each group is an expression of that person, her gifts and talents and abilities. And that we are slowly but surely reaching towards healing.

# Prejudice Against Survivors

I had been out of the cult for almost 8 months and felt alone and isolated. I had been going to a large metropolitan church in the city that I was living in, and had seen a Bible Study for survivors of sexual abuse advertised in the church bulletin. It was just starting up for the fall, and I decided to visit it.

During the first meeting there were 14 people present, and they were asked to introduce themselves and share a little of their background, whatever was comfortable for them.

The survivors one by one shared why they were there; some were very explicit and graphic in their discussion of the sexual abuse they had undergone.

When it was my turn, I simply said, "I can relate to almost everyone here. I am a survivor of ritual abuse, and was molested by everyone in my immediate family at one point, and I'm glad to be here."
That was it for me.

The next day, I received a phone call from the leader of the Bible Study. "Please don't come back," she said. "The other leader and I can't handle the fact that you came from this background."

I was devastated. Apparently it was okay to have been sexually abused in this church, but they set the line with ritual abuse.

Unfortunately, this was only the first of several experiences that I went through, until I finally learned my lesson. To not share my past with anyone in the church, because they can't handle it.

I had gone to one church until a few months ago, and had privately shared my past with the pastor when asking for prayer for my children to help him better understand how to pray for them.

He literally backed away from me, and said, "This is more than I can handle knowing about." He never spoke to me again.

In another church, I visited the deliverance team, who told me that DID and alternate personalities are really demons to be exorcised. I was "holding onto demons" if I had personalities.

I joined another Bible study at another church for those struggling with sexual brokenness. The leaders of this group would interview those entering the program.
I was getting smarter by now, so I told them, "I have a background of ritual abuse but I won't bring it up at all during discussion times, I promise."

"Are you multiple?" I was asked in accusing tones.
"Yes, but I can control my switching and won't be inappropriate during meetings."

I was allowed to visit on "probation" and told that if I ever switched once, I would be forced to leave the study. I went, and after four months the leader was surprised and amazed. "You've been a real blessing to us here, "she exclaimed. "I thought all multiples were strange!"

But I made a mistake. A few weeks later, when discussing why I felt broken sexually although I had male tendencies, a *different* male alter who was quiet yet appropriate came out and discussed his emotional pain. The only problem is, he had a slight Irish accent and so others could tell that I had "switched."

The leaders met with me and told me this was unacceptable since he was "demonic". I was devastated.

***I have not found a church yet in my own life that understands or accepts the reality of ritual abuse.***

I wish that I were not alone in this. I believe that this is one of the number one problems today for a survivor leaving a cult group. They are literally giving up everything emotionally important to themselves in their lives: their family of origin, their closest friends, even spouses who are members of the group.

Survivors are looking for understanding and support, and instead are met by unbelief (as if to profess this stuff doesn't happen in this day and age), or else intense rejection.

In most churches, it is okay to be a recovering alcoholic, a recovering addict, or even the victim of domestic violence, but it is not okay to have been the victim of ritual abuse. It frightens people. They don't want to see living proof that it *really does* happen, and will turn their heads the other way.

This doesn't mean that all churches respond this way, but a very large percentage of them do (the majority in fact; the ones that don't are the rare and encouraging minority).

Others have shared their pain when the body of Christ, called to minister to its wounded, instead either adds to the wounding, or worse yet, isolates and ignores
them.

Karen is a wonderful, loving, and compassionate Christian survivor who has helped to found a support group for other ritual abuse survivors and was told that her dissociation and DID were "attention seeking" devices.

Here is her response:
*"You know I love it when I hear people use the 'attention seekers' routine. I think to myself (someday I may have the nerve to actually say it). "Yeah, I just love the
rejection of it all."*

She said that sometimes she wants to respond back in kind," Maybe something like saying to these people, "I didn't know you were such an advocate for Satan. He
too, likes to bring condemnation to people!" I better stop now. .before I really get going and forget the One who never rejects or condemns us." Karen has found, like many other survivors that God loves her and cares for her even when His body can't.

Alice shares her experience within her church: "He (her pastor) even chose this woman to be my "care giver", well, after a few years of what I thought was a wonderful, loving relationship, come to find out she was casting out demons when I left, blaming everything that went wrong in her life and her children's on ME! I'm surprised she was able to hug me as she did without shuddering in disgust. "

She tried going to a deliverance seminar to become free of the demonic and to find healing:" Another thing were these "Cleansing Streams Ministry" retreats/seminars that I would go to. my gosh, they talked about freedom from bondage from SRA and all sorts of things. I mean I thought they covered it all, but because I was acting out/alters acting out.

I mentioned this before, they said that they would not pray for me because I was uncooperative. And again, I got called names and shunned. I mean once is bad enough but I went to about four or five of these "retreats" with the promise that the next time would be a charm. And each one was a disaster, and I got yelled at, shunned, and people would not pray for me.

Heck, the last one I couldn't even get a ride home!! I scared the couple off that were supposed to take me home. (It was out of state), my caregiver came and reamed me out, and another told me to quit game playing, and I blew up at them. I left in tears with my bags packed and roamed the city and met up with someone who helped me catch a bus back home. What should have been a 7 hour trip for me, took at least 15 hours by bus, because I was some kind of leper.

Yeah, they talked about freedom from SRA, but apparently, I was the only one dealing with that and mind control and DID, and to them, I was a *super possessed demon* and they couldn't cast me out of myself, and since those "demons" wouldn't flee, I was ostracized!"

Experiences such as this clearly do not bring healing, deliverance, or the feeling that the survivor can trust the body of Christ when they are trying to become free of cult control and the demonic influences within.

It is fairly obvious that this ministry did not understand DID or how to help someone with alternate personalities who are wounded.

Joann's experience was more subtle, but a common one that survivors of severe torture and ritual abuse in the church frequently face. She faced the denial of those in the church, and intense pressure to be normal and functional in spite of great emotional pain. People in the church thought I was acting and should be able to hold down a job.

I was a mess then, more so than now. The Pastor said I HAD to get a job and prove to everyone that I was stable. He and lots of other church members harass me all the time about being stable. I couldn't be, I was a mess, full of lots of programming and breaking down big time.

He would call demons to the forefront and have littles look at them in the mirror to prove that they had demons. He did all kinds of things like that that totally horrified my littles inside."

This was an extremely traumatizing situation for her child alters, but there is more:
"My Pastor's wife at the present called women in the church and told them I was just acting. I have been accused of being a plant in the church, being there to destroy the church and everything else, all the while I was cleaning the church, going witnessing with the church twice a week, doing all the typing for the church, everything I could do to serve God.

I to this day still am fighting against serving God. Not because of God, but because I don't trust what anyone says God wants me to do. I now only want to hear it straight from God. I was misled *soooo many times* by people using God's will against me. How would they know? God will guide me!

Guess I am pretty angry, too, at all these Christians who *know* I am a demon supposedly, and am acting and everything else. Oh yes, and that I am going against
God's Word for dealing with memories, wanting truth about my memories and everything. I am wrong according to them for needing memories to have my identity back that my identity is in Christ. They do not understand that that goes along with programming.

I feel like all I do is run into walls and blocks and cannot get anywhere. How can I live in truth and face truth if I am not allowed to deal with all the lies they programmed into me? I am so fed up with hearing this stuff all the time. "

Joann finishes with her conclusion on why she went through this at her church: "It is so hard to understand. People don't want to know what is really going on out there, they like their safe made up worlds, and don't want the reality. They don't want to come out of their sheltered boxes they made and have to deal with anything outside of their own selves."

Kylie agrees with the above assessment and shares her opinion on why there is prejudice against ritual abuse survivors in the church and society at large: *"I have had similar things happen to me with the church. It seems most people. . not just church people. . .don't want to know about the dark side of things and prefer to think that it does not really exist. . . so they do not hear what I have to say and avoid talking about it. Most prefer to hide their head in the sand. I am learning to wait until the Lord leads me to speak with those who have ears to hear. It is a great disappointment. It does freak people out that SRA exists. . I think it did just about that to all of us.*
*I think it is too shocking for many to hear about suddenly. I believe education can help; but most cannot handle too much too soon. When that happens, they end up saying we are crazy because they cannot cope with our stories."*

Finally, Sally shares her pain at not being able to share with others her past and find understanding: *" It boggles my mind that all our lives we were taught to be quiet, keep it quiet and we get away and we still can't talk!!!*

*No one wants to hear that. Reminds me of a lady i used to have to work with. She refused to watch news or read the paper because she didn't want to know what was going on in the world. She wanted to believe none of that existed. So she continued to live in her little world."*

Sally shares her experiences at church: *"Well, they balk at me for one thing. While some truly seem compassionate. Most actually fear me. They never call me, I have called some and they are so nervous to talk. I know I come across quite strangely here, but in a normal and not "frenzied" state, I do not bite, I do not have fangs, I do not drink blood .But you would think it the way they avoid me like the plague.*

*I get the sideway glances at church and murmurs.*
*I have had some come up to me and accuse me of "playing games". Another accused me of seeking attention and acting out! I mean things like that stay with you.*

*I'm sorry, but this is a touchy subject for me too. It took me years and years to get the courage to attend church and then I was made to believe that Christians were this special breed, so full of love and compassion and they will just take me under their wings and accept and love and care for me like never before.*

*What a joke and what kind of breed are they? I don't mean to be so critical sounding, but I have encountered so many hypocrites in church people, that i am almost ashamed to even call myself one.*

*I am a terrible Christian by the way, in case you haven't noticed by now. I have a lot of pent up resentment, but I still keep plugging through."*
Jackie has worked through for herself why there is such a lack of acceptance of survivors and shares her insights:
*"I think what I have learned in therapy is that not everyone has the capacity to "hear" the intense pain that we have experienced from the extreme abuse we have suffered. My therapist has admitted to me that even though he is trained to hear, to listen, it is sometimes hard for him to know that someone could be so horribly abused in this country in this time period.*

*Last summer he worked with trauma survivors in Bosnia and the Ukraine with a group of therapist volunteering time in these war torn areas. There are children there that have seen many atrocities. there are parents there who have seen their children murdered. the difference in my mind is that the humanity is willing to document these sorts of traumas. So in my mind it is not that no one hears, but that people choose not to believe.*

*I have learned to accept that some people will never hear, never believe, but there are also people who will never hear about Jesus or believe that Jesus is God/*
*Savior, but that doesn't negate the fact that Jesus is Lord and Savior."*

These are quotes from just a few survivors, myself included, who have experienced the at times extremely wounding prejudice against survivors. It appears that society at large, and all too often the church as well, are not willing to acknowledge the reality of ritual abuse, or the special needs that survivors have.

My greatest hope is that as time goes on, this can change. That more churches other than the isolated few will have a desire to learn more about this, and to help those who are struggling to get out of a coercive and controlling group.

I personally believe that within the next ten years there will be a literal flood of people leaving this group, a kind of "last chance to get out" as it were because of the group's agenda. But my question is, will the church be ready with trained, equipped, and most of all, compassionate people to help them? I leave this as a matter of prayer and hope that the answer will be "yes".

# Eating Disorders
# And Ritual Abuse

"You're putting on a little weight," my stepfather noted. I had gone away to school that year, and had gained five pounds. He was teasing me when I came home to visit.

I was 14 years old, and decided to start dieting. I was an instant success at dieting strenuously, since my iron self-control and discipline had taught me to ignore my body's signals since early childhood. I was proud of my ability to eat tiny amounts in spite of severe hunger. I lost weight quickly.

"You're too thin, I can see every rib," my roommate at school that year told me. "I'm getting worried about you." "No, I'm fat," I insisted. I looked in the mirror and saw someone who was obese, who had to lose more weight to be okay. Why couldn't others see how fat I was?

Several weeks later, my mother had to come and get me. My liver had shut down, and I was hospitalized. I was 5 feet 10 inches tall and weighed 90 pounds. I was still insisting that I was too fat. I came close to dying from this disorder as I entered my teen years and it would be years before I came close to a normal body weight. I never received treatment from a therapist for it, because my parents didn't believe in therapy.

Instead, I was given a programming command to "eat, don't die" from my mother when I refused to eat after I was discharged home. I shook and shook for hours, and finally picked up the spoon and swallowed some soup.

*When a young child is systematically deprived of food and water to teach them a lesson or to break them down and make them more accessible to programming messages, it has a long-term psychological effect.*

**Starvation and deprivation are all primary parts of many programming sequences that are done on children starting as young as age 2 in the Illuminati.**

The child will be desperate to eat once the deprivation is over, and will associate eating with the comfort of the adults around him/her. *Food becomes one more area that is controlled by the adults and the trainers, and the child early begins to realize this.* While very young, the child cannot control how much food they are allowed to eat, or if they are allowed to eat.

Cult parents, building upon the lessons learned at night, may also systematically starve the child during the daytime, or punish the child who dares to eat because they are hungry. Later in life, it is not surprising to find that many survivors of ritual abuse and cult programming have eating disorders.

There are several types of eating disorders. One is *anorexia nervosa*, in which the person struggling with this disorder starves themselves. Anorexia has many causes, but a root need for control and underlying depression has been noted by therapists who work with it, combined with a negative self-image and self-hatred.

The self-hatred becomes focused on body image and fat. Some survivors with this disorder have confided that they starved themselves as adolescents *to delay the onset of menstruation, to delay the development of breasts*, or other characteristics.

Others with male alters wanted the flat chest that being thin can bring. And others starve themselves to numb the pain. Current research into anorexia is showing that high serotonin levels are associated with anxiety and feeling distressed, and some researchers have theorized that starvation decreases this excess serotonin and effectively helps to block these uncomfortable feelings.

Another eating disorder is known as bulimia. This disorder is characterized by swings between bingeing, and eating large amounts of food (often past the point of discomfort) within a short period of time, and then purging the body of the calories or food.

Purging is accomplished by taking laxatives, vomiting, taking diuretics, excessive exercise, or starvation after bingeing. Often the person with bulimia feels that they cannot control their binges, and feel ashamed afterwards. The purging is "punishment" for eating.

Janna struggled with bulimia for years. She never told anyone, not even her sister or best friends. It started her senior year in high school when she had gained some weight. Desperate to shed pounds, she began vomiting after eating large meals.

She also began using laxatives to "clear out" the calories. *"I knew I needed help,"* She states, *"But I was ashamed to tell anyone."* Finally, at the age of 27, her bulimia was out of control. It seemed to get worse when she was stressed, and being promoted to a management position made it intensity. At that point she entered counseling, and began looking at some of the causes of the depression and pain that had filled her life for as long as she could remember.

The third eating disorder recognized by experts is known as *binge disorder*. Like bulimia, the person has uncontrollable food cravings, and will binge to the point of abdominal pain in some cases. Favorite foods are hoarded, and the binge eater will often binge in secret, eating very little in front of others.

The person struggling with this disorder is often highly distressed because they feel that they can't stop themselves from bingeing. Usually this person is overweight, and struggles with the problems that this causes.

Sarah hides donuts in her house, and also has other favorite foods. "I once ate a whole cheesecake at one sitting" she admits. She hates being overweight, and acknowledges, *"My doctor said that this weight is killing me, putting my life at risk. I would give anything to be able to slim down."* But she also struggles with other feelings. *"Being this large makes me feel safe, though"*, she confides. *"I know that men won't look at me."* This is important to her, since she has been sexually abused by all the men in her family of origin.

Cult programming, sexual abuse, and the pain of trauma all contribute to the eating disorders that survivors often struggle with. The reasons for coping with an eating disorder are often complex, and frequently unconscious. A child who was starved during preschool years may be left with "food anxiety", hoarding food around the house to ensure that they will never go hungry again.

Child alters who are chronically hungry due to these experiences may switch out at night, and the survivor wakes up to an empty candy bag or plates with leftover desserts on the night table.

In some cases, in spite of the health risks (all eating disorders are dangerous) the survivor will persist in an unconscious desire to punish their body, and to inflict illness or pain on themselves. In others, the desire can even escalate to a *death wish* and be part of a suicide program.

Cindy is 34, model beautiful, and bright. Her heart is failing because she continues to starve herself. *"I know I might die, that I have to eat, my doctor has told me this over and over"* she shrugs and smiles. *"It wouldn't be a big loss, would it?"*

She finds it difficult to believe that she is cared for and considered a wonderful person by others, as she struggles with the internal messages of degradation and pain inside. *"My mother beat me over and over if I ate too much when I was little,* "She shares. *"Maybe that's one reason I have trouble giving myself permission to eat now."*

Healing from an eating disorder is often a lengthy process that involves overcoming the denial that exists (the survivor often feels that there isn't really a problem, that friends and family members are worrying too much).

Therapy with someone who understands both the underlying trauma, and also working with a registered dietitian, can be invaluable. Learning how the survivor feels about food, and what has shaped those feelings, and how they feel about themselves, is part of the process.

If programming is driving the disorder, it is also important to look at how it was done, and why. Survivors have reported programming to "overeat to death" or to "starve to death" in many cases, especially if they try to leave the cult group.

Healing a distorted body image, and learning to love themselves in spite of their weight, and learning normal eating patterns can help. Traumatized child alters can be reassured that the survivor won't allow them to go hungry, and planning meals to allow these parts a chance to choose favorite foods can help cut down on night time or amnesic binges.

Each person is unique, and will have their own individual issues to deal with as they heal. In partnership with a qualified therapist, and with increased cooperation inside, healing is possible.

**Resources:**
There are many excellent resources online for information about eating disorders. The following are just a few:

The Alliance for Eating Disorders Awareness This site created by Johanna S. Kandel contains excellent articles and information about different types of eating disorders, with special sections for teens and parents.
http://www.eatingdisorderinfo.org

The Body Cage This site contains a highly personal look at eating disorders as well as links and information on diagnosis and treatment. **http://www.bodycage.com**

Escapees of Illuminati handlers report "Black Mass" rituals such as these take place in the homes of elite and often well-known members all over the country and even the world!

# Satanic Ritual Abuse: The Evidence Surfaces

**Contributor(s): Article originally published in the ICCRT Newsletter Published on: September 19, 2001**

The following lyrics are from a song about Satanic ritual abuse off Joan Baez's latest album, Play Me Backwards. Incidentally, it's the lead song.

*"You don't have to play me backwards to get the meaning of my verse. You don't have to die and go to hell to feel the devil's curse..."*

It's not only the "devil's curse" survivors of Satanic ritual abuse have been feeling of late. They have also been feeling the curse of a pronounced societal backlash.
In some circles now, the stories of some of the most heinous abuse imaginable - sexual abuse, brainwashing, torture, murder/sacrifice - are being labeled as "patently false."

Therapists are being accused of planting these memories. And, for instance, the FBI has come out debunking the phenomenon, saying, unequivocally, there is no tangible evidence organized Satanic ritual abuse exists at all.

However, my research shows it does exist. And indications are we are only seeing the tip of the iceberg of a social phenomenon that, when totally exposed, will rock the core of societal beliefs.

For the last four years, I have crises-crossed the country interviewing cult researchers, ritual crime investigators, task force members, therapists, investigative reporters, cult survivors.

As part of an in-depth investigation on the issue of Satanic ritual abuse. And, the research has yielded some extremely eye-opening things. The most eye-opening hasn't been the mutilated backwoods remains of a cult victim's body in Massachusetts.

It wasn't the bloody pentagram carved into a cult victim's corpse in San Francisco. The most eye-opening, has been a widely cited Law Enforcement Perspective report out of the FBI's Behavioral Science Center in Quantico, Virginia.

The report was written by supervisory special agent Kenneth Lanning. It has gone out to law enforcement agencies around the country; and has been cited consistently throughout the media the last several years.

The report states, in regards to "organized" Satanic ritual abuse homicide (that is, two or more Satanic cult members conspiring to commit murder): "The law enforcement perspective can't ignore the lack of physical evidence (no bodies, or even hairs, fibers, or fluids left by violent murders."

**No bodies?**
The following is an excerpt from a March 13, 1981, UPI article:
*"Fitchburg, Mass. -- The alleged leader of a devil worship cult was found guilty of first degree murder Friday in the ritual killing of a young Fall River, Mass. Prostitute last year. Carl Drew, 26, stood pale and expressionless as the verdict was announced.*

*He was immediately sentenced to life imprisonment by superior court judge Francis W. Keating. Miss Marsden was allegedly killed, mutilated*

*and beheaded by Drew and two others in a blood-soaked night time ritual in a wooded area <u>because she wanted to leave the cult</u>."*
In 1993, House Bill 1689 was introduced in the Massachusetts Legislature. It is a bill prohibiting
*"Certain Ritualistic Acts."* Some of these acts include: ritual mutilation, dismemberment, torture, the sacrifice of animals, humans.
(A similar bill was passed in Idaho in 1990).

Also, in the 1993 Avon Books release: *Raising Hell*, author/investigative reporter Michael Newton writes, *"While some cult apologists may be forgiven their ignorance of current events, (FBI) Agent Lanning -- with access to nationwide police files -- should know better.*

*As this volume amply demonstrates, cult related killers stand convicted of murder in 23 states and at least nine foreign countries.*

*Numerous other occultists are now serving time for practicing their "faith" through*
*acts of arson, rape, assault, cruelty to animals, and similar crimes."*

The organization, Looking Up, founded initially as a nationwide support/referral program for incest survivors, serves approximately 15,000 people a year, 40% of whom now are reporting they are dealing with ritualistic or cult related abuse.

According to a spokesperson for JUSTUS Unlimited in Denver, a non-profit referral and resource center, they are currently receiving more than 7,000 Satanic ritual abuse related calls a year. (What's more, they are also hearing from all over the world: Australia, New Zealand, England, The Netherlands, Germany, Israel, Canada.)

Given the tangible evidence now surfacing, and given the volume of people reporting Satanic cult related abuse, it would seem curious the FBI would come out with such a definitive stance attempting to discredit the increasing phenomenon.

Of course, then again, it was the same FBI that for more than the first half of this century consistently said there was no evidence whatsoever of another type of "organized" criminal activity. That is -- Mafia related crime.

Actually, Satanic cults are somewhat similar to Mafia crime families. There is, for instance, extreme secrecy through code of silence programming. This is usually initiated with the signing of a "blood" contract. Wendell Amstutz, author of Satanism in America, said these contracts are generally signed in the initiate's own blood.
The contract, said Amstutz, usually demands life-long obedience. And breaking it means death.

And that's exactly what it meant for the four California Satanic cult defectors one fateful night in 1990. The defectors were tracked to an apartment on, of all places,
Elm Street in the small town of Salida.

The defectors were beaten and stabbed. Finally, they were decapitated. What was left behind rivaled the carnage of the Tate-LaBianca crime scene. The trail led back to five Satanic cult members, and the story began to unfold. The five who were indicted were part of a 55-member Satanic cult that was operating out of a compound in Salida.

Cult members stretched across a three-county are, with a number of them holed-up in a Salida compound (homes and trailers), somewhat similar to Waco's Branch Davidian complex. Except for one thing: What was going on in the Salida compound for the most part made what was going on in Waco seem like a Disney production.

Randy Cerny, Director of the Northern Chapter of California's Ritual Crime Investigator's Association, had followed the cult closely. And after the indictments, he interviewed several of the cult members and reviewed extensive diaries they'd kept.

He said the cult worshipped Satan, followed the teachings of renowned Satanist Aleister Crowley, engaged in sexual abuse, ritual torture including electric shock, child abuse, murder.In other words, many of the same things Satanic ritual abuse survivors have been consistently reporting.

Cerny also said it was reported cult members were from all walks of life. This even included a dentist, a minister, and a woman enrolled in a law enforcement class at a local community college. (Satanic cult members aren't, by any means, always tattooed teen bikers who have listened to one too many Metallica albums, Often,

*Satanic ritual abuse survivors report their cult perpetrators are respected members of the community: doctors, law enforcement officials, PTA members, little league coaches.*

This all, apparently, is part of the facade.) One of the Matomoros cult members responsible for some of the 13 grisly murder/ sacrifices in Mexico a few years back, was majoring in law enforcement at Texas Southmost College at the time she was arrested.
"The California cult was a very secretive, close-knit, sophisticated group," said Cerny.

The Satanic cult was run under the iron fist of charismatic leader, high priest, Gerald Cruz. And, as David Koresh had done in Waco, Cruz *used sleep deprivation, brainwashing, and torture. to keep members in line.*

At a trial in Oakland in December, 1992, cult expert and psychologist, Daniel Goldstine, would characterize Cruz as "evil and sadistic."

The jury thought so too. Cruz and two other cult members were sentenced to death for the murders. Two other cult members got life.
*"Now let's project this 20 to 25*
*years down the road," Cerny continued. "Say someone walks into a police department or therapist's office and says, 'I'm starting to have memories that my dad was a leader of this Satanic cult in California. And they would brainwash people, torture them with electric shock, sexually abuse me, sacrifice animals, kill people. '"*

Cerny wondered if that would all be passed off as a "false memory." Nationally syndicated columnist Molly Ivins might well have passed it off as just that. In a May, 1994, column, Ms. Ivins wrote: *"Social workers who deal with child abuse have nightmares about the people who come up with patently false recovered memories of Satanic ritual abuse."*

Monika Beerle seemed to be nobody's "false recovered memory." The following is a February 18, 1992, Newsday article excerpt: New York -- Members of a cult here killed ballerina Monika Beerle in August, 1989, and then dismembered her and fed her flesh to the homeless as part of a Satanic ritual, law enforcement sources said yesterday after arresting a cult member in connection with the slaying. *"The public isn't generating enough momentum to get police mobilized around this (Satanic ritual abuse) issue at this point,"* explained Akron, Ohio Police Captain Jerry Foys.

And John Hunt, Sherman, Texas ritual crime investigator says that "because of the FBI report, the stigma around Satanism and other factors have made it hard to get internal police department support in following up on the ritual aspects of a crime."
Hunt and Foys both said they believe the Satanic ritual abuse *is quite widespread* -- and extremely dangerous.

It definitely proved dangerous for an alcoholic drifter known only as John Doe No. 60, whose body was found in San Francisco. According to a May 6, 1988, San Francisco Chronicle article: *"The victim had a pentagram carved into his chest, lash marks across his buttocks, a stab wound to his neck, wax in his right eye and hair, and a sliced lip. The naked body was virtually drained of blood."* Clifford St. Joseph, 46, was eventually convicted and sentenced to 34 years to life for the killing.

In his book, *Raising Hell*, Michael Newton writes when police came to St. Joseph's apartment nine days after the body was found, they found St. Joseph dressed in a black robe, companion Michael Bork, 26, stripped to the waist, his face daubed with cosmetics, and another man, Edward Spela, 26, passed out from drugs. In the middle of the room was a 19-year old man, who was laying on the floor, handcuffed and surrounded by candles.

According to the San Francisco Chronicle: *"Investigators said that St. Joseph appeared to be part of a Satanic cult that involved men of means in San Francisco's gay community."*

Again, John Doe No. 60's mutilated body was real. It was nobody's false memory.

A term popular culture has latched onto tightly in the last couple of years is the very clinical sounding, **false memory syndrome**. It is a term coined by the Philadelphia, Pennsylvania based *False Memory Syndrome Foundation (FMSF),* which is an advocacy group for people whose children have accused them of either sexual abuse and/or Satanic ritual abuse.

Despite its scientific sounding title, there is actually no such thing as a clinically acknowledged category for "false memory syndrome," reports Judith Herman, an associate clinical professor of Psychiatry at Harvard Medical School, and author of the book, Trauma and Recovery. "

The very name FMSF is prejudicial and misleading," said Dr. Herman. "There is no such syndrome, and we have no evidence reported memories are false. We only know they are disputed."

Many professionals dealing with Satanic ritual abuse believe we are seeing the beginnings of a phenomenon that might well mushroom into staggering proportions. And they draw a parallel to the amazing evolution of the sexual abuse field. "As recently as the 1970s," said Herman, "rape was considered rare, and incest was regarded as a universal taboo.

Less than twenty years ago, for example, the Comprehensive Textbook of Psychiatry estimated the prevalence of all forms of incest at one case per million population. And popular and professional literature [as in the case with SRA survivors now] routinely questioned the character of victims, and disparaged the credibility of women who made claims of assault.

Today, however, widespread sexual abuse/incest has been extensively documented." In the case of false memory allegations, perhaps we should be spending a bit more time actually questioning the character of some of those accusing the "alleged" victims of confabulation. And perhaps we should start at the False Memory Syndrome Foundation itself.

The following is an excerpt from a February 29, 1992, FMSF Newsletter where the organization claims it is: *"not in the business of representing pedophiles. We are a good-looking bunch of people: graying hair, well-dressed, healthy, and smiling. Just about every person is someone you would likely find interesting and want to count as a friend."*

Joan Baez's song goes on:
**Let the night begin There's a pop of skin And a sudden rush of scarlet There's a little boy riding on a goat's head And a little girl playing the harlot It's a sacrifice in an empty church Sweet little baby Rose.**

A Fall 1989 Cleveland Plain Dealer article excerpt reads: Three Norwalk area residents charged with opening two graves, beheading the corpses and stealing the skulls, were part of a cult that had recently gotten instructions on how to sacrifice babies to Satan, Norwalk police said yesterday. "We're taking this very seriously," he [Police Chief Gary Dewalt] said. "Maybe society should take the police chief's lead, in a lot of different areas regarding this problem.

For one, many youth are bombarded with Satanic symbols, images, lyrics. One area where it is probably the most prevalent is in the heavy/black metal music scene. For instance, the heavy metal band Venom sings:
***"Candles glowing, altars burn Virgin's death is needed their Sacrifice to Lucifer my master Bring the chalice, raise the knife Welcome to my sacrifice."***
**Just a passing phase kids go through? Just lyrics?**
May 5, 1993 -- Three eight year old boys were riding their bikes down a country road in West Memphis, Arkansas.

Suddenly they were forced off the road and horribly killed. One of the suspects accused in the murders, Jessie Lloyd Miskelly, Jr., 17 according to wire service reports, told police that the murders were tied to a teen Satanic cult sacrifice.

"Miskelly said the children were lured into a wooded are of West Memphis known as Robin Hood Park, choked until they were unconscious, then brutalized in various ways -- including rape."

According to a March 8, 1994 article on the trial appearing in the West Memphis The Commercial Appeal: "A witness last week told him Baldwin (one of the accused) told him he sucked the blood from one victim after he mutilated him." Diaries indicated the Satanic cult in Salida, California, followed the teachings of renowned Satanist Aleister Crowley.

In his book, *Magick in Theory and Practice*, Crowley wrote,

*"The blood is the life. Any living thing is the storehouse of energy. At the death of the animal this energy is liberated suddenly. The animal should therefore be killed within the Circle, or Triangle, so that its energy cannot escape. For the highest spiritual working one must accordingly choose that victim which the greatest and purest force. <u>A male child of perfect innocence is the most satisfactory and suitable victim.</u>"*

There's a good bet that seven year old Yvando Caetano, like most seven year olds, was living a life in "perfect innocence" in the small town of Guaratuba, Brazil.

This may well have been the precipitating factor in his death. According to a July 28, 1992, Cable News Network (CNN) report/transcript, Yvando was found in a shallow grave. His arms and legs had been dismembered, his internal organs cut out.

Ritual implements used during the ceremony were also found near the body. Investigator Jose Moscic Favetti said police believed the mayor's wife and daughter were involved with a Satanic cult, and that the wife had paid five cult members to sacrifice Yvando to Satan -- in return for the mayor having a good political year.

*"The stories (about different aspects of cult rituals) are very much the same, whether it's someone reporting about a ceremony in Melbourne, Australia, Vermont, Utah."* said Dr. Judianne Densen-Gerber. *"This leads me to believe, not only are the cults all over, but because of the similarities, many are also networked."*

Dr. Densen-Gerber is a New York Psychiatrist who has treated a number of SRA survivors since 1980. She also has a law degree, and is the founder of PACT (Protect America's Children Today).

Are American children in danger because of these Satanic cults? Well, the small town in Brazil might provide some clues. Besides the death of 7-year old Yvando in July, 10 other children had come up missing in Guarutuba since January of that year.

According to Brandon Perez, initial Development Director of the National Missing Children's Center, based in Houston, Texas, **there are currently some 4,000,000 abductions a year in the United States of which, said Perez, almost 50% of the children are never found.**

Perez added that many of these cases are not adequately tracked.

In his book, *The Franklin Cover-up: Child Abuse, Satanism and Murder in Nebraska*, author and former Nebraska State Senator John DeCamp interviewed 28 year veteran FBI agent Ted Gunderson. Since his retirement from the FBI, Gunderson has been actively investigating reports of Satanic ritual abuse.

DeCamp writes: *"Evidence from Gunderson's investigations has convinced him tens of thousands of children or young people disappear from their homes each year, and that many of them are ritualistically sacrificed. Nobody knows the true figure because the FBI doesn't keep count.*

*Gunderson observes, 'The FBI has an accurate count on the number of automobiles stolen every year. It knows the number of homicides, rapes, and robberies, but the FBI has no idea of the number of children who disappear every year. They simply do not ask for the statistics.'*

*Gunderson goes onto say he believes they don't ask for the statistics, simply, because they don't want to see them.* "They would be confronted with an instant
public outcry for action, because the figures would show a major social problem that would demand action.'"

And it's not just the tragedy of the missing children that come up dead as a result of this savage cult abuse -- there are many children that are "*walking wounded.*"

Pamela Hudson, LCSW, a child therapist with a county health outpatient department in northern California began to identify the symptoms of

SRA in several children who had been referred to her in 1985. What was to follow was a most frightening phenomenon.

Throughout the remainder of 1985 and into 1986, twenty-four children, all from the same day care center, all exhibiting varying degrees of ritual abuse symptoms, were brought to her by concerned parents. (What was even more amazing, said Hudson, was that the cases came to her individually, without the parents initially talking among each other.) Some of the symptoms included frequent night terrors, night sweats, extreme separation anxiety, uncontrolled vomiting, 3,4, and 5 year olds acting out sexually in bizarre, sadistic manners. All indicators of significant trauma.

As Hudson continued to work with the children, the Satanic ritual abuse stories started to surface: the children reported being locked in cages, buried for short periods in coffins, injected with drugs, defecated and urinated on, sexually abused, forced to watch animal and human sacrifice.

Hudson took the information to authorities, but the District Attorney's office decided not to prosecute. A disappointed Hudson said she attributes the decision to the lack of physical evidence, and the children being perceived as too young, and also considered too emotionally traumatized for the stories to appear credible to a jury.

However, several years later, a jury in Austin, Texas, did find children's stories of sexual and Satanic ritual abuse credible enough to put Fran's Day Care directors,
Fran and Dan Keller, in prison for extended sentences. (The Kellers became eligible for parole in 2004.)
As with the case in California, the children talked of extreme forms of abuse: being threatened with guns, being buried alive, forced to make pornographic movies, watch an infant sacrifice.

In addition, my research has also turned up similar day care and school SRA cases in Florida, several more in California, Massachusetts, New Jersey, and in
Christchurch, New Zealand.

The longest trial in American history, California's McMartin Day School case, was one of the first day care center cases to claim Satanic ritual abuse. There were some 500 separate reports filed at the Manhattan Beach Police Department in connection with the case. The children's stories matched those of other cases cited.

However, there was an additional component to the McMartin case. The children consistently talked of being abused in an *underground tunnel* below the day care center. A highly qualified archaeologist, hired by the children's families, talked about a series of what he says were highly questionable incidents in the search for the elusive tunnels.

Archeologist Gary Stickle, Ph.D., has worked extensively in the United States and in Europe, including heading the largest underwater archeological sonar survey ever conducted in Europe. In addition, he has been a consultant to Lucas Films in the development of the Indiana Jones movie series.

He has also been professor of Archeology at the University of California at Long Beach. Stickle said initially a private investigator went to the day care center site and did some preliminary informal digging.

It is reported, said Stickle that this investigator found some rabbit bones in the soil. (The children talked about rabbits being sacrificed.) However, the day before he was to testify, the private investigator was found dead from a gunshot wound. It was determined to be a suicide. But Stickle said that determination was questioned by more than a few people, given the timing.

Eventually, said Stickle, the prosecution hired an archeological firm that dug seven pits clustered *outside* of the building. (This was curious, said Stickle, because the children were reporting the abuse had gone on in tunnels *below* the building.)

Stickle said a remote sensing device was also used at the time, but it was reported that no tunnels were found. That was 1985. The lack of a tunnel damaged the credibility of the children's stories tremendously.

Stickle's firm was hired by the parents in 1990. Using a sophisticated ground penetrating radar, Stickle said *a tunnel was found, right where some of the children had told his staff it would be.*

However, even though evidence of the tunnel was found in May of 1990, while the trial was still in progress -- the evidence was never introduced in court, said Stickle.

*"Finding such a tunnel was highly relevant (to the case)," said Stickle. "Because it (prior lack of physical evidence of a tunnel) was a major thing used to discredit the children."*

The accused McMartin Day Care Center staff were eventually acquitted. However, some of the McMartin parents haven't quit fighting.

A two hundred page report on the tunnel findings has recently been released by the parents, in an ongoing effort to keep the case before the public.

As with these children, it is becoming more and more apparent that there are many adult SRA walking wounded as well. As a result of the trauma, these are people often afflicted with things like severe paranoia, schizophrenia, multiple personalities. They are people almost off the scales in terms of addictions/ compulsions, depression, self-mutilating behavior.

However, an advancing therapeutic field has developed highly sophisticated techniques to help survivors. And the prognosis for recovery is often good. In addition, parts of society are also rallying around these survivors.

- The County Commission for Women has a Ritual Abuse Task Force in Los Angeles;
- There is a state-wide Minnesota Awareness of Ritual Abuse group;
- Jireh, headquartered in Arlington, Texas, is a national program to create safe-houses for cult survivors breaking away;
- The International Council on Cultism and Ritual Trauma, in Richardson, Texas;

…and a number of cult survivor resource and referral organizations; ritual abuse twelve-step programs are evolving.

**As much as we don't want to believe it as a society -- Satanic ritual abuse is a reality.** And, as was done by the parents in the McMartin Day Care Center case, we need to be rolling up our sleeves and digging deeper to get at the whole truth.

***May 25, 1994 was designated National Missing Children's Day***. Those postcards that come to our homes so very often don't represent anybody's "false memories." Those are real children, with real fates.

-------------------------------------------------------------

*Daniel Ryder*, an investigative journalist and a counselor, is the author of *Breaking the Circle of Satanic Ritual Abuse*. The above article is based on material from Mr. Ryder's newest book ***Cover-up of the Century (Satanic Ritual Crime and Conspiracy)***.

# Retraumatization

This chapter addresses how we, as therapists and counselors can inadvertently retraumatize our patients, even when they have told us clearly this is what we are doing. The question will surely be asked, *"How could I continue to damage my client in such a way if they have told me this is happening?"*
The answer is obvious. *You weren't listening!*

I have written an article on listening that might help in illustrating this statement but if it hasn't been read, then I will add that if we are not truly listening and attuned in to where our client IS and the message he/she is telling us both verbally and nonverbally, then we can be guilty of retraumatizing again and again with disastrous results for our patient and the therapy.

If we cannot think of an incidence in which we have thus treated our patient, it might be helpful to review some of the ways in which it could be done.

I am not speaking to overt retraumatization such as unprofessional loss of control where there has been yelling at the client, inappropriate sexual behavior towards them, or sudden termination of therapy without explanation or closure. I have dealt with the aftermath of all of these, the last being perhaps, the most damaging when a therapeutic alliance has been formed, and there has been good rapport between counselor and client(s) with progress being made. I am remembering when in the position as Clinical Supervisor at an Adolescent Day Treatment Center, one of the staff simply did not return.

The subsequent effect on his clients and the whole group was devastating. But this is overt retraumatization.
I am speaking to the more subtle, and insidious ways in which we, as therapists can miss our cues and do harm to our patients unwittingly and unawarely unless we keep in mind the pitfalls and potential of causing unnecessary suffering to an already suffering patient.

It would be impossible to name all the ways in which we can rehurt and throw our clients back into reliving former traumata. The ways are as diverse and numerous as there are individuals, simply because what is traumatic for one person is not necessarily true for another.

However, there are commonalities in the therapy arena we could use for general headings which could be explored. I will touch only on four and leave it to the reader to do some honest and rigorous self-examination to discover others.

1. Triggers
2. Reenactment.
3. Transference/Countertransference.
4. Failure to truly listen.

## 1. TRIGGERS

Triggers can be myriad and often are. They may be people who resemble past abusers, surroundings similar to places where abuse occurred, sounds reminding the patient of a certain tone of voice used before or during abuse, certain music that was playing during abuse, sights and smells encountered that evoke conscious or unconscious memories of past traumas.

*For victims of Mind Control, colors, numbers, words, phrases, gestures, (e.g. hand signals) etc. can be very triggering and set off programs layered one on top of another.*

In the case of DID (Dissociative Identity Disorder) alter personalities might come out in an effort to cope with, protect from and resist, what is perceived as a potential or real danger or unbearable pain. Again, different things can trigger different alters depending on the experiences they hold.

I addressed Triggering Procedures in an article about Emergency/Casualty Guidelines where hospital per se with its personnel, equipment, smells and procedures are vivid reminders of torture and abuse for Ritual Abuse, Satanic Ritual Abuse and Mind Control survivors.
(See website: www.survivng.org.uk under Dissociative Identity disorder)

In the Therapist's Office any one or more of these triggering catalysts can be found, spoken or seen. Therapists who treat cult survivors need to be very sensitive to anything that could remotely resemble ritual activity.

Having masks hanging on the wall, pictures depicting any kind of sacrifice whether mythological or
ancient art form, burning incense of particular fragrance, blood red coloring in decorations and furnishings, wearing a black robe-like garment, etc.

This is not saying a therapist should redecorate their office or minutely change any POSSIBLE trigger! I am saying that we, as therapists, should be sensitively aware of our client's body language, facial and eye expressions, anything that denotes terror, unease, dissociation, and not MISS these cues but inquire what is going on.

To miss these cues because the client cannot verbalize the fear, and continue to allow an easily removable object to remain during session time is retraumatizing at a level that can put the healing process back months. To continue to ignore any verbalization of fear around any object is willful retraumatization unworthy of professional standards.

A client of mine told me a picture I had threw her into a state of panic, so I turned the picture round to face the wall for session time and that worked fine.

I, personally believe, that to insist on keeping an object or anything that is obviously triggering for my client, and in so doing retraumatize them, reveals only that I have a control issue, my own agenda and the erroneous belief I can change in the mind of my client the memory that object reminds them of.

Whatever memory a trigger taps into, the patient relives that memory as though it were today. It is the sad delusion of some therapists to think they can erase a memory by attaching a new meaning to the trigger object.
NOTHING can replace the memory. It is the MEMORY that needs working through, not a substitution for it.
This applies to ritual dates.

It is futile for a therapist, however well meaning, to think they can change the meaning of a date to something better, safer or different. For one thing, a therapist cannot change ANYTHING. Change comes from within the client with the help of their counselor.

Trigger dates whether ritual ones or anniversaries of trauma such as rape, murder, accidental death and so on, require the therapist to remember when such dates occur. To schedule session, activities or other events on trigger dates is retraumatizing - willfully so if the dates are remembered and still kept as a scheduled plan.

I am notoriously bad at remembering anniversaries and birthdays but I try to keep up with the traumatizing dates of my clients and be sensitive to special needs surrounding them.

**The vital lessons here are:**

   a) Do not MISS the trigger through preoccupation, lack of observation, insensitivity, or having ones own agenda.
   b) Explore what the trigger is connected to if possible.
   If the client is not ready to process whatever the original trauma was, file it away and return to it later.
   Never force a recollection of a trauma triggered that does not come into consciousness without fear.
   If the connection is recognized and accepted then it can be worked through.
   c) Work through the memory and don't try to "make it better" or substitute another experience.
   d) Remember at all times that mishandling of triggers is retraumatizing.

## 2. REENACTMENT

We, as therapists, have a great responsibility and task in our commitment to our clients. They teach us, criticize us, commend us, frustrate and anger us, bring out the best and the worst in us. But it is easy to look only from this perspective and omit realizing what we can do to them!
We all make mistakes, say the wrong thing, make a wrong judgment, assume, guess and be miles off track. Sadly, in many of our weaknesses and failings we retraumatize our patients who have experienced just such weaknesses and failings in those who are the reason for them being in our office.

We reenact for our clients, the rejecting parent, and the loved one who does not hear the child's cry of unmet needs. They find we do not truly listen so they are thrown back into the place of unimportance, invisibility and Therapist Attention Deficit!

We are apt to talk too much, to theorize, interpret and explain things and effectively silence our clients as they were silenced by abusers and adults who "knew better."

We put on the paternalistic or maternalistic cloak of authority and retraumatize those who will do anything to please their therapist just as they did anything to please their abusers, and as long as we continue this role they come back to be retraumatized over and over again.

Nothing is accomplished except lengthening the healing process and time, but far more damaging, is that our patient will never gain an insight into something DIFFERENT.

While we as therapists do not recognize the power position we hold and because of this non-recognition manipulate, control and dictate to our clients, we retraumatize and the fault is OURS, not theirs.

It is good to be brutally honest with ourselves in looking at the interaction between us and our clients. Is there an equality of give and take, of respect, of openness to the other's views and perceptions? If there isn't, we cannot but retraumatize through reenactment.

## 3. TRANSFERENCE AND COUNTERTRANSFERENCE
It might be interesting to note here that there is the possibility not only of retraumatizing our clients but also ourselves if we do not deal effectively with our countertransference. I hope there is not one therapist who would deny a history of personal trauma in one form or another.

When I write that we can retraumatize ourselves I mean that if we do not recognize what our clients have raised in us positively or negatively, if we do not see how to keep the boundaries in the transference of our patients and we do not seek skilled supervision, we are in danger of losing perspective, insight and growth. In so doing, whatever traumas we may have sustained in the past or present there is the potential of remaining STUCK in their effects.

We wouldn't be experiencing countertransference if our past has been worked through. We experience countertransference because it hits us where it hurts the most, where we are the most vulnerable and where we HAVEN'T healed ourselves. So it is good to remember what we can do to ourselves as well as our client.

One of the most traumatizing thing we can do to our clients is to project our own countertransference on to them as being their transference. In so doing, we not only retraumatize them by reenacting previous experiences in which, and because of which, they feel blamed and that they are to blame for whatever is happening, but the saddest part of this phenomenon is that the therapist remains blinded to their own issues and the need to self-examine.
It is one of the easiest cop-outs for a therapist to avoid looking at him/herself by turning errors back onto their client, e.g. "due to your abuse, I can see how you think this, behave in such a manner, perceive me as doing whatever". How often have we relieved a twinge of guilt by projecting onto our clients, what we need to look at in ourselves? We retraumatize ourselves and don't even know it!

I am not proud of the fact that I have done this.
Retraumatizing a client who transfers to us all the emotions, reactions and behaviors that were felt and shown to significant figures long since removed from their life either literally or figuratively, occurs in different ways.

It can be in not recognizing at what developmental stage such feelings belong; in the therapist garnering adoration to her/himself because of the need to be idealized, needed, admired etc.

There could be an inability to handle intense and sometimes primal emotions such as rage, terror, indescribable emotional pain and in the response to any of these on the part of the therapist by unrecognition, avoidance, neglect, dismissal, denial of them being real, said therapist can reenact the exact responses shown to their patients. Shown at a time when they were too small to comprehend such lack of understanding from those they loved, or too afraid to question what didn't make sense in the abuse, punishment and total lack of love and nurturing.

Retraumatization of a client in the deepest phase of transference is decimating and simply relives in them all the horror, disbelief and terror of someone they either love to desperation, fear to the point of paralysis, or both. If the therapist cannot handle, recognize or appropriately care for their client in this stage, the damage caused is irreparable.

Reenactment doesn't need to be a physical repeating of a past trauma, a broken heart is far more traumatizing and difficult to heal than a broken limb. In the delicate and sensitive condition of a patient in the throes of emotional transference it behooves the therapist to treat their client as they would a container of Dresden China".

FRAGILE. Handle with CARE". If we do not do this, we are guilty of retraumatization.

## 4. LISTENING
In an article I wrote about *Listening*, (www.surviving.org.uk),
I posited that perhaps the greatest gift we could give our client, friend or stranger is the ability to truly LISTEN and to enable them to feel without a shadow of a doubt that he/she has been HEARD.

It is my belief that the worst thing that can be done to someone is to ignore them. Ignoring is an umbrella for rejection, silencing, making another feel invisible, less than nothing, unimportant, unrecognized, unloved, unheard and unwanted.

Ignoring is TOTAL dismissal and recognition of a person's presence and being.
If we, as therapists are not fully present and focused on our client in their session time, if we are preoccupied, wandering off on some thought and agenda of our own
(Even if it concerns our client) we are, in reality, ignoring them.

We are ignoring what they are telling us because we hear only part of what is being said, and sometimes none at all, our attention is somewhere else and often our eyes are likewise.

Our clients are not stupid and they sense how present we are with them, how much we are paying attention, and it is easy to convey the feeling that in one sense they are being ignored. Our response to their questions, our comments on their affect and the content of what they are relating, our body language, and expressions all tell a tale.

It is my firm belief that the worst kind of retraumatization I can commit upon my patient is to in any way ignore them by not listening with 100% of my mind, heart and attention. If I am not listening carefully, I will miss the triggers, fail to recognize the transference process and reenact traumatic responses already experienced by past abusers - it is the culmination of how to retraumatize a client.

The positive thing about all this is that NONE of it need happen! It depends entirely on how willing we are, as committed therapists to work on our own "stuff", with honesty and integrity, to take our concerns to a skilled supervisor and train ourselves to be constantly self-aware of how we are with our clients.

It is when WE get in the way that our clients get OUT - out of the place of healing, progress, understanding and growth.

I do challenge my colleagues to test their honest integrity in self-examination from which we are so prone to run. May we remember the emotional, psychological and sometimes physical life of our clients depends on it.

May we give sober and serious thought and consideration to how we can better help those we work with that we do not add to their dilemmas and suffering by willful or unaware retraumatization.

Aurora Colorado shooter James Holmes' strange post incident behavior as well as his oddly detached courtroom demeanor (complete with bright orange hair) lead many to believe he was an mK Ultra mind control patsy, put into play by CIA/Illuminati insiders to fuel public outcry for further gun control legislation.

# Dealing With PTSD

Ritual abuse is one of the most severe forms of physical, psychological, and spiritual trauma that a human being can undergo. During the trauma itself, the victim is silenced and taught to ignore his or her own internal feelings about events, and in many cases is taught to dissociate their trauma away.

Once safety is achieved, or in later life when the survivor experiences events that remind them of former painful events, they often wrestle with the symptoms of ***Post***
Traumatic Stress Disorder, or PTSD.
In fact, dissociative identity disorder, which is common in ritual abuse survivors, has been labeled by some therapists and psychiatrists as "a chronic form of PTSD".

**What are the Symptoms of PTSD?** The symptoms of PTSD can begin soon after the trauma, or may resurface years later, depending on the coping style of the trauma survivor. The main symptoms include: ***re-experiencing the trauma***, and the symptoms related to the event(s) and ***avoidance*** of remembering the trauma.

Re-experiencing the trauma can include any of the senses, and for the survivor may mean brief visual flashbacks (such as of a ritual scene or a long suppressed event), feeling emotions tied to the traumatic event (such as terror, nausea, or rage), and feeling physical sensations, or body memories. These can include feeling that the hands or feet are tied up, that the survivor has a gag over their mouth, or even re-experiencing the sensation of being shocked or sexually tortured.

Bad dreams and nightmares may mean sleepless nights, or nights with interrupted sleep, as the survivor wakes up with a feeling of terror. In some cases, the survivor may fully re-experience the event and act as if it is happening again (abreaction).

The remembering can cause feelings of severe anxiety, defensiveness, or even combativeness in some survivors, as anger, terror, and physical feelings recall the original trauma.

These re-experiencing the trauma are as if the brain and psyche are trying to struggle through the trauma that occurred and was forgotten.

The survivor may not have total conscious recall, but their body never forgot what happened to it.

Remembering can be triggered by sights, smells, tastes, sounds, or a situation that in some way reminds the survivor of their trauma. Some survivors are triggered when they have children who are the same age that they were when they underwent certain abuse; the sight of their child reminds them of their own pain history. Others may be triggered by holiday decorations, or the anniversary of a painful event.

The survivor with PTSD may struggle with hypervigilance, or feeling that they are constantly on the lookout for danger. They may feel unsafe, and their body will react to loud noises with and outpour of adrenaline (causing panic and sweating).

And some survivors of RA have been known to reflexively tackle or hit anyone who walks up suddenly from behind, as a protective mechanism. With avoidance, the survivor will try to avoid remembering the trauma, and may feel that they are in danger if they do begin to remember. This will often be reinforced by cult programming for the ritual abuse survivor.

The survivor may avoid triggers either consciously or unconsciously. They may avoid family members who were involved in their abuse, or any activities that remind them of their trauma. Some survivors become completely numb, or "shut down" to avoid feeling or thinking about their painful history.
The problem with avoidance is that in the long run, it doesn't work well, and the person will continue to experience symptoms related to their trauma if they are not dealt with.

Other symptoms often occur along with PTSD as a consequence of the hypervigilance, re-experiencing, and avoidance. Frequently, loneliness (feeling "different" or "marked") and a lack of trust in others because of the betrayal and severe abuse results in poor relationships with others and the survivor can become isolated.

Deep bitterness due to the loss of innocence and faith (and feeling cut off from God) is also very common and is reinforced by cult programming to ensure that the survivor believes that God has abandoned them. They may also feel deep anger or rage towards others and turn on family members, spouses, and others, causing personal relationships to deteriorate.

The survivor may also experience extreme guilt and shame, and wonder why they survived when others didn't (survivor guilt), or because of shame at the abuse that they experienced.

Children will often blame themselves if they are abused, and when they grow up, fear reaching out for help for this reason. In fact, many survivors are reluctant to ask for help, even when they are in crisis, and must be taught this skill in therapy.

Because PTSD symptoms can last for years and years, especially with chronic abuse such as ritual abuse, the person may struggle with the fear that they will never get better, or that they are "hopelessly damaged." Depression at the length of time the survivor must struggle with symptoms and work at healing can also occur, and cause lowered self-esteem.

Poor health and various addictions, including food, alcohol, drugs, or smoking can also occur in an attempt to cope with the anxiety that occurs with PTSD.

Treatment of PTSD For treatment to be successful, it is best if the person is safe, or removed from their ongoing trauma (although many survivors begin treatment while their cult abuse is still occurring, and finding afety may be a process that takes time for some).

Safety issues are usually addressed first (ie stopping cult contact, dealing with severe depression or suicidality). Factors that could slow healing such as addictions to drugs, alcohol, or sex may also be addressed fairly early in therapy, and the use of positive, healthy coping skills in place of numbing behaviors will be taught.

Education about PTSD, what it is, and the symptoms, what causes it is also done and can help both the survivor and their family cope with the effects of trauma better.

Coping skills such as slow breathing, anxiety containment, positive distraction (the use of a positive or healthy method to distract from the memories to avoid being overwhelmed), and grounding techniques will often be taught.

Intrasystem cooperation will be used, and as the survivor of ritual abuse gets to know his/her internal people, they will learn to slow down memories to avoid flooding.

Therapy may include both talk therapy (telling the therapist about the painful events, and discussing the feelings the survivor has; often just learning to have permission to feel at all will be addressed early in therapy since the cult often teaches members to not feel or show emotions), the use of imagery to reaccess traumatic memories, or cognitive restructuring (discussing the survivor's beliefs about him or herself caused by the events that they underwent).

Learning new social and interaction skills may also be taught, to help make the "here and now" better for the survivor and to help them develop a good support system. Learning to ask others for support, and giving and receiving it from others is often a large part of the healing process. This can help to decrease the sense of isolation and "differentness" that often occur.

EMDR (Eye Movement Densensitization and Reprocessing) is another technique that has been used to help survivors reaccess trauma memories.

Medication can also help survivors with PTSD deal with the terror, depression, sleep problems and other symptoms that frequently occur.

The survivor will need medical follow-up to find out which medications can help the best. Often, as the
"edge" is taken off of symptoms with medication, the survivor can work better in therapy to resolve memories.
Group therapy is also helpful to many survivors in finding a safe place to process their memories with others to understand.

Because ritual abuse is such highly charged material, it takes a therapist experienced with both groups and working with ritual abuse to successfully lead a group. Mixed groups of RA survivors with non-RA survivors may or may not work, dependent on the group members and the therapist.

Once concern in mixed groups is that those with less traumatic material to process may feel overwhelmed, or as if their own abuse issues are minimized when a survivor of RA shares their memories.

The ritual abuse survivor may also feel that they are not understood, are not believed, or may fear traumatizing those who have no background of understanding this type of abuse. But some therapists have reported success with mixed groups if the group dynamics are handled skillfully.

Learning healthy methods of distraction (while working on trauma with a therapist) can also help with coping. For many survivors, this can include hobbies, artwork, or enjoyable activities that are relaxing.

Finding meaning in the trauma, and helping others, can also be a method of coping. Each survivor will find their own unique coping method to both process the trauma, and deal with the aftermath.

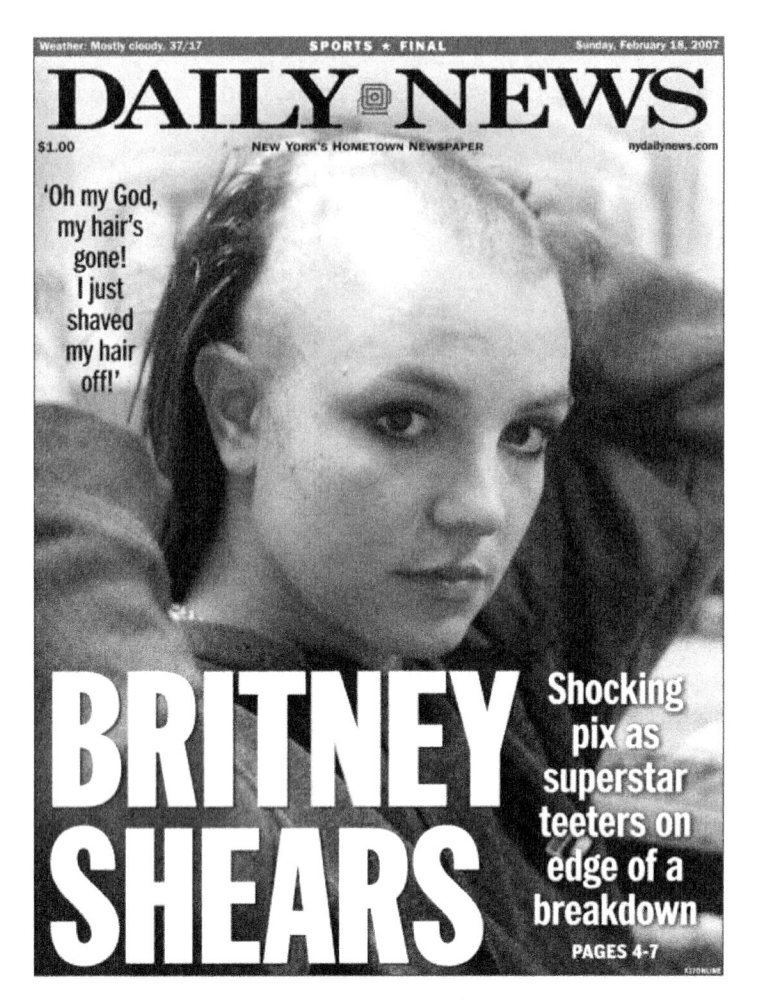

Long thought to be a "Beta" mind control slave for the Hollywood Illuminati, Brittney Spears shocked the world in 2007 by shaving off her hair and exhibiting strange behavior very reminiscent of PTSD symptoms caused by years of mind control programming breaking down.

# A Day In The Life Of A Trainer

A lot of people have written and asked questions such as, "When did you go to meetings?" or "What about your children when you were in the group?", and even "How did you divide the cult activity from your normal life?"

This chapter is an attempt to answer these questions and to better promote understanding of how dissociation works in the person who is *cult active*.

This "day" is based on over 12 years of therapy, and is a collage based on several different memories of what life was like roughly seven years ago when I was still active in the San Diego group.

Hopefully it will help those who are support people and therapists understand better how severe the amnesia is between cult activities and daily life, and will explain how a member of an abusive and occult cult can be a kind Christian person in their day life.

7:00 a.m. I wake up tired, as always. It seems as if tiredness dogs my steps even when I go to sleep early. I wake to the buzzing of the alarm clock, and get up.

I am already dressed, because over the past two years my wife and I have started going to bed with our clothes on. We laugh and say it saves time dressing in the morning. I am in the uniform of every American housewife: baggy sweat pants and matching top, and tennis shoes with foam soles. I change into a nicer outfit for work.

I get my two children up and prepare breakfast, which is simple: cereal and toast. Afterwards they prepare for school, and I drive them to the small Christian school that they attend. I am the teacher for first grade there; my daughter is in fifth grade.

I have a nagging headache that I ignore as we arrive at the school. 8:45 a. m. School starts. I teach first, second, and third grade at a multigrade Christian school that my children attend. Before this, I had home schooled my children for several years.

I was asked to substitute at this school when one of the regular teachers left, and soon was asked to teach fulltime. I enjoy teaching and I multitask well; I go from first grade to second to third, giving each activities to do.

I have lesson plans set up for the whole semester. I am considered a kind and patient teacher; the kids like me and I like them, although I wish the headaches would go away. Sometimes by the end of the day, they are intense.
3:30 School is out.

My daughter has invited a friend home to play, so I remind them all to buckle up for the drive home. I am tired, but I also realize that it's important that my children have an opportunity to reach out. I worry sometimes at their tendency to withdraw, and encourage them to have friends over.

We practice riding our horse in the penned field in our back yard. My son comments, "Gee, Mom, you're a lot nicer to me at home than when you're my teacher," and I laugh and say, "That's because I don't want to play favorites at school."

5:30 I drive the friend home. Dinner is in the oven.
At this point, my day has been exactly that of any other person who is not DID or in a cult group. This is because my presenters, or day people,

have been out. They are kind, caring, Christian, and completely unaware that there is another life that I live.

If you stopped me at this point and asked, "Are you involved in any activities at night?" I would have absolutely no idea of what you were talking about. I was created specifically to look, act, and be normal in every way during the day.

You could follow me around all day to this point, and there would be absolutely no indication that I lead another life at times. The only hint is the headaches, and occasional bouts of unexplained depression that I can't seem to shake. I have had both all of my life.

6:30 My wife comes home and we all eat dinner. He and I have a good friendship, although we are distant in some ways: he lives his life and I live mine.
We rarely argue or even disagree openly. I help the children with homework while he works on a business plan for a client.

7:45 A call comes, and when I pick up the phone, someone says, "Is Samantha there?" This is one of my code names, and I immediately switch. "Call back in a little," I tell them. "Fifteen minutes," the voice says. I send the kids upstairs to take their baths.

8:00 The call comes again. "Samantha?" I instantly change. My voice goes flat, and I reply in a wooden voice. "Yes, what is it?" "Remember to bring the items we discussed tonight," I am told. I then recite a key code to this person, who is the head trainer that ensures that I will remember his message. I hang up after he does.

8:30 I read my children a bed time story. They are very, very afraid of the dark even at six and ten years of age, and insist that a light stays on in their room all night. As the evening progresses, they become more and more anxious. "Dad, I'm afraid," my daughter tells me. "Of what?" I ask. "I don't know," she answers. She says this a lot, and I worry about my overly sensitive and anxious young daughter.

Deep inside, I feel that these fears aren't normal, and that there is something wrong, but I don't know why. My wife tells me I worry too much, and that our daughter picks it up from me. I stay with both children until they fall asleep. This is our nightly routine, and I feel it is the least I can give them.

9:30 I get ready to go to bed. I have to get ten to twelve hours of sleep a night, or I am completely exhausted. Many times, I fall asleep reading to my two children.
Just before falling asleep, I say to my wife, "Remember" and give her the code that lets us know we have to wake up later. She replies in German that she remembers.
1:00 am. My wife wakes me up. He and I take turns being the one to wake up the others. We don't need an alarm, because our internal body clocks wake us up.

I am in my sweats, I fell asleep dressed to make it easier when I rise in the middle of the night. I am finally me, I can come out now and see the outside world, not locked inside as I am during the day. "Get the kids," she says in a low tone.

I go upstairs and tell them, "Get ready, now." They are up instantly, completely obedient which is very different from during the day. Quickly, silently they put their shoes on and I take them down to the car.

My wife drives, I am in the passenger seat. She drives with the headlights off until we are on the road so we won't wake our neighbors up. We live in the country on a dirt lane and there are few houses to worry about. My job is to keep alert, looking for anyone following us, to alert him if anyone is coming.

Once we are down the road and turn onto the paved road, he turns the headlights on and we go to the meeting. "I didn't finish my homework," my son says. My wife and I turn briefly to him, enraged. "We don't talk about day at night, EVER!" we remind him." Do you want to be beaten?" He looks hurt, then the rest of the drive is in silence, the children looking out the windows of the car as we glide silently to our destination.

1:20 am We are at the first checkpoint at the military base. We drove in the back entrance and are waved through, the lookouts recognize our car and our license plates. They would stop anyone who wasn't familiar or authorized to be there.

We will pass two more checkpoints before coming to the meeting area. It is at a large field on a major marine base that includes hundreds of acres. Small tents are erected, and temporary bases set up for the night's exercises. We come either here, or to one of three different meeting places, three times a week.

People are chatting and drinking coffee. There are a lot of friendships here, because everyone is working towards the same goal. The work is intense and the friendships are just as intense.

I join a group of trainers, who I know well. "Looks like Chrysa is missing," I say. *"I bet the lazy bitch couldn't get out of bed."* I am very different at night.

I use words that would horrify me during the day, and I am very catty and mean. The others laugh. "She was late two weeks ago, too," says another. "Maybe we will need to REPORT her." He is joking, but partly serious. No one is allowed to be late, or sick. Or too early, either. There is a ten minute window of time when all members are supposed to report to meetings.

If not, then they are punished if there isn't a good excuse. High fevers, surgery, or an auto accident are considered excuses. PMS, fatigue, or the car not working aren't.

We drink coffee to stay awake, since even our dissociated state doesn't stop the body's protest at being awake in the middle of the night after a full day's activities. I go to the tent to change into my uniform. We all wear uniforms at night, and we all have ranks too, based on how high we are in the group and how well we do.

1:45 am We start going to our assigned tasks. I have brought the log books with me, the "item" that I was asked to remember. I keep them hidden in a closet at home, locked in a steel box. These books contain data about different "subjects" that we have been working on.
I go to the head trainer's room inside a nearby building. I work with him, since I am the second trainer under him. He and I despise each other, and I suspect he would love to undermine me since I have made many cruel jokes at his expense. I am supposed to be afraid of him, and I am, but I also cannot respect him, and he knows it. I point out his mistakes to him, in front of others, and he often tries to get back at me.

1:50 am The room inside the warehouse-like building is set up to work on the subjects. It has a table, a light, and equipment. The room is apart from the activities going on outside, so that others will not be distracted by what we do here.

The subject is there, ready to be worked on. Another, younger trainer is there to help, and I tell her to administer the medication. We are working on medications to help induce hypnotic states, and are studying the effects of these medications, combined with hypnosis and trauma.

The medication is injected subcutaneously, and then we wait. Within ten minutes, the subject is drowsy and his breathing is slower and heavier, but his eyes are open which is what we want. (I will not describe the rest of the session here, it is too painful for me to describe at this time. I believe that human experimentation is cruel and should be stopped, but the group that I was in did it on a continuous basis).

We record information in the logbook throughout the session, and I have a laptop computer into which I am putting the information as well. We are profiling not just the medication, but also this person's individual response.

We have profiles that are very complete and thorough on this person, started when he was an infant. I can pull up a special profile that tells me everything about him: his favorite colors, foods, sexual preferences, soothing techniques, and a list of all the codes that will elicit a response from him.

There is also a diagram of his internal world that has been created over the years. This subject is easy to work with and things go quickly. I correct the young trainer at one point, when she starts to do something too soon. "You have to learn patience," I chide her in German.

At night, we all talk German, it and English are the two *ligua francas* in this group. "I'm sorry, I thought it was time," she says. I then teach her the signs to look for when the subject is ready. This is why I am a head trainer. I train the younger ones, because after years and years, I know human anatomy, physiology, and psychology inside out. Luckily, I caught this young trainer before she made the mistake; if she had made one, I would have had to punish her.

At night, mistakes aren't accepted, ever. Once a child is two or three, they are expected to perform correctly, or they are brutalized. This continues into adulthood.

2: 35 The session is almost over and the subject is recovering. The medication is quick acting and he will recover in time to drive home. I leave him in the care of the younger trainer and go to the coffee room to take a break.

There I smoke a cigarette and having coffee with the other trainers. During the day, I have never smoked and coffee makes me ill, but here, at night, it is completely different.

"How's your night going?" Jamie, a friend, asks. I only know her as Jamie, it isn't her real name, but we all go by our nicknames at night. She is also one of the teachers at the school during the day, but we aren't friends there. "Slow. I had to correct another stupid kid," I say. I am not kind at night, because no one has ever been kind to me. It is a very dog-eat-dog and political atmosphere where the cruel win.

"How about you?" I ask. She grimaces. "I had to march some brats around", she says, referring to military exercises with children ages 8 to 10. Every night there are military exercises, because the group is preparing for the eventual takeover. The children are divided into groups by age, and different adults take turns teaching. We chat for a few minutes, and then go back to our "jobs".

2: 45 This is a short session. It is a "tune up" for a member who is one of the military leaders. I take his profile out and review it before starting. The head trainer and one other trainer are working with me. The hypnotic induction goes quickly, and he remembers his programming. It is reinforced with shock, and we check through all parameters.

They are all active and in place. I sigh with relief. This was an easy one, and he doesn't fight us. Afterwards, I am soothing and kind. "You did well, "I tell him. Inside a little trickle in my stomach revolts at the use of brutality to teach. He nods, still slightly dazed from the session. "You can be proud of yourself," I tell him, and pat his hand. He is given his reward afterwards, and spends time with a child. He is a pedophile and this is how he is comforted after his session.

3:30 We have changed out of our uniforms, which are placed in a special hamper to be cleaned. My clothes, which were neatly folded on a shelf are back on, and we are all in the car on the way home. My daughter speaks. "I get promoted next week," she says, her voice proud. "They said I did really well in the exercises tonight."

She knows that I and the other adults will be at the ceremony to honor the promotions. "I'm glad," I tell her. I am weary for some reason. Usually, I would be glad, but tonight, although it was a routine night, was hard. I have been feeling little cold trickles inside me lately, twinges of terror.

Sometimes, I hear a child inside, deep inside, screaming, and I sweat as I work on children or adults. And I wonder how long I can keep doing this. I have heard of trainers who broke down or couldn't do their job, and I also heard whispered stories of what happened to them. It was the essence of nightmares, and I shove down my own anxiety.

4:00 am We are home and collapse into bed, instantly asleep. The children fell asleep before we got home, and my wife and I carried them to bed. We all sleep dreamlessly and deeply.

7:00 am I wake up to the alarm, tired. It seems I am always tired, and this morning I have a slight headache. I hurry to get the kids up and get ready to teach another day. I wonder if there is something wrong with me, since I seem to need more and more sleep and still wake up tired. I have no idea that the night before, I was up and living my other life.

It may seem unbelievable to some readers that a person can live another life and have absolutely no idea, but this is the nature of amnesia. If programming is done correctly, it is almost undetectable and the person will be completely amnesic to their other activities. This is called dissociation, and it is present in most members of abusive, generational cult groups such the one I describe.

# The End Of The Illuminati

With the recent events that have created fear and concern about the implementation of military rule and/or the ushering in of the NWO for many, I wanted to add some thoughts.

Will the NWO take over? It appears that way, as, occult groups are heading in that direction. They are joining hands and resources, and differences have been overcome.

But what is their fate? What will happen to the Illuminati and other groups? I want to take a look at this, because it is very encouraging. And the Bible clearly shows the fate of this new order.

Daniel was one of the greatest prophets who has ever lived. He was an administrator and ruler during the time of king Nebuchadnezzar of Babylon, and became one of the highest rulers in the Babylonian kingdom. He was also a man who sought God and was faithful during the rule of an occult- based world kingdom.

This was an age when the king consulted wizards and necromancers for help, and an age when the person who openly worshipped God encountered hostility from these workers of darkness.

But in the midst of this darkness, Daniel prayed and sought God's counsel, and God defeated his enemies.
God also shared with Daniel His plan for history.
In Daniel chapter two, King Nebuchadnezzar has a disturbing dream which only Daniel is able to interpret with God's help.

The king dreamed about a large statue made of different materials (a head made of gold; breast and arms of silver, a belly and thighs of bronze, legs of iron, and feet of mixed clay and iron). These different elements represent different kingdoms that would arise and God was showing the king what would happen over the next few years. These would try to rule and subdue the earth (the Greek and Roman Empires almost succeeded).

But look what happens to these kingdoms in Daniel 2:34-35: "A stone was cut out without hands, and it struck the statue on its feet of iron and clay, and crushed them. Then the iron, the clay, the bronze, the silver

and the gold were crushed all at the same time, and became like chaff from the summer threshing floors; and the wind carried them away so that not a trace of them was found.
But the stone that struck the statue became a great mountain and filled the whole earth." What is this stone that defeated and crushed the greatest earthly kingdoms and reduced them to rubble and then filled the whole earth?

Later on, in chapter 2, verse 44, Daniel explains: "And in the days of those kings the God of heaven will set up a kingdom which will never be destroyed, and that kingdom will not be left for another people; it will crush and put an end to all these kingdoms, but it will itself endure forever."

The stone is the Kingdom of God, established by Jesus that God states will be set up as a kingdom which will never be destroyed and will crush the occult kingdoms.
We now know the end of the Illuminati and any other occult groups that try to set up a kingdom here.

They are already defeated: we know who the winner is!
In Daniel, chapter seven, verses 13 and 14, God even gives us a glimpse of the coming of Jesus in glory, and the establishment of His rule here on earth (which began when Jesus came to earth and His church was established).

Again, the Bible is clear: "And to Him was given dominion, Glory and a kingdom that all the peoples, nations, and men of every language might serve Him. His dominion is an everlasting dominion which will not pass away; and His kingdom is one which will not be destroyed."

The Illuminati and other groups that are organizing to create a world order based on the occult are hoping that this won't happen. But history is against them. They base their principles and spirituality on the occultism of ancient Rome, Crete, and Babylon.

But look what happened to the original practitioners! Their rules ended, and God brought those rulers filled with pride to dust. I know that this is the end of the Illuminati and any other occult groups as well; God has given us a wonderful glimpse in Daniel of their eventual fate.

There is only one rule, one kingdom that will last forever, and that is the reign of Jesus. His reign has already begun in His church, and this gives me hope and joy, and takes away the fear of what the occult "planners" can do. I've placed my bet on the winning side, and moved from darkness to His kingdom.

# The Washington Times

THURSDAY, JUNE 29, 1989 • WASHINGTON, D.C. • 25 cents

## Homosexual prostitution inquiry ensnares VIPs with Reagan, Bush

### 'Call boys' took midnight tour of White House

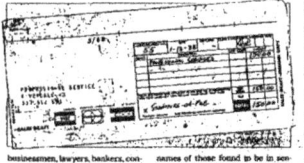

By Paul M. Rodriguez and George Archibald
THE WASHINGTON TIMES

A homosexual prostitution ring is under investigation by federal and District authorities and includes among its clients key officials of the Reagan and Bush administrations, military officers, congressional aides and U.S. and foreign businessmen with close social ties to Washington's political elite, documents obtained by The Washington Times reveal.

One of the ring's high-profile clients was so well-connected, in fact, that he could arrange a middle-of-the-night tour of the White House for his friends on Sunday, July 3, of last year. Among the six persons on the extraordinary 1 a.m. tour were two male prostitutes.

Federal authorities, including the Secret Service, are investigating criminal aspects of the ring and have told male prostitutes and their homosexual clients that a grand jury will deliberate over the evidence throughout the summer, The Times learned.

Reporters for this newspaper examined hundreds of credit-card vouchers, drawn on both corporate and personal cards and made payable to the escort service operated by the homosexual ring. Many of the vouchers were run through a so-called "sub-merchant" account of the Chambers Funeral Home by a son of the owner, without the company's knowledge.

Among the client names contained in the vouchers — and identified by prostitutes and escort operators — are government officials, locally based U.S. military officers, businessmen, lawyers, bankers, congressional aides and other professionals.

Editors of The Times said the newspaper would print only the names of those found to be in sensitive government posts or positions of influence. "There is no intention of publishing names or facts about the operation merely for titillation," said Wesley Pruden, managing editor of The Times.

The office of U.S. Attorney Jay B. Stephens, former deputy White House counsel to President Reagan, is coordinating federal aspects of the inquiry but refused to discuss the investigation or grand jury action.

Several former White House colleagues of Mr. Stephens are listed among clients of the homosexual prostitution ring, according to the credit-card records, and those persons have confirmed that the charges were theirs.

Mr. Stephens' office, after first saying it would cooperate with The Times' inquiry, withdrew the offer late yesterday and also declined to say whether Mr. Stephens would recuse himself from the case because of possible conflict of interest. At least one highly placed Bush administration official and a wealthy businessman who procured homosexual prostitutes from the escort services operated by the ring are cooperating with the investigation, several sources said.

Among clients who charged homosexual prostitute services on major credit cards over the past 18 months are Charles K. Dutcher, former associate director of presidential personnel in the Reagan administration, and Paul R. Balach, Labor Secretary Elizabeth Dole's political personnel liaison to the White House.

In the 1970s, Mr. Dutcher was a congressional aide to former Rep. Robert Bauman, Maryland Republican, who resigned from the House after he admitted having engaged in sexual liaisons with teen-age male

*see* PROBE, *page* A7

How far does the Illuminati's reach extend? All the way to the highest levels of government! Its members blackmail, threaten and manipulate elected officials into unspeakably treasonous behavior coercing them to sell out the public's best interest and as they continue to lull them into a false sense of security.

# Book Review: People Of The Lie

**People of the Lie (The Hope for Healing Human Evil)
By M. Scott Peck, M.D.**

Occasionally, a book is written that transcends normal categories and deserves a category of its own. The book *People of the Lie* is one such.

While this book is not directly about ritual abuse, the topic it covers, the existence of human evil, is very closely related. The author, Dr. Peck, is a psychiatrist of many years who early in his therapy took the normal psychological approach to his clients.

But over the years, as he was confronted with both the best and basest in human nature, he believed that a new diagnosis should be created for the DSM: the category of evil.

This is a bold approach for a clinically –based doctor of psychiatry to take. To state that in his professional opinion, and based on his contact with certain patients (or their parents), that a true diagnosis of evil can be made.
He uses case studies to underline his argument. These studies are clear, recognizable, and include one man who made a pact with the devil (then later took it back at Peck's urging), two children with emotionally brutal parents whom Peck considered candidates for this diagnosis, and others.

I believe that this book is worth reading for the ritual abuse survivor for this one classic paragraph alone: To come to terms with evil in one's parentage is perhaps the most difficult and painful psychological task a human being can be called on to face. Most fail and so remain its victims.

Those who fully succeed in developing the necessary, searing vision are those who are able to name it. For to "come to terms" means to "arrive at the name (evil)." As therapists, it is our duty to do what is in our power to assist evil's victims to arrive at the true name of their affliction."

This is the emotional task that every victim of generational occult abuse must also face, and try to work through in therapy. If only every therapist understood the reality of evil, the capability that can work through parents to children, as Peck so clearly does.

Peck goes on to delineate the face of evil, to show what evil looks like. His contention is that evil does not often look like what we expect; those who are most evil will often appear most "together" or wholesome at first glance.

The picture he draws of evil people is all too familiar to the child raised in such a home as he delineates the "evil personality disorder":

He states: "In addition to the abrogation of responsibility that characterizes all personality disorder, this one would specifically be distinguished by:
(a) consistent destructive, scapegoating behavior, which my often be quite subtle.
(b) Excessive, albeit usually covert, intolerance to criticism and other forms of narcissistic injury.
(c) Pronounced concern with a pubic image and self-image of respectability, contributing to a stability of life-style but also to pretentiouslness and denial of hateful feelings or vengeful motives.
(d) Intellectual deviousness, with an increased likelihood of a mild schizophreniclike disturbance of thinking at times of stress.

What child, raised in a generational cult family, has not been exposed to all four of the above in high degree in their family members?

I remember well the day that my sister disclosed to me the fact that she went to our school guidance counselor (she was 17 years old) and told him just a little of the events ongoing at home. He became concerned, and stated that if this was true, she would need to be put in foster care.

My sister agreed, jumped at the chance, and then found out that she needed my mother's permission to be placed in foster care (this was rural Virginia in 1975). She asked that night, and my mother unequivocally said "No" to her daughter's request to be placed in a foster home. Her rationale? "What would the neighbors think if this happened?" she asked. "I can't have them thinking I'm an unfit mother."

This illustrates point c above, and became the basis of the title of the book; "people of the lie" cannot stand to have the truth of who and what they are uncovered, it is intolerable to them.

My sister did run away from home and lived with a teacher two months later, but she never forgot our mother's response to her request, either.

At no point was there remorse, or concern, or asking why she felt she could no longer live at home, which illustrates point b above. And my sister was labeled a "horrible, vicious, terrible child," for wanting to leave home and later running away, which illustrates *point a* above.

I believe that any therapist who works with survivors, and survivors themselves, should read Peck's classic work. It is an eye-opener to say the least, and will validate the survivor and their instinctive feelings about their family of origin. And most of all, it gives a label to what they have endured, at the hands of people of the lie.

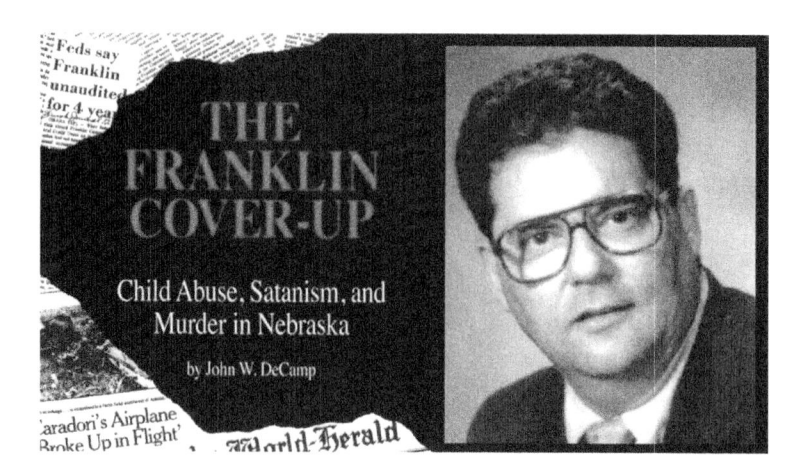

The Franklin Cover-Up Documents the depth to which illuminati / Satanist ties proliferate our everyday lives. Author John DeCamp Gives an unflinching look behind the pillars of power and their twisted alter activities.

# Christmas In The Cult

Christmas is a time when people think warmly of family gathered around the Christmas tree, sharing laughter as presents are opened and sleepy-eyed children excited see what Santa has brought. Adults share egg nog and cheer, and happy traditions are followed.

But for the child raised in a generational satanic cult, Christmas has a very different meaning. In the daytime, the normal activities of shopping for presents and going to parties occurs, and the family may have a large "warm" gathering of its members in the day.

But at night, things are quite different. The child who in the daytime looks forward to Santa and presents under the day, quakes with terror at the thought of what will come at night.

The winter solstice occurs on December 21, and this is one of the highest pagan/ celtic holidays, since the "New Year" begins after this date for the cult. Special ceremonies are planned to ensure the coming of a new year filled with power, and the return of the sun's lengthening days (many occult ceremonies are also based on ancient sun deity worship). Added to this is the Christian holiday in celebration of Christ's birth, which the occult group despises, and special ceremonies are planned to desecrate and twist the meaning of this day.

For many families in the occult, the whole week from December 21 to December 26 is filled with activities, since family members are naturally gathered together, and there is no need to explain missed days from school for the children.

The cruelty surrounding Christmas and the solstice is intense. Children are often abused by cult members dressed as Santa; or a mocking of the nativity occurs with the end result that "Herod" succeeds in slaying the baby Jesus (with ritual murder of an infant occurring). The child may be sexually abused under a Christmas tree, and paraphernalia of the holiday are given a new and dark meaning.

Instead of a celebration of birth, Christmas for the child raised in a cult family becomes a time of horror and death. Programming may occur, with images associated with the holiday implanted, and the child told that seeing these images (such as a lighted Christmas tree, or nativity scene) will mean contact with "family" or other messages placed in under trauma.

Children (and adults) may receive presents with hidden meanings that remind them of Christmas past and the trauma that is meant to bind them to "family".

A mock "holiday feast" may occur, but instead of egg nog and ham, the meal is gruesome.

These are just a few of the associations that occur in the dissociated alters of the child raised in a cult family, and why many survivors feel a mixture of anticipation and fear when the holidays come around. Added to this, once the child grows up, intense efforts by cult family members to recontact will occur during these holiday times at which all family members are expected to be present.

Panic and anxiety can occur for the adult survivor on these anniversary dates of intense trauma and rituals, and they may wonder why a holiday that is associated with good cheer for them means the desire to hide and cower.

It can help if the survivor learns for themselves where the panic is coming from, and which triggers were placed in. This usually will occur in therapy, or from journaling.

If a survivor has stopped contact with family members, then receives a flood of Christmas cards or gifts, they should be cautious, and aware that these items could be intensely triggering. A desire to "call and recontact" family members will often be awakened as a result, and the survivor will need to work through this in therapy.

Child alters often hold the most horrific memories, and listening to them, allowing them to process their trauma and fears in therapy, journaling, and art work can also help.

Creating new holiday traditions that feel safe can also help. Some survivors celebrate Christmas by doing things very differently than their family of origin to help reinforce that they are able to break free of all the traditions that their family held. And having outside support and safety help most of all during this time.

Christmas is an especially difficult time for many survivors. But as adults, survivors can choose to break free from the traumatic meanings it once held, and to create a safe Christmas for themselves.

# Your Tax Dollars At Work

I am writing an article that is somewhat angry, but I can't help myself. I am angry that my tax dollars are being used, and yours as well, to fund certain projects. I am risking my articles here at this site being pulled for writing this, but I can't stay silent.

The projects are under the umbrella of the Central Intelligence Agency in Langley, Virginia. These projects are investigations in the techniques of different forms of mind control and how easily "subjects" can be coerced, drugged, hypnotized, traumatized, or otherwise brought under "control" and turned into willing workers who believe fully that they are doing a "good thing" for either their "country" or their "family".

I should know. I was a victim of these brutal experiments, and later in life I was an experimenter on others.
There is a ton of documentation and evidence both through governmental records and online that this stuff really happens.

That *MK-ULTRA, BLUEBIRD, ARTICHOKE, MONARCH* and other projects funded by our tax dollars were and **are** being covertly used to abuse and torture innocent children and later adults through these programs.

The fact that there IS documentation available in the face of the notorious amount of governmental paper shredding that goes in shows the sheer volume of the documentation and notes that were kept and that could not be completely erased from the public record.

With project PAPERCLIP, it is known that Nazi doctors (you know, the ones who did those experiments on people in Germany during WWII) were imported into the
United States.

While ostensibly they were there to help the US increase its technology, many of them also shared their knowledge of human neurophysiology, and were recruited into overseeing ongoing experiments.

***Enough third person. I will share my own personal memories of this.***

At night, by age 8, Dr. Timothy Brogan of George Washington University, my main trainer, and my mother would take me to Langley, Virginia. I remember there were dark trees in the fields behind the long buildings at one end, and that we always went to the same building. Underneath there were classrooms, used for training. I would sit in a group with other children, and watch films on : How to kill someone (we were forced to analyze these films, asked by the "teacher" what the "subject" or "mark" who was killed did wrong, and how the kill was set up.

We would analyze and discuss everything, including wind direction, type of firearm used, scope used, etc.
Target practice: there was a shooting gallery there and we would do literally hours of target practice. We learned to take a gun apart and put it together again in ten seconds or less. We were timed.

Training films: projectors showed different films on every conceivable topic, including ones on "These are your leaders" with a conference table, and then the top Illuminati leaders in the US rising when the top one entered the room.

Films that were sexually explicit, violent films, and films that discussed loyalty. We practiced how to "drop a tag" (someone following us) and how to follow someone without being detected. In one room was an isolation tank.
It was NOT used with group exercises, but for special training sessions. Usually the room was sealed off when not in use. Language training: different people would come in and both in class and one on one teach different languages.

At times, my mother would sit and chat with her friend, Sidney Gottlieb (who was very, very egotistical in this setting), or with Dr. G. Steiner, a medical doctor who was working on this project with children.

I don't know who the other children were, or where they came from. Their families would come and pick them up afterwards, usually a mother or father or family friend. The exercises would be done by 4:30 am.

At Tulane Medical Center (home of "The Institute", considered one of the top research facilities in the United States for mind control techniques and exploration of the paranormal, near death experiences and using recorded messages to repeat a message over and over were used.

They believed that the near death state would engrave a message or belief into the deepest levels of the unconscious, and the "rebirth" experience (which created a new alter at a very deep level) created a very, very loyal "subject". It did. The subject was terrified and told that if they ever disobeyed, they would go back to the "near death" state, so few thought of being "disloyal" under those circumstances.

The equipment that our tax dollars bought for these organizations working under a governmental umbrella was very sophisticated: VR equipment, and use of the most sophisticated neurolinguistic techniques available.

And people who were taught in how to use it all to maximum effectiveness. By the time I was 23, I was a head trainer in San Diego. At night, I continued to experiment on others, under the supervision of Jonathan Meier and eventually Col. Aquinos, who was a regional director over our group.

And sure enough, each evening after we were done, we would upload our data that was heavily encrypted to the data banks at Langley, Virginia. We had to go through six levels of security passwords at the CIA data center before we came to the area where data could be uploaded.

They wanted to know the results of experiments ongoing everywhere, and there were strict protocols to report any unusual reactions, anomalies, or new medication combinations that were especially effective.

I believe that most of the American public has no idea that certain governmental organizations are using their money this way. I also believe that most who read this will disbelieve that the CIA and a respected medical center could be the site of such experimentation on the minds and psyches of both children and adults (we did it on both). But it is the truth, and I am sorry that it is, because I am angry that part of my taxes taken out when I work goes to support ongoing abuse.

My only hope is that someday, this will be discovered, brought out into the open and the public will be able to scrutinize what occurred and still occurs, and it can be stopped.

# Shadow Government And Mount Pony

**Author: Carol Rutzi**

While the news media feigns surprise and continues to report on the "Shadow Government" deployed outside of Washington to run things in the event of an attack, we who have written about this "Shadow Government" know that this is nothing new. I have to believe there is some purpose to this revelation now, as little is published without the blessings of those in power to use for their own personal agendas.

There are many underground facilities throughout the United States which are set up to house those people that are considered "*Essential.*" It would be interesting to view the master list, wouldn't it? What secrets might truly be uncovered if we were to find out who in this nation is truly worthy of surviving a catastrophic incident.

When I saw the news article published by *the Federation of American Scientists (from the FAS Project on Government Secrecy, Volume 2002, Issue No. 17, March 4, 2002)* in which they cited the Washington Post and the Cleveland Plain Dealer and their claims of breaking the news on the "Shadow
Government, I became so intrigued that I had to read these stories.

One of the sites that was mentioned was Mount Pony in Culpeper, Virginia. One more piece of the amazing puzzle of my own experiences of being experimented on as a child during the Cold War as told in my book "A Nation Betrayed," suddenly came together.

Sidney Gottlieb who retired from the CIA in 1973 after 2 decades with the CIA, owned a small farm near Boston, Va., about 10 miles northwest of Culpeper, Virginia. The location of his farm seems to be well planned when you understand its proximity to Mount Pony in Culpeper, Virginia.

Mount Pony was a 140,000 square foot radiation hardened facility with a 400 foot long bunker, built of steel reinforced concrete a foot thick and covered by 2 to 4 feet of dirt. Until July 1992 the bunker served as a Continuity of Government facility.

The facility was designed to support an emergency staff of 540 for 30 days. Some features of the facility were a cold storage area for maintaining bodies unable to be promptly buried (due to high radiation levels outside), an incinerator, indoor pistol range, and a helicopter landing pad. Until 1988 the facility stored a $1 billion stock of currency to be used to reactivate the American economy following a nuclear attack.

Gottlieb's choice of a home seemed to be no coincidence. Such a highly placed, valuable asset would be privy to many secrets other than those having to do with "Mind Control." As Ted Gup reports in the Washington Post, "Gottlieb had emerged as a kind of Dr. Strangelove. He had overseen a vast network of psychological and medical experiments conducted in hospitals, universities, research labs, prisons and safe houses, many of them carried out on unsuspecting subjects-mental patients, prostitutes and their johns, drug addicts, and anyone else who stumbled into the CIA's web.

Some had been subjected to electroshock therapy in an effort to alter their behavior. Some endured prolonged sensory deprivation. Some were doped and made to sleep for weeks in an attempt to induce an amnesia-like state. Others suffered a relentless loop of audiotape playing the same message hundreds of thousands of times." Gottlieb's obituary in the Times of London began, *'When Churchill spoke of a world 'made darker by the dark lights of perverted science' he was referring to the revolting experiments conducted on human beings by Nazi doctors in the concentration camps.*

But his remarks might with equal justice have been applied to the activities of the CIA's Sidney Gottlieb.' Along with Gottlieb's close proximity to Mount Pony, we have another key figure who lived nearby.

Intimately involved in MKULTRA intrigue and the emigration of former Nazis into the US. through the CIA-funded OPC (Office of Policy Coordination) in the State Department was Carmel Offie. He lived less than 20 miles from Sidney Gottlieb on a sizable farm in Markham, Virginia. He handed me over to Allen Dulles and Sidney Gottlieb in 1952 for my first experiments and torture when I was 4 years old.

In 1946 Offie was putting together reports on the movement of German scientists from the American Zone into France, individuals who had eluded Paperclip.

In the spring of 1948 Carmel was working in Frankfurt at USPOLAD. Burton Hersh reports in The Old Boys, that "One of Offie's functions at POLAD had been to rake
through the flotsam churned up by the postwar disorder—the defunctive Nazi exluminaries and cutthroat émigré politicians and paper mill impresarios of promise —and help the CIC and others plug legitimate experts in around the emerging Cold- War bureaucracies."

According to Hersh, Carmel Offie was "doubling as a kind of booking agent for many of the refugee scholars" that the U.S. was interested in obtaining. He went to work for Frank Wisner who got Congress to pass the One-Hundred-a Year CIA Act, which allowed Offie to bring in, unmonitored, a hundred refugees each year with their dossiers "Sanitized." Offie was Wisner's special assistant for labor and migratory affairs. He personally oversaw the National Committee for Free Europe, which passed OPC money to anti-Communist unions in Europe.

John Loftus reports that Offie worked for the DDU (Document Disposal Unit), which took orders from Dulles. He calls the DDU the OSS "Political Intelligence" experts who wore Army uniforms but were paid through the State Department. In 1949 Offie became responsible for the care of a number of Bloodstone émigrés'.

Bloodstone was the codename for the operation, which proposed that 250 Nazi collaborators be brought into the United States who would otherwise be barred by the Displaced Persons Act. Simpson also reports that a special Bloodstone subcommittee had been created to supply false identities, government cover jobs, and secret police protection to selected Bloodstone immigrants.

Carmel Offie was also handling another project employing Nazi collaborators through a U.S.-financed "think tank" named the Eurasian Institute. The Institute was enlisting men who were important members of the German espionage network in Central Asia from 1931 to 1945. Wisner and Offie were still working together in
1950, when Joseph McCarthy referred to Offie as a State Department veteran who "has now been assigned to the Central Intelligence Agency.

These people were true spineless cowards who made sure they would have a safe place to run if there were threats to their survival. Many "Continuity of Government Facilities" were built during the cold war. As reported by the Cleveland Plain Dealer. "One such facility built into a mountain in Virginia has a hospital, crematorium, emergency power plant, and sleeping cots for 2,000 people.

A bunker in a Pennsylvania mountain, known as "Site R," can accommodate 3,000 people." Sabrina Eaton reports that "it included a reservoir, medical and dental facilities, dining hall, barber shop and chapel" and
that "the government decommissioned similar bunkers at the Greenbrier resort in West Virginia and at Mount Pony in Culpeper, Va., in recent years."

Another report in taking a Tour of Cold War Baltimore,
, "Gimme Shelter Or, Last One Underground Is a Rotten Egg", "Greenbrier opened in 1962 under a posh resort in White Sulphur Springs, W. Va., this capacious bunker -- code name *'Project Greek Island'* -- was where Congress was to duck and cover when all the big, bad buttons were pushed. The vast complex includes chambers large enough for both House and Senate to meet.

The article goes on to say that Mount Weather near Berryville, Va., is a vast underground facility, complete with streets, multistory buildings, and a lake large enough for water skiing.

A host of governmental higher-ups have sleeping quarters here, including Supreme Court justices. The Federal Emergency Management Agency runs a multitude of disaster-response operations from under the mountain today.

Two more sites described in this article are Olney in Montgomery County and Raven Rock. A substantial 1971 bunker that now serves as an Alternate National Warning Center (designed to get the word out when bad things happen) and a Satellite Teleregistration Facility lies beneath what used to be a cow pasture in Olney.

Raven Rock also known as "Site R" and colloquially referred to as "the underground Pentagon," is a 48-year-old megabunker which lies under a mountain just north of the Maryland line near Waynesboro, Pa., close to the presidential retreat at Camp David.

For those of us who have endured the silence of those years following the secret experiments carried out on an unwitting public in the name of "National Security," such revelations come as just another footnote in our untold stories. In the epilogue to a congressional committee report headed by Sen. Frank Church, the committee concluded: *"The United States must not adopt the tactics of the enemy. Means are as important as ends.*

*Crises make it tempting to ignore the wise restraints that make men free. But each time we do so, each time the means we use are wrong, our inner strength, the strength which makes us free, is lessened."*

Let us remember this when we start giving up our freedoms under the guise that it is necessary for this brave country of ours to survive. It appears that those who really are important already have a place to escape to.

Will we?

DAILY MIRROR, Wednesday, February 13, 1980   PAGE 9

## DAY TWO of a dossier on the quiet men who control our destiny

THE Daily Mirror yesterday revealed the power of the Trilateral Commission as a group of global manipulators. The Trilateral Commission—known as the Kingmakers—stands second to none in power, prestige and influence. But not far behind comes the Bilderberg Group, a circle of the elite and wealthy whose hush-hush meetings determine how the Western nations should run their affairs.

# SECRET MEETINGS TO SHAPE THE WORLD

**by ROBERT ERINGER**

*An American journalist who has spent four years investigating the all-powerful groups that aim to influence our lives.*

EVERY year 120 of the world's most powerful and influential men come together, lock themselves away for three days and decide what policies the democratic nations of the West should follow.

They are members of the Bilderberg Group and their meetings are always kept a closely guarded secret.

But I can reveal that this year they will meet in the spa city of Aachen, just 45 miles from the German capital, Bonn, from April 18 - 20 inclusive.

I can also reveal that former German President Walter Scheel has been invited to replace the ageing Lord Home as chairman of Bilderberg. Scheel has accepted.

Top of the Aachen agenda will be world politics and economics following the Russian invasion of Afghanistan.

Bilderbergers represent the elite and wealthy establishment of every Western nation. They include bankers, politicians, diplomats and leaders of the giant multi-national corporations.

Among British politicians who have attended their meetings are Edward Heath, Harold Wilson, James Callaghan, Denis Healey, Margaret Thatcher and Enoch Powell.

Other influential members of the British Establishment include Lord Roll, of merchant bankers S. G. Warburg; Sir Reay Geddes, chairman of Dunlop; John Harvey-Jones of ICI; and Sir David Steel, chairman of British Petroleum.

Everything about the group is shrouded in mystery.

Their meetings, which take place at a different location each year, go unannounced, their debates unreported, their decisions unknown.

Ideas and suggestions made at Bilderberg.

C. Gordon Tether, the distinguished former columnist of the Financial Times, wrote: "If the Bilderberg Group is not a conspiracy of some sort it is conducted in such a way as to give a remarkably good imitation of one."

Walter Bedell Smith, then director of the CIA.

One of the most intriguing aspects of the Bilderberg group is its steering committee's amazing ability to invite politicians to join the group who later reach the pinnacles of power in their respective countries.

TOP: Margaret Thatcher and David Rockefeller meet in London.

Make no mistake: The Illuminati agenda for total control is very real, it's organized and it's often times right in your face if your eyes are open to it.

# Easter In The Cult

There are certain times of the year that are particularly difficult for survivors of generational occult. These are "holiday dates" that correspond to rituals celebrated by occult groups. While the actual rites and practices may vary somewhat from group to group, there are certain similarities among many.

Easter is one such time. In the group that I grew up in, during the daytime I was allowed a normal experience. Easter was a celebration of springtime, of lengthening days, and the new flowers signaling winter's end. I often enjoyed playing with waving palm branches during Palm Sunday, and hunting for Easter eggs on the church grounds. And of course, every year a small Easter basket appeared with a chocolate rabbit or lamb.

But at night, the holiday time was celebrated in a very different manner. The preparation leading up to it often lasted during the week before (there was no school during Easter week when I was a child, in the years before "Spring break" became common. Most schools let out for a week to ten days during this week).

The events of this time were quite painful, and including brutalization, sexual abuse and other rituals surrounding fertility rites, culminating at the end of the week with a mock crucifixion.

Often a child would be chosen to undergo crucifixion in a grim mockery of the Christian celebration, and the adults would state that this ritual was an offering to debase the Christian tradition and show its lack of meaning.
I do know that young boys were chosen for this ritual, and it was horrible to see.

At times, a mock "resurrection" ceremony might occur, but the resurrector was not Jesus, but a demonic entity who would enter into the person brought to a near death state.

The spiritual roots of these ceremonies were created to allow the passage of the demonic into the participants, and to "seal" them as they participated in the ceremony. At times, a golden chalice was passed between participants, and the child's blood filled the cup that participants drank.

I am finding in my healing that more and more of what was done to me involved dark occult ceremonies as a child, such as I describe here. These ceremonies allowed the entrance of the demonic, and one of the hardest parts of the group programming to break has been the hold that these memories, and the spiritual destruction that ensued, has had on me.

Part of my own healing process is involving undergoing deliverance, and replacing the gruesome, negative spirituality of my childhood with a faith that includes love, mercy, and forgiveness, the antithesis of the harsh and punishing ceremonies that I saw.

One of the most important tasks for the survivor when remembering these types of events, (and anniversary dates often bring memories) is to find healing and self-forgiveness for participating, and to reach out for a belief system that can replace the negative.

For me, that belief is Christianity, and my hope is that others will know its comfort during this difficult time of year.
It can also help to realize that so often the group makes certain things sound final.

"You are sealed for life", they tell the children, or "You agreed to this, and now you are one of us forever." This is nonsense. No contract is binding forever, especially one created under coercion, and once a person has free choice, they can choose to break childhood spiritual contracts made under duress.

The group during holidays and ritual events tries to inculcate helplessness and a feeling that "Now I can never leave", but this message is absolutely false and plays on a small child's fears. Instead, as an adult, the survivor has choices, and can choose to break those covenants and enter into freedom.

This is a battle, and I don't want to make it sound as if it is easy. It isn't, and I am still battling this is my own life, but it is well worth breaking free of the hold that these ceremonies and demonic entanglements have in the life of the survivor.

# Dealing With Threats

I am at work, and one of my responsibilities as office manager is to answer the phone. In this age of privacy, almost one fourth of my customers have 'private' or 'caller unknown' as their identification on my caller i.d. machine. So I think nothing of answering the call identified as 'caller unknown'.

"Why aren't you dead yet?" the voice asks, then hangs up.
I sit there, feeling as if I have been kicked in the stomach. It hurts most because the call comes from a source close to me: my mother, a leader in the group that I left, who is very angry with me for my decision.

Apparently she would rather have her child dead than out, and this hurts. One of the issues that most survivors leaving an abusive cult must face is that of receiving threats from the group.

These threats can take various forms, including:
-Hang up calls. These can occur in sequences meant to trigger a survivor, or else the cult escapee may be literally flooded with dozens of hang up calls, one after another.

The message is obvious: the calls communicate to the survivor silently that the cult knows where they are.
-Phone threats: these are verbal messages meant to intimidate and harass.

For instance, when I first considered leaving the cult, I got a phone call from San Diego. There was a baby crying in the background, then the sound of a young child screaming. The caller, a man, then said, "Isn't it nice to know that your children are still alive?" My children were in San Diego, living with my wife, and I was being told that there safety depended on my decisions.

-Accessing calls: these are similar to the hang up calls, but when the survivor answers, tones are played, music may be played, or a name spoken which is meant to trigger an alter to come out. For instance, the person calling may ask, " Is Karen there?"

This is an alter created in the person who is supposed to be triggered out. If for some reason the alter is not triggered out (i.e. the survivor is working in therapy to break this programming) then the caller will say, "I'm sorry, I have a wrong number."

This makes it sound innocent, but a survivor should be suspicious if there are 50 'wrong numbers' in the period of a day or two. Phone threats and messages are the first level of threats that a survivor will face.

But if for some reason they anger individuals in the group, or if the group wants the survivor back badly enough, then the next level of threat can occur. This is abduction and harming the survivor. I should know. This happened to me two months ago, and is one reason I have not posted here as frequently in the past weeks.

But I also refuse to be intimidated by this group, and so am choosing to speak out in spite of what happened.
When the group believes that they are truly losing control over the survivor, they may step up their efforts beyond phone threats.

Instead, they will look for a time when the survivor is alone and vulnerable. Or, they will call and trigger out an alter, and tell them to meet a 'friend'. This is often done to littles, who are trusting, and keep hoping that they will receive love or a 'treat' from those they look up to.

Once the person is lured or found alone, then abduction is usually easy for the cult to do. The person will be forced into a van, or vehicle. They may be driven to a house, or the abuse may occur in the back of a van with windows drawn.
These people are able to brutalize quickly and swiftly in a small space, and have the equipment with them when they make a "call".

The victim will be told things such as 'You haven't been doing your job', or other threats. Their internal programming will then be reinforced, with torture or even rape as punishment for disobedience.

The victim will be gagged during the punishment to prevent others from hearing what is occurring. This will also usually occur in an isolated area, far from houses or intrusions.

The victim will then be returned to a nearby area, or to their car, and told to "remember what they learned". When it happened to me recently, I was told, "See how easy it is to find you? Think about your children, and how easy it would be to do the same to them."

**What Can Be Done** I immediately reported the abduction and abuse to my therapist, my wife, and my pastor. I considered calling the police, but wondered how they would receive the following: "I was abducted by a man who I don't know in a cream colored van with a temporary license plate, so it probably isn't the real one.

He used a halt command on me given to him by my mother and my trainer from San Diego, since they are the only two who know this, that's why I didn't fight him when he tied me up.

He shocked me, so there are no bruises, and sexually abused me with an instrument, so there's no semen." He wore gloves the whole time, so there are no fingerprints. I blocked this all out for five days, and just remembered it today."

My husband, pastor, and therapist all felt the police would probably not follow up on this report, so I didn't file it. But what happened also shows how careful those who threaten and abuse are to cover their tracks and to make identification difficult.

At the same time, I am taking steps to be safer.

1) Don't be alone: I am being especially accountable for my time, and don't drive in isolated areas.

2) I have quit answering 'unknown caller' calls at work. Instead, I told my boss that I
have been receiving harassing calls from unknown callers, and will only take calls
that are identified and with a number.

3) I am working hard in therapy to look at how I was triggered, the codes that were used, and how, and to undo them. I am also dealing with the immense amount of panic and suicidality that this incident caused, which was the first clue that something HAD happened.

I have been calming down littles, and reminding older parts inside that they don't have to believe lies or do what these people tell them.

4) I have asked for help, which is very difficult for me, from my support system, including my church and my husband and children. Their encouragement, prayers, and help has made a huge different to me.

They told me to be silent. I refuse to. They told me not to tell. I refuse to agree with them. They told me I'm not 'doing my job'. I plan to continue to not doing it, because they aren't my owners, and have no right to tell me what to do.

Only by breaking the power of the lie, can a survivor break free of the control of these people. And this is my goal: to become, and to stay, free.

Easter, originally a Pagan celebration is still seized upon by occultists as an opportunity for ritual programming of members.
Note the *white rabbit* imagery to the right (The same used in Alice in Wonderland) its significance it that of a "spirit guide" and you'll often find it in occult literature.

# Education Matters: Denial In Dissociation

**Author: Diane W. Hawkins, M.A.**
*"...when denial is no longer needed, neither is dissociation."*

Once considered merely an annoying appendage to the diagnosis of Dissociative Identity Disorder (DID), denial is now being recognized as the glue that holds the dissociation in place. The fact is that DID would not exist without the mind's need for denial. In other words, when denial is no longer needed, neither is dissociation.

DID originates when severe, repeated childhood trauma produces intolerable conflicts which the young psyche, under extreme duress, resolves by splitting itself into separate identities. This enables part of the person to encapsulate the unbearable event so that other parts can live as if it had never occurred.

Intolerable conflicts arise whenever seemingly vital beliefs are threatened. These beliefs may involve survival, safety, functionality, identity, morality, religious commitments, or any other issue that is viewed as unable to be compromised.

For instance, most young children, because of their extreme vulnerability, believe that they cannot survive without a protective parent or caretaker. Therefore, if
Daddy violently hurts the children, this creates an intolerable conflict with the child's belief concerning what is necessary for survival.

The child resolves the conflict by creating a dissociative split in its own mind, which allows part of him/her to "not know" about the event and thus continue believing he/she has a protective caretaker and therefore the means to survive.

The same kind of intolerable conflict arises when a person is faced with an absolute need to function and yet is too overwhelmed by the impact of the trauma to do so or a person committed to high moral standards is forced to participate in "unthinkable" activities.

Again dissociation provides the means by which part of the person can be separated from knowledge of the trauma and thus be able to do such crucial things as function normally or maintain its moral identity. Perpetrators who understand the mechanism of dissociation may deliberately create such conflicts for their victims whenever their agenda calls for another split off part or extreme secrecy.

They can readily do this by subjecting the victims to trauma which seems unsurvivable or evokes intolerable emotions, such as life threatening terror, humiliating shame, or unbearable guilt, or by forcing them to participate in activities which drastically conflict with their own moral or religious beliefs.

Each of these situations will generate an intense need to deny that the event ever occurred, which will invariably create the dissociative wall the perpetrators desire.
They can usually rest assured that the person will also be deeply invested in never taking it down as that would mean confronting the unbearable reality or emotions.

When the key role which denial plays in both the origin and maintenance of dissociation is recognized, it creates a profound shift n therapeutic focus. No longer is it sufficient to possess traumatic memories with the parts that experienced them.

Instead the need for the dissociative barriers between the trauma-bearing an denial maintaining parts must be addressed if true healing is to occur. This entails identifying and resolving the intolerable conflicts which seemingly demand their existence.

This can be a very threatening process, but it will bring the focus of therapy to the true issues maintaining the dissociation.

Giving up denial can be a process for the survivor, passing through progressive stages. Often in the beginning the whole idea of being multiple may be denied.

When the reality of the split-off parts is finally accepted, the reality of some, or all, of the trauma may be denied. Perhaps abuse by one perpetrator is accepted but not by another, or the memories of sexual abuse are finally accepted but not those involving anything Satanic.

Eventually the reality of the trauma in its entirety may be accepted, but "owning" it may be resisted. In other words, the primary denial-bearing identity accepts that all the horrible things happened but wants to continue to remain separated from them.

Only when this key identity is willing to identify personally with the events and their implications can the dissociative barriers come down.

Since this involves a major change for the denying Core/Host rather than the trauma-bearing parts, the therapeutic focus belongs much more heavily on these identities than previously recognized. Somehow their threshold of tolerance must be raised at a deep psychological level.

What was once considered absolutely unacceptable must be embraced as "*ownable*". Changing this perspective will involve identifying, challenging, and correcting many false beliefs. It will also mean coming face to face with horrendous emotions and deep-seated identity issues.

The truth is that becoming whole requires tremendous motivation, ego strength, and courage on the part of the survivor. When God is your partner, however, He promised to supply the grace and strength to enable you to do "all things."

------------------------------------------------------------

Article originally printed in 'Restoration Matters', Fall 2001, vol. 7, #1, online at http: www.rcm-usa.org . © Diane W. Hawkins, M.A., reprinted with the permission of the author.

3. A San Diego county policy of not interfering with the academic freedom to teach about ritual abuse and treatment of ritual trauma.
4. The convening of a task force to study the problem of ritual crime and to develop an interagency coordinated response.

It is time for San Diego County to review its position regarding reports of ritual abuse. To accomplish this, many segments of the community must join together and support each other in much-needed reform.

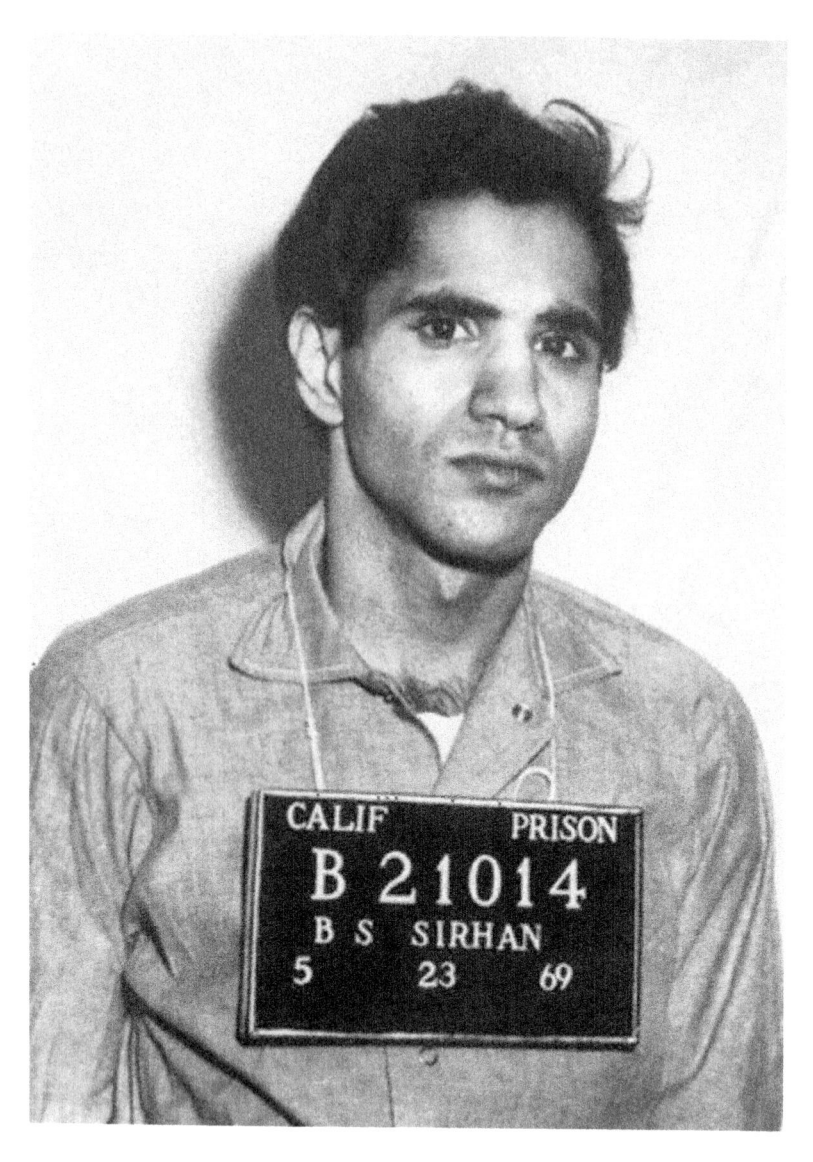

Alleged assassin Of Bobby Kennedy. Sirhan Sirhan claims no memory of the incident even to this day, leading many to believe he may have been a victim of early mind control operations conducted my CIA/Illuminati operations.

# The European Roots
# Of The Illuminati

Until recently, I have mainly written about programming and methods to work through and attempt to resolve it. But as I am working on my own healing, I am coming to realize that while breaking programming is important (and often lifesaving), that eventually it becomes important to deal with core issues. Core issues go beneath and behind programming, and often not only drive it, but sabotage the therapy process as the survivor attempts to heal.

These issues will be different for each survivor, since we each have a unique history. I have received emails from survivors from around the world, and have found that:

*The Illuminati is certainly not the only occult group in the world; there are many other well-organized groups that do methodic, repetitive abuse of an occult nature.*
*But in these groups, often the core issues are different than for the Illuminati.*

Even within the Illuminati, each individual will need to discover their own personal history, since parentage, bloodlines, and programming methods will differ, as well as the child's eventual role in the group. This article is not meant to address all methods, or all survivor's histories in the group.

I can't speak for everyone who was abused in the group; I can only speak of what I myself am discovering about my own personal history, in the hopes that it will help other survivors through either validation, or to help supporters better understand some of the issues that they face during the process of remembering and healing.

The Illuminati are based in Europe, which is where their power base has always been. I remember being told as a young child that America was basically considered their "mission field" or the "land of opportunity" by those whose roots extend for hundreds of years or more into the ancient European dynastic bloodlines.

This is why their power hierarchy around the world, whether in the U.S., Asia, Australia, Canada, or elsewhere will always point back to Europe, where the 13 rulers (they also call them "lords") are based. Each ruler represents an area of Europe held under his sway; and each one represents an ancient dynastic bloodline.

For example, the Hapsburg bloodline (Merovingian) is still active in Europe, although hidden, as well as the Rothschild and Battenberg bloodlines. In many modern European countries, the heirs of these bloodlines are immensely wealthy, and secretly are the "power behind the throne", if not the actual rulers.

This is one reason why those of high Illuminati rank/descent in the U.S., for example, can always trace their bloodline or parentage to members of this ruling
cabal in Europe; members of leadership councils in the States are always direct descendants, whether legitimate or illegitimate.

Whether at the lowest levels, or the highest, though, this group operates with the same methods: instilling intense fear and terror to control their members. Often this is done through the fear of death, and at the core level, the person who has undergone their training will have an immense fear of dying because of the "death and resurrection" experiences, or near death experiences, that they have undergone.

During these experiences, the very young child or even infant core will be faced with intolerable choices: to allow themselves to be extinguished, or to embrace the demonic and the beliefs of those in their bloodline parentage. I believe this is dissociation at its deepest level, since the desire to survive is one of the deepest instincts that God has given us, and will override intellect, cognition, and even well thought out beliefs in an adult-much less in a very young child.

When faced with certain death and terror, or life, albeit at a price that is much too high, the infant or child almost always chooses life (I have never heard of one that hasn't to date, although my own knowledge and experience are limited).

Then the one who offers life to the infant becomes their "savior", and worshipped virtually as a deity in the child's mind and heart for "saving" them in one of the wickedest set ups imaginable.

In many cases, this is one of the child's parents, and most often, their biological father. The biological father may not be the person that the child consciously remembers raising them during childhood; and once again, this encourages deep dissociation: the consciously remembered "Daddy" may not be the survivor's real father.

Identity confusion is also layered in. The name the child goes by during the daytime may be quite different from their "real" name, or even the name on their birth certificate. A child of high lineage may discover that they weren't born in the United States, but in Europe, if the ties to the European bloodlines are great enough; or even that their American birth certificate was forged, to cover their European one.

Each situation is different, and different bloodlines practice different methods of raising, mentoring, and training their offspring. For instance, those of German descent may be taken to Germany, and spend time with those of this bloodline learning the ways of this country, and developing a loyalty to what they consider their "true homeland", before going back to another country to live under a different identity.

Because above all else, children are called back to their European roots at frequent intervals to develop loyalty to their family home and name, and to undergo ceremonies meant to instill terror and ongoing cooperation, alternated with loving bonding experiences meant to instill deep love for the parental figures.

A child may live in Japan, but they will always know that their true home is in Germany or France; the child in Canada may know that their true home is the U.K., or Russia, and the child in the U.S. will long to return to "home" in Europe with the loyalty that is instilled, whether "home" is Germany, Bavaria, France, Moscow, the UK, Spain, or another country ruled by one of the 13.

This terror, this training, and the bonds of not only loyalty, but caring and nurturing that the child experienced through their true parentage, are often the most difficult and insidious to break.

Deep terror combined with loving rescue and nurture create deep loyalty through trauma bonding, and breaking these ties at the core level is the most difficult task that many survivors face.

My prayer is that by explaining some of this, it can help others know that this does occur, which is the first step to uncovering it and working on it. I believe that deep prayer and support from others are the only methods of both uncovering these ties, and of breaking their hold.

I am still working on these issues, and welcome others to share their experiences of undoing the hold of loyalty at this core level to the original perpetrators, and of breaking the spiritual and emotional ties to them.

I will be more than happy to publish here anonymously any articles on this topic, as an encouragement to others who are breaking ties to the power centers in Europe.

Because, ultimately, these men must lose in their bid for power. Scripture tells us that there is only one king on the throne: Jesus Christ, and that eventually, even the European roots of the Illuminati and their coming "prince" or antichrist, will be cut down, when Christ reigns over the earth.

Blessings to you all,
**Archangel**

Printed in Great Britain
by Amazon